SCOTTISH ISLANDS

SCOTTISH ISLANDS

Ian Grimble

BRITISH BROADCASTING CORPORATION

With gratitude to
John Lorne Campbell

Co na mise do'm bu chàra
Is co a b'theàrr na thu thoill?

Published by
the British Broadcasting Corporation
35 Marylebone High Street, London W1M 4AA

ISBN 0 563 20361 7

First published 1985
© Ian Grimble 1985

Set 11/13 Times by
Rowland Phototypesetting
Printed in Great Britain by
St Edmundsbury Press
Colour separation and printing by
Belmont Press Ltd, Northampton

Contents

Preface

This book follows the transmission in 1984 of seven television documentaries filmed by BBC Scotland. They were commissioned by James Hunter, head of television in Scotland, under the executive production of David Martin. Barry Toovey directed most of the filming on the spot, after Bill Hook left the team to take up another appointment. So I found myself working again with old friends and colleagues with whom I had enjoyed so many other ploys in the past.

Since I have been broadcasting with the BBC for over thirty-five years, and served for a time as a sound producer both in London and in Scotland, only the younger members of our team were not associates of long standing. Among these was Margaret Mutch, who came from Aberdeen to act as Barry Toovey's personal assistant, and our film editor, Jock Clark.

The films were made in all the extreme varieties of weather that the Scottish islands afford, a challenge to a succession of outstanding cameramen: Dick Johnstone, Stuart Wyld, Norman Shepherd and Douglas Campbell. The fortitude of assistant camera-persons, trundling heavy equipment up steep escarpments, is likewise missing from the screen: Colin Godfrey, Rahina Qureshi, Paul Kerrigan, Susie Neilson and Susanna Shaw. The sound recordists and lighting boffins also have their crosses to bear, not least extraneous noises to silence and sudden cloud or sunlight to circumvent: Alan Cooper, Les Booth, Roy Argyll, Peter Brill, Mike Donald and Garry Coleman; Alan Marshall, Alan McClellan, George Thompson, Graham Walker, Willie Cadden and Kenny Laird.

As for our message, expanded in the pages of this book, this is only what I have learned from my betters over the years, pre-eminently Dr John Lorne Campbell, Professor Derick Thomson and Scotland's Historiographer Royal, Professor Gordon Donaldson. The extent of my debt to these and many others will be apparent to anyone who turns to the bibliography. Less evident to the reader will be the debt I owe to Hilary Duguid, who has prepared my text for publication. I have enjoyed the help of other patient editors in the past. I intend no disrespect to any of them when I offer the prize to Hilary Duguid, with my gratitude.

Introduction

Our environment is man-made, though nature has also played a dominant part in moulding the landscape. Mountains have been denuded by human agency as well as by the weather. Ancient forests were destroyed before new species of trees were planted. Birds and animals are extinct where others have been introduced. Successive races of people lived in lands that preserve only broken fragments of the things they made, and not a whisper of the languages they spoke. This process continues to this day, and the Scottish islands are crucibles in which it can be examined. Not one, but many crucibles, as many as there are inhabited islands.

The islands vary more than in the relative height of their mountains, the fertility of their soil and the safety of their harbours. All of them have significantly different stories to tell, as well as the experiences that each island's inhabitants have shared in common.

Tracing this story from the earliest human footprint on an island shore involves a great deal of initial guess-work. Only the sparsest evidence remains of simple inventions which helped the early colonists to master their environment. Yet this is still relatively true of life in the islands in quite recent times. Only during the past century or two has detailed information been assembled, giving us anything like a complete picture of the lives of ordinary folk.

All too little evidence remains, for instance, of the era in which the Scottish islands did share a common experience, and one that was to affect their inhabitants profoundly – government by the mainland Scots. This began in 1266, when the Hebrides were ceded by King Magnus VI of Norway to the Scottish Crown, and ended in 1707, when the creation of a United Kingdom of England and Scotland moved the seat of authority to London. From that date the common experience continued in a modified form.

The records of Scottish rule in the islands are lamentably incomplete. Yet it is often the earlier events, ones that can be discerned only in a dim light, which nevertheless cast the longest shadows. The story of the Scottish islands contains a fundamental peculiarity that sets them apart from others to the north and south, east and west, and has affected the lives of their inhabitants more than any war, epidemic or accident of climate. It cannot be explained by recent happenings, however richly documented. It must be sought in the dark recesses of a remoter past, from the time when the islands first passed under the dominion of mainlanders speaking a different language from the islanders, and for the most part of entirely different ethnic origins.

The peculiarity does not consist in the fact that the islands were governed from Edinburgh or London. The Isle of Man and the Channel Islands were also governed by mainlanders during the same period. What is unique to the story of the Scottish islands is the *manner* in which they have been governed. The mystery to be explored is *how* they came to be governed as they were. To this day the Channel Islands and Man also owe allegiance to the Crown of the United Kingdom, but unlike the Scottish islands they possess their own parliaments and are self-governing. The Shetland Islands bear a far closer resemblance to the Faroe Islands that lie to the north-west of them than they do to any Scottish islands, except in this same respect. The Faroe Islands belong to the Danish Crown and are self-governing like Jersey, Guernsey and Man. So are the Finnish Aaland Islands to the east of Shetland. Like Faroe, Aaland has a language different from that of the parent country, and this is also true of the Hebrides. Yet in both Faroe and Aaland their native languages are fully protected by law as the Gaelic language of the Hebrides has never been.

This is the story of islands in which prehistoric peoples raised monuments that still fill us with wonder, in times in which they possessed few assets except one that appears to have been the most effective of all. They enjoyed an autonomy in which they controlled their own destinies. The story relates the manner in which the Scottish islands were transformed into unsceptered isles, and what the consequences have been.

1

Islands before History

First footers reached the Hebrides perhaps more than a thousand years before Britain was separated from the continent of Europe by the English Channel. The galaxy of the British Isles was still in the making as the sea-level rose in the wake of the last ice-age. Those who landed on Jura from their dug-out canoes found its beaches between 50 and 120 feet above their present level, while those who paddled on to Oronsay reached an island far smaller than its present size. Anyone driving round Arran today can see the old sea caves on one hand and the shore on the other, 25 feet below its former level.

The height of the raised beaches varies in this way according to a see-saw motion that has continued throughout the ages. When water was taken from the sea to form ice sheets the level of the ocean fell: when the ice melted, it rose again. The land had its own responses. Where the ice lay thickest, it rose farthest after the weight had been removed. The mean level has been reached a number of times in the past, between periods in which the sea was either higher or lower.

The earliest settlers came up from the South in extremely small numbers, perhaps not more than a hundred all told, widely scattered about this region. The presence of these original tourists can be traced largely because, like so many of their modern descendants, they left their rubbish lying around. This included massive shell-heaps. It takes 140 limpets to provide the food value of a pound of meat, so comparatively small numbers of people assembled all these shells. Their tools have also been found, stone hand hammers and antler mattocks, harpoons and bone fish-hooks, and they learned to make use of the pitchstone of Arran and the bloodstone of Rum.

They adventured north beyond these islands to Skye and as far as Lewis. Today we may make such a journey in a matter of hours. In their dug-out canoes the voyage of discovery could not have extended far in each generation, especially in an age when few people lived longer than twenty-five years, and scarcely any reached thirty.

About 2000 years after the appearance of the earliest mesolithic food gatherers, others arrived in the islands with new skills. These people brought with them cattle, sheep and goats, and their precious store of seed grain. They looked for the most fertile areas and discovered these in North Uist and Orkney. In Orkney they found that in addition to the rich soil there was a kind of stone which splits easily into flags, an ideal building material. With this they began the tradition that was to endow Orkney with the most impressive concentration of prehistoric monuments in all Europe. Here the earliest domestic settlement to have been discovered dates back over 5000 years, yet it is preserved better than many buildings erected in this century. It stands on the Orcadian isle of Papa Westray, and there is another complex, larger but less well preserved, at Noltland on neighbouring Westray.

The most spectacular of all these settlements is Skara Brae, which lies by the bay of Skaill on the Orkney mainland. When the earliest boat people came to Scotland the sea-level was far higher than it is now. Yet by the time the farming folk built Skara Brae, thousands of years later, the sea had sunk below its present level. Today their homes have had to be protected from the waves by a concrete wall, and there may be lost sites beyond, under water, which originally lay at a safe distance inland. Those that survived were discovered after a storm that blew out of the bay of Skaill in 1824, stripping away the grass and sand that covered the site. Archaeologists discovered that a similar storm, thousands of years earlier, had driven away its inhabitants and sealed it for posterity. It seems they escaped in a hurry. One woman broke her necklace as she ran through her narrow doorway, scattering beads along the passage as she went. In the deserted rooms cups of shell and whalebone remained, holding their cosmetics of red, yellow and blue pigment. Bone pendants and fine necklaces were also found, together with articles for use as well as ornament, such as pins and awls, tools of stone and flint.

Today, ten excavated houses with their connecting passages have been laid out so the visitor can look down on those living rooms with their box-beds and dressers, their wall cupboards and hearths, while some of their artefacts are on display in the nearby museum. It is one of the most rare and remarkable sights in Europe.

However, neolithic man's sepulchres for the dead are a great deal more imposing than his amenities for the living. Arran possesses an exceptionally early example, dated by the charcoal found beneath its forecourt to about 4000 BC, and others have been found throughout the Scottish islands. They vary in design, like the Christian churches of a later age, yet reveal a similar underlying unity of purpose and style that link them to others throughout Europe. They suggest a similarity of beliefs, though their exact nature remains a mystery.

Once again it is Orkney that contains the most spectacular of these monuments, not only among the islands but in all Europe, with the exception of Mycenae in Greece. It is called Maes Howe, and it stands not far from the Loch of Harray on the mainland. It was built in about 2800 BC, while Skara Brae was occupied from before 3000 BC until its destruction in about 2400 BC. Although the two sites·lie many miles apart, they have given rise to much speculation about a possible relationship between them. What appears to be beyond dispute is that Maes Howe represents the culmination of a long building tradition. The tomb of Quanterness, containing over 150 burials, was erected before 3000 BC, centuries earlier than Maes Howe and before Skara Brae was first inhabited. Yet Quanterness itself stands midway in the period of tomb-building that reached its magnificent climax in Maes Howe.

All these tombs, whatever their peculiarities, belong to a European tradition. But Orkney also contains two examples of structures found only in the British Isles, the stone henges of Stenness and Brodgar. By definition, a henge is a circle of stone or wooden pillars surrounded by a ditch. The supreme examples are Stonehenge and Avebury in England, beside which the Orkney examples are relatively small. But they stand next in importance, and their position overlooking the Stenness and Harray lochs within sight of Maes Howe invests them with a singular majesty in those wide surroundings. Work on them began soon after Maes Howe was completed, and an enormous labour it must have been, since the ditches surrounding the stone circles were cut deep into solid rock.

Orkney alone among the Scottish islands contains these henge monuments. But many of the western isles possess stone circles without surrounding ditches. There are two on Tiree, others at Lochbuie on Mull and Kilchattan on Bute. Arran has no less than ten and North Uist preserves a rich collection. Eccentric Shetland possesses none.

Besides the circles, the islanders erected other tall stones, either singly or in groups, that still dominate the landscape. North Uist has three known as *Na Fir Bhreige*, the Liars. In Mull, Coll and Tiree they are particularly plentiful, while the moors of Lewis are dominated by

Clach an Trushal, a monolith standing to a height of nearly 19 feet. But Lewis contains a far greater marvel in the stones of Callanish.

The complex consists of a flattened circle of stones on a high ridge overlooking Loch Roag, with a monolith over 16 feet high in its centre. A long processional way approaches it between a double line of stones, while single lines of them extend in other directions from the circle, forming a cross. It was observed long ago that anyone standing on a natural outcrop to the south and looking along the line of stones that form the head of this cross could see the Pole Star directly above the central pillar on a clear night. These stones are aligned due north, although it was not, in fact, Polaris, today's Pole Star, but Thuban in the constellation of Draco that indicated due north at the time when they were erected. Whereas Stonehenge is situated in a latitude especially suitable for establishing the calendar of the sun which governs the farming cycle, Callanish is well sited for observing the movements of the moon, governess of tides.

About two thousand years after the stones were erected here, the Greek historian Diodorus Siculus wrote in 55 BC, after thirty years of travel, that there was an island called Hyperborea (which means 'Far to the North') where a round temple stood from which the moon appeared only a little distance above the earth every 19 years. In fact the lunar cycle repeats itself during every 18.61 years of the solar cycle, and when it does so the moon skims less than two degrees above the southern horizon at Callanish, precisely as Diodorus described. No other temple has been found on any island in the north where such a phenomenon can be observed.

Professor Alexander Thom is a leading scholar to have explored the possible significance of Callanish, the henges and monoliths as astronomical observatories. But the archaeologists, Graham and Anna Ritchie, express caution that 'astronomical observations should not be given too great a prominence in our appreciation of life in the third and second millennia BC, and that they ought not be used to imply a stratified society, a theocratic élite, or a gene pool of mathematically gifted people'.

What is certain is that the folk who raised those stones possessed an astonishing vitality, imagination and skill in the far-off days before people in the islands learned to dissipate their energies in fighting one another. It is equally certain that they received the stimulus of fresh immigrants with new ideas, all the more fruitful because it seems that there was no strife between them.

Identified by the distinctive kind of pottery they made as the Beaker folk, the most portentous new technique they brought with them was metallurgy. The arrival of the Beaker folk in Britain has been dated to 2500 BC, a few years later than the building of Maes Howe, and it was perhaps another 500 years before their knowledge of metal-working spread among the islands – the secret of mixing copper with tin to form a less brittle alloy called bronze. The Beaker folk settlements at Northton in Harris and Staneydale in Shetland date from as late as 1500 BC, and this corresponds with the antiquity of a bronze dagger blade discovered at Blackwaterfoot in Arran. ·

Whether or not the earlier, stone-using islanders had been organised in an entirely egalitarian society, the Beaker folk evidently introduced a more stratified one. It appears especially in the individual interment of top people with rich grave goods, in contrast to the old communal burial practices. As usual, Orkney possesses outstanding examples, notably one of the barrows of the Knowes of Trotty, in which four gold sun-discs were found, judged to have been fashioned from Irish gold, and an amber necklace of a style found also in the tombs of Mycenae in Greece. The same people also left testimonies to their skills in their tools, buildings and stone carvings, as well as in their ornaments and pottery.

But from the year 1500 BC there was a decline in all these activities, caused by a deterioration in the weather. Increasing rainfall made arable farming less productive, peat began to envelop the stones of Callanish, and still the climate became colder and wetter as the centuries passed. There are intimations that privation and scarcity had their effects on human behaviour. The skills in metal-working, by this time well established, were used to produce bronze weapons in what looks like an arms race. The gold hoard found at Whitefarland on Arran and the 36 gold armlets buried on Islay help to create an impression that those with wealth to save looked for what equivalent they could to a numbered account in a Swiss bank.

Such were the circumstances in which a new set of people established themselves at Jarlshof near the southern tip of Shetland soon after 1000 BC. Like other coastal sites, this one has been eroded by the sea, but enough remains to prove that it was first occupied by earlier stone-using folk, whose building style was copied by the latest arrivals. Six of their houses may still be seen here, and they contain the earliest evidence of the stalling of cattle anywhere in the British Isles. These people also bred the Soay sheep whose descendants still inhabit Shetland, while the bones of ponies suggest they may also have domesticated this animal. Certainly they fished for cod, collected shellfish and hunted seals, and, while the levels of lakes were rising throughout Europe and peat accumulating in lowland areas, they could still grow barley here.

In about 600 BC the first metalworker of whom there is any record in Shetland came to live among them. He was a bronze-smith from Ireland, and perhaps he had emigrated because the use of iron was understood in that country by then, making his trade obsolete. He set up his workshop in an abandoned house, turned a cubicle of the original entrance into a rubbish dump and threw on it the clay moulds that tell us of the axes and swords, gouges and ornaments that he manufactured.

Europe was in turmoil by this time, as the deteriorating weather contributed to land hunger, and the discovery of iron gave a sharper edge to discord. A warlike folk of Indo-Aryan origin had moved into the heart of Europe and were fanning out in all directions. They had passed south of the Caspian Sea perhaps as early as 1500 BC on their migration westwards, and here they are commemorated by the province of Gilan in Iran. The Greeks called the district where they settled in Asia Minor Galatia, and the part of Spain that they occupied is known as Galicia. Julius Caesar knew the country in which he defeated them as Gaul. Their language, in the form in which it is spoken in Scotland to this day, is called Gaelic. But the Greeks also called them Keltoi, and this was the term chosen by the sixteenth-century scholar George Buchanan to define people who spoke any of the Celtic family of languages. It has been in general use ever since.

The earliest Celtic immigrants, who were arriving in the British Isles from 600 BC onwards, spoke an archaic form of the language. It contained elements of the two branches that have evolved into today's Welsh and Gaelic, presumably before these had diverged on the Continent. In the north of Scotland it became corrupted by contact with earlier, lost languages, and in the islands from Shetland at least as far south as Skye this hybrid speech came to be known as Pictish.

Those who spoke the Celtic language brought with them a novel form of architecture, forts of stone or earth laced with beams of timber. When the wood embedded in them caught fire, the heat concentrated in the stonework caused it to vitrify in a semi-molten mass, so that they have come to be called vitrified forts. However, by no means all the fortifications of this violent age used the timber-lacing technique. The isle of Mull contains the remains of some 35 forts of different shapes and sizes, of which only one near Tobermory appears to have been vitrified.

On the Continent the undisciplined Celtic tribes were defeated by the arms of Rome. Britain was also conquered and remained for four centuries under Roman rule. A Roman fleet sailed round the north of Scotland in about AD 84 while an army marched into the heart of the Grampians to defeat the Picts at Mons Graupius. However the legions retired, and Scotland, beyond the narrow waist formed by the Forth and Clyde, remained outside the *Pax Romana*.

During this age a most remarkable form of defensive building was in use throughout the islands. It was shaped like a cooling tower, with no external apertures apart from a small, well-protected entrance, and it contained a hollow or double wall, in which a staircase circulated to the summit. It was built of stones without mortar, beautifully fitted. Colin Renfrew has excavated a building at Quanterness in Orkney, occupied between 800 and 200 BC, which he considers to be the precursor of these towers, known as brochs. It would not be surprising if the inventor of this brilliant and original form of construction was an Orcadian, the latest in a long line of outstanding, anonymous architects. What is generally agreed is that the style originated somewhere in the northern isles.

Yet the brochs were being built long before the Roman fleet appeared over the horizon, from about 100 BC, and whatever the emergency was that called them into being, it had evidently passed by about AD 100. Over forty years before Agricola's army marched into the Highlands, the chieftains of Orkney had sent a deputation to the Emperor Claudius in Rome, asking to be received into the Roman peace and thus qualify for imperial protection. Against whom? Whatever the menace, the quantity of brochs throughout the islands suggests that they were found to be effective deterrents. The most perfectly preserved of them stands on the little Shetland isle of Mousa, and there is a fine example at Carloway in Lewis.

After the danger had receded, many brochs were partially dismantled to provide dwellings within and around their walls. There are coastal brochs at Gurness and Midhowe in Orkney that were converted into veritable shanty towns of wheel-houses and small huts and partitioned accommodation within the ruined towers. It was during the period of their occupation that the Roman legions eventually sailed away from Britain, in about the year 400. North of Hadrian's wall they left behind satrap kingdoms of Welsh-speaking Britons. The nearest of these to the Scottish islands was Strathclyde with its capital of Dunbarton, the Fort of the Britons, and perhaps their Welsh language penetrated to such adjacent islands as Arran and Bute, while Pictish was spoken in all the others. Then, in about 500, colonists arrived from Ireland and set up their kingdom of Dalriada in Argyll. They brought with them the name of Scots, by which they had been known in Ireland, their Gaelic language, and the art of writing. This last gift brought the Scottish islands into the light of history, which depends upon the written record.

2

Isles of the Saints

The Roman legions still occupied Britain when Christianity became the official religion of the Empire, so naturally it was the Welsh speakers who were the first to receive the Christian message north of Hadrian's wall. Scotland's earliest Saint, Ninian, grew up in the kingdom of Strathclyde towards the end of the fourth century, and he was said to have been trained in Rome before establishing his See at Whithorn in Wigtownshire. He was said also to have conducted a mission among the Picts, while later church dedications carried his name as far north as Shetland. But Saint Patrick, born in the fifth century, wrote of 'the most unworthy, most evil and apostate Picts', which suggests that whatever success Ninian achieved, they had soon relapsed into paganism.

Patrick is the earliest native of what is now Scotland whose own writings have survived, and they tell us in Latin how he had to change his speech from Welsh to Gaelic in order to preach to the Irish. Saint Columba was to face a similiar difficulty, as a native Gaelic speaker, when he was obliged to converse with the Picts of Skye through an interpreter. The three forms of the Celtic family of languages were no longer mutually comprehensible.

It was a few decades after Patrick's death when King Fergus, son of Erc, transferred his seat of government from Dalriada in northern Ireland to what was to become known as Argyll on the west coast of Scotland, bringing the Gaelic language and the term 'Scot' from which the country takes its name. His society was organised in kindreds, of which that of Angus settled in Islay. The kindred of Gabran occupied Kintyre, the isle of Gigha, and perhaps Jura as well. The branch of Comgall gave its name to the district of Cowal on the western mainland, and its members spread to the nearby islands, including Bute and probably Arran. So Columba found himself amongst compatriots only recently settled in Scotland when he sailed from Ireland in 563 to embark on his Christian mission here.

Columba was a Prince of the house of O'Neill, and himself eligible for the Irish kingship. He possessed the imperious temper of his family, the love of literature of his race, and the piety that was to earn him the epithet *Colum Cille*, Dove of the Church, by the time of his death. The events leading to his exile in Scotland illustrate the contradictions in his character. He had copied without permission a psalter that belonged to his teacher Saint Finbarr, and when the King uttered his famous judgement, 'to every cow her calf, to every book its offspring,' Columba refused to surrender his manuscript.

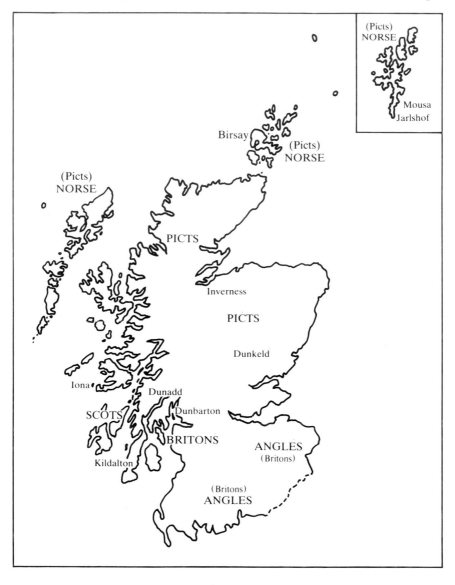

Instead he took up arms against the King, as a result of which he was obliged to leave the country.

It is not certain whether he had already founded his monastery at Derry when he sailed for Scotland, or at Durrow either. He returned to Ireland often enough in later years to have done so subsequently, but he always retained a special affection for Derry, as though it was his first, according to a Gaelic poem that was attributed to him. 'The reason I love Derry is for its peace, for its purity and for its crowds of white angels from one end to the other.'

The monastic organisation that he planted on Iona stemmed from a Mediterranean tradition that appears to have reached Ireland independently of Saint Patrick or of the British Church's links with Rome. Emulating the Desert Fathers, the Celtic monks sought communion with God in the wastes of the ocean, settling on remote islands where they could practise their austerities undisturbed. They carried with them the same particular veneration for Saint John that can be witnessed to this day on the island of Patmos. The high cross of Saint John on Iona still stands, where so many have fallen, in memory of that devotion.

The search for solitude, combined with a spirit of enquiry for which the Celtic monks were celebrated in this age, carried them to islands never before visited by humans. The Shetlanders had lived for thousands of years in their Ultima Thule, and if any of them ventured out of sight of land into the ocean beyond there is no record of their journey. But the monks followed the flight of birds until they reached the uninhabited Faroe islands, where they incised the cross of Christ on stones, as it were baptising the rocks for want of people to convert. They sailed on further to discover the great empty wastes of Iceland, and it may have been on Iona that Dicuil wrote his description of what they saw.

When they settled on treeless islands they built little round beehive cells of unmortared stone in which to dwell. On the rock of Skellig Michael off southern Ireland there remain the only complete surviving buildings of this kind, six cells on their narrow ledge above a steep precipice. One Scottish island preserves the same kind of hermitage. On Eileach an Naoimh, in the Garvelloch group north of Jura, is a stone cell with its doorway still intact, though its corbelled roof has fallen in. The neighbouring cell is far more dilapidated, and unless something is done to protect those of Skellig Michael it will not be long before they are reduced to the same condition.

For the most part the monasteries of the Scottish islands now consist of little more than outlines in the soil. The Brough of Deerness on the mainland of Orkney is typical of the sites that the monks preferred. This projecting headland can be reached only by a narrow path, beyond which the monks built a wall to define the sanctuary area. Ruins of their little rectangular oratory remain, whose resemblances to Saint Ninian's chapel on the island of Bute suggests that this was an extremely early foundation. The traces of other buildings, most clearly seen from the air, recall a community that possessed its cells for the monks and presumably its guesthouse, library and functional structures, such as a kiln for drying corn.

As a rule, it is in the most remote places chosen by the monks that the best material evidence of their lives is to be found. In the case of Canna, the smallest of the island group between Skye and Mull, a grassy terrace above the rocky south-west coast of the island contains the relics of a nunnery. Sgor nam Ban Naoimh, Ledge of the Holy Women, preserves the remains of three structures within a sanctuary defined by a roughly circular wall, and four more outside it, all of drystone.

By contrast, the most famous of all foundations in the Scottish islands, the monastery which Columba established on Iona, is marked by nothing more than the traces of its surrounding earthworks, a rampart and ditch that enclosed the sanctuary area. Within this must have stood a timber church, cells, refectory and scriptorium, all of wood and wattle. The fact is that stone churches were not typical of the period, although they were built where wood was scarce, as in the islands. The material of these has contributed to their survival, but the wooden ones are likely to have been very much larger.

Most of the thousands of pilgrims who flock to Iona today are unaware of the original site of Columba's monastery. But they carry away with them a vision of the surroundings he knew, the pink rocks and green-blue sea, the quality of space and light experienced by the monks who sought peace for meditation here, and a release into the world of the spirit. Many visitors participate in the religious services, held in buildings of a later date that bear witness to the enduring influence of the founder.

Columba's posthumous reputation, indeed, has been such that many of his most distinguished contemporaries have been eclipsed by it. Apart from the personal qualities that help to explain this, there has also been the intervention of providence. Columba's career was recorded soon after his death by no less than three authors, Cuimine, Adomnan and Bede. Of these, Adomnan's *Life of Columba* is Scotland's earliest biography and by far the most important of the three sources. Yet it survives only in the sole copy that was carried abroad to Europe, and might easily have disappeared entirely like the Chronicle of Iona.

Among the most influential associates of Saint Columba was Saint Comgall, who is of particular interest because he was neither a Briton nor a Gael, but a Pict. Born in 517, so that he was only a little older than Columba, he studied at the seminary of Bangor in Ulster and went on to found a monastery on the isle of Tiree. The Irish Saint Moluag, who founded the monastery on Lismore, was trained under him, and his pastoral staff was preserved by its Dewars, or hereditary guardians.

But the details of his life are uncertain, and the dedications to him have not been accepted without question as evidence of his activities. One of these is Kilmoluag in Raasay, where a cross of unique design was cut into a rock surface beside the island's most convenient natural harbour, facing Skye. It has the appearance of a Maltese cross within a square frame, and its handle contains a bulge as though to provide the grip when it was carried in procession. Not far away, a free-standing stone has been carved with a cross of identical design. But both have been dated to the late seventh century, after his time. Moluag is also thought to have taught on Mull, and there are dedications to him on Tiree and in the extreme north of Skye.

Skye is the most distant island to the north that Columba himself visited, according to Adomnan. There he baptised an aged native chief called Artbrannan, presumably a Pict since the Saint required an interpreter. As for the monasteries he may have founded in Skye, there are the remains at Loch Choluim Chille, and also the site of Annait in the parish of Duirinish. Annait is the oldest ecclesiastical term in the islands, probably denoting the earliest religious centre in the area, wherever it occurs.

Columba did not cross the Minch to the Outer Hebrides, and it is not entirely clear whether Moluag made the journey. There were dedications to him at Europie near the very Butt of Lewis, as well as another on Pabbay (Priest's island) off Harris. And beyond the Long Island there is irrefutable evidence that somebody in Holy Orders reached even as far as North Rona, a tiny island well to the north of the Butt of Lewis. Here, there is a stone chapel which the Royal Commission on Ancient Monuments listed with Annait in Skye and the nunnery on Canna as the three oldest structures of the Celtic Church in their inventory. But who Ronan was remains a mystery. Donegal's records contain twelve saints of this name, the Scottish calendar, two. Islay and North Uist both preserve dedications to one or another of them.

Adomnan tells the story of a Pict named Taran, a refugee of noble family who placed himself under Saint Columba's protection. Columba entrusted him 'to the protection of a certain Feradach, a rich man who lived in the island of Islay, earnestly requiring that Taran should for some months live in Feradach's retinue as one of his friends'. But Feradach killed him treacherously, whereupon Columba pronounced a divine judgement on him, which was fulfilled according to his biographer. On the other hand it has been suggested that Taran was no Pict, but the Irish Saint Ternan or Torannan, whose influence was certainly greatest in mainland Pictland, and who is commemorated by Banchory-Ternon on Deeside.

Another saint who may have been Pictish, and whose missionary activities in the islands appear to have been independent of Iona, is Donan. He was trained at Whithorn, the British seminary associated with Saint Ninian. There are several dedications to him in south-west Scotland, as well as Kildonan as far north as Sutherland. The tidal island called Eilean Donan in Loch Alsh is crowned by a castle that may cover the relics of a religious site. Eventually he seems to have established his monastic centre on the island of Eigg, not far from Canna with its nunnery. Beyond, his name was planted in the Outer Hebrides on South Uist, and on Little Bernera in the Uig parish of Lewis, as well as on Skye. The Irish annals record that he was murdered on Eigg in 617, with fifty-two of his monks another source adds, which gives some insight into the size of his establishment.

The island on which it would have been least surprising to find a substantial Columban foundation is large and fertile Islay, midway between Iona and Ireland. Islay's simple early crosses carved in stone bear witness to the Christian activities here in Columba's time, yet there is no evidence that a large community was established on the island. It was on Tiree that Columba's cousin Baithene founded a monastery after they had settled on Iona, an island that was favoured by Comgall and Moluag also. Perhaps the explanation lies in the meaning of the term Kildalton, which defines a dependent church, and suggests that this one belonged to the ecclesiastical domain of Iona. Two centuries after Columba's death the high cross of Kildalton was erected on Islay, a supreme masterpiece which forms a trio with those of Saint John and Saint Martin on Iona itself. And this despite the fact that there is no record of a monastery in the neighbourhood.

Perhaps there was occasional jealousy between monks trained in different seminaries and divided by differing languages. But islanders who had endured centuries of conflict before the saints appeared must surely have been struck by the spirit of amity that accompanied the Christian message. In a troubled world, the monks who announced it might well have appeared to ordinary folk as the 'crowds of white angels' of Columba's Gaelic poem. Comgall the Pict, trained in the monastery of Bangor, accompanied Columba on at least one of his visits to the Pictish King Brudei at Inverness. Here Columba confounded the Druid and obtained Brudei's permission to send his disciple Cormac to the Orkney islands.

It is believed generally that King Brudei gave Iona to Columba for his monastery, although the Irish records do not concede this. When the Saint extended his missions to the predominantly Pictish islands of the west, such as Mull and Skye, he may well have found his labours eased in them by the activities of Moluag. Mull preserved many crosses on pillar slabs and smaller stones that may have been carved during the lifetime of both men, notably at Calgary and Carsaig. Here as elsewhere, they give no hint of demarcation between rival sects.

But the most notable achievement of the Celtic Church was its love of letters, and there can be no doubt of the dominant influence of Columba, so abundant is the testimony to his literary enthusiasm. Whether or not the document called the Cathach is the actual copy of Finbarr's psalter that occasioned the action for breach of copyright, it has been preserved and venerated from his time to ours as the handwriting of Saint Columba, the earliest Irish manuscript of its kind in existence. Whether or not the Gaelic poems attributed to him really are his own compositions, they attest the general belief that he was a poet, as well as illustrating his enthusiasm for the written word. 'I send my little dripping pen unceasingly over an assemblage of books of great beauty, to enrich the possessions of men of art, so that my hand is weary with writing.' The poems attributed to Columba may well be apocryphal, but they reveal how he was remembered, even though he had played the part of a belligerent prince during so much of his life.

According to Adomnan, Columba was still writing after he had given his final blessing to the monastery he had founded. 'After these words he descended from that little hill, returned to the monastery, and sat in a hut, writing a psalter. And when he came to that verse of the thirty-fourth psalm where it is written, "But they that seek the Lord shall not want for anything that is good," he said, "Here, at the end of the page, I must stop. Let Baithene write what follows."'

It was his cousin, Baithene, who succeeded him as Abbot, and only fifty years later Cuimine was writing the founder's first biography. Legend tells that Cuimine was asked what he desired most to see in a church. 'I should like to see it full of books,' he replied, 'for them to go to students and to sow God's words in the ears of everyone.'

The ancestors of these men had invented an alphabet of their own in Ireland, long before they adopted their own distinctive version of the Latin one. This was called ogam. It consisted of a line, marked with groups of strokes that either crossed it or were incised on either side. Such writings could easily be notched along a strip of wood with a knife, though surviving texts have mostly been found in the form of funeral inscriptions on stones.

One extraordinary feature of ogam is its use to preserve texts in some pre-Celtic language that cannot now be deciphered. Ogam was adopted throughout Pictland for this purpose, as far south as Fife, and 28 inscriptions have come to light in this region. But no less than 10 of these are located in Shetland. Here, they seem to say, lived survivors of aboriginal stock, relatively immune to the influences of the Celtic peoples who had been pouring north since 600 BC. But apart from the few Celtic words embedded in the inscriptions, they contain nothing more that is intelligible. In the western isles, by contrast, only one ogam inscription on stone has been found, a Gaelic memorial message on a four-sided granite pillar in the isle of Gigha.

It is curious that the Picts did not employ ogam to preserve their own language. From first to last they reveal none of the Gaels' passion for the written word or love of literature. They did produce a Latin chronicle in due course, but this is scarcely more than a list of kings. The Picts constituted the most numerous element in the Scottish population over a period of centuries, yet Gaelic and Welsh remain living languages to this day while Pictish has disappeared leaving not one complete sentence behind.

However, in the visual arts, the Picts expressed themselves with an eloquence unmatched by the Gaels or any other peoples in Europe. Their picture album in stone of the society of this age is unique, with some of the finest artists at work in the northern isles. Burra island in Shetland contained particularly expressive examples of their craft. It has been suggested that the monastic centre of Shetland's southern mainland may have been planted here at Papil at quite an early period, and certainly its sculptures are worthy of such a status. While Orkney has yielded only three ogam inscriptions, it contained more Pictish sculpture.

Just as remarkable as this portrait gallery, and no less mysterious than the ogam writings, are the symbols carved on the same stones. There were fourteen of them, of three kinds: stylised animals, abstract designs, and artefacts such as combs and mirrors. None is a Christian symbol except the fish, yet they could not have been inconsistent with Christian beliefs, since they were carved on stones containing the cross. They convey only one message with certainty: wherever they are to be found, they define the boundaries of Pictland.

The isle of Skye contained relatively few stones, and of comparatively poor quality. The most impressive in this neighbourhood is that of the Raasay stone, with its highly original cross on one side and symbols on the reverse. Lewis and Harris present the greatest mystery. The inhabitants of Scotland's largest island had erected the stones of Callanish in remote times, and built Carloway broch to repel the invader. Yet they contain extraordinarily little evidence of the achievements of the Celtic Church; and no Pictish symbol stones, ogam inscriptions or carved pictures have been found here. It is as though the island was asleep under its blanket of peat.

Elsewhere, the arts of the different islanders poured into a common pool of inspiration. The stylised carving of the Pictish wolf on the Papil stone in Shetland resembles a lion painted on vellum in the gospel book of Columba's monastery of Durrow in Ireland. The Maltese cross on the Papil stone recalls another from Ardwall island off the coast of Kirkcudbright in the British sphere of influence.

Then there is the contribution of the Angles. After these had established themselves in Northumbria, monks from Iona were invited to found a Columban monastery on the tidal island of

Lindisfarne, where they taught the English to read and write. These responded with more enthusiasm than the Picts, and presently produced those wonders of the age, the Latin history of Saint Bede and one of the most beautiful books in existence, the Lindisfarne gospels. Anglian styles and motives became entwined with those of the Gaels, the Britons and the Picts.

It might appear that such achievements could only have been the fruits of people united by a common faith and living at peace. In fact life was not so idyllic. A dispute between the Celtic Church and that of Rome caused the Columban monks to abandon Lindisfarne. The controversy spread north, and in 717 the Pictish King expelled his monks from Iona. Here the biographer of Columba, Abbot Adomnan, left his monastery when he could not persuade all his brethren to accept the authority of Rome, and retired to Ireland. There he composed the code of laws that was endorsed by the assembly of Tara in 697.

In Ireland, unaffected by the controversy involving the authority of Rome, people found their own source of conflict. Here, everyone's loyalties and obligations began and ended with their own tribes, and since each monastery belonged to a particular tribe, even this sacred institution of an enemy tribe could become a legitimate target in the event of strife. On occasion, monasteries actually went to war against one another, as did Saint Ciaran's foundation of Clonmacnoise against Saint Columba's Durrow in 759. On the other hand, Columba had distanced his monastery of Iona from this kind of discord when he founded it in Scotland and there is no record of involvement in any feuding with another monastery.

On the contrary, Iona and the other establishments of the same kind introduced into the Scottish islands a quality of life such as they have rarely enjoyed subsequently. At a time when the secular leaders of society were tribal headmen to whom administrative obligations were unknown, it was the Church that discharged the responsibilities of a state. Its monasteries were not only the centres of religious instruction and craftsmanship. They dispensed medical care, organised a system of communal husbandry, provided in seasons of want, offered sanctuary and dispensed the Law of Adomnan. Like their arts, their social services had perhaps reached a peak when the Vikings appeared in about the year 800, bringing a new and terrifying threat.

3

Isles of the Vikings

The Scottish islands had been dominated by the Celtic Church in varying degrees for about three hundred years. It was the culminating influence at the end of a long, intermittent colonisation by different branches of the Celtic peoples, ever since they had discovered the islands during their migration period. Now these same Celts were to find themselves at the receiving end of a similar process. Another European folk were to discover the Scottish islands at the climax of their migration period, and dominate them in turn for centuries.

The Vikings were Scandinavians, a term that can be applied to them all, despite the fact that they were divided into three main groupings of Swedes, Norwegians and Danes. Then, as now, they spoke different dialects of a common language that was more or less comprehensible to them all, and their earliest runic inscriptions reveal that this had been so at least since the third century AD. In addition to preserving a greater linguistic cohesion than the Celts did, they were also united by the pagan Norse beliefs that they shared.

They possessed a powerful weapon enjoyed by no other people during the period in which they made the Scottish islands their own. It was an incomparable skill in seamanship, based on their invention of the keel and their mastery of rudder and sail. This, above all else, united the diverse Scandinavians and brought about the achievements of the Viking age. All their raids were launched from the sea, and it was this that took their victims so completely by surprise, as the Northumbrian scholar Alcuin makes clear in his description of the destruction of Lindisfarne in 793. 'It is some 350 years that we and our forefathers have inhabited this lovely land, and never before in Britain has such a terror appeared as we have now suffered at the hands of the heathen. Nor was it thought possible that such an inroad from the sea could be made.'

Iona suffered the fate of Lindisfarne a year later, and the Vikings returned in 798 and 802, giving the impression that they were allowing their victims a respite in which to restore their shrines and restock their barns before they struck again. But after this the Abbot decided to move his monastery to the relative safety of Kells in the centre of Ireland. The Breccbennach was saved, an eighth-century reliquary in the shape of an early Celtic oratory, made of wood decorated with metalwork and thought to have contained the relics of Saint Columba. It is preserved in the National Museum of Antiquities at Edinburgh.

Another treasure rescued from the Vikings was 'the great Gospel of Colum Cille, the chief relic of the western world,' as it came to be described. Tradition tells of its narrow escape in a shipwreck on its way from Iona to Kells, probably before the year 806, when 68 monks who had remained to tend the sanctuary were slaughtered in the next orgy of burning and rapine. The Vikings responsible are considered to have come exclusively from Norway, by way of the more northerly isles.

Of course there were many Scandinavians who did not share the spirit of adventure of the Viking age, who lived in the isolation of their Swedish forests and in the recesses of the Norwegian fjords, tending their farms generation after generation, and desiring only to be left alone. Among the emigrants the principal objectives were better land and a kinder climate, and all who sailed west, whatever their motives, were likely to have seen Shetland first. Except in rough weather, the journey made comparatively slight demands on their seamanship, since Shetland lay only a day or so away under sail, and for half of this time they were not even out of sight of land.

Beyond Shetland lay the Faroe islands, uninhabited except by Celtic monks. Dicuil the Gaelic geographer wrote in about 825 that these had now left 'because of Norse robbers'. This descriptive term was carefully chosen, but it could hardly apply to Norsemen who wished to settle in virtually uninhabited islands, so remote from the arena of profitable piracy. Clearly the intention of these was to colonise a little world that they could call their own. They held what may fairly be claimed as Europe's first parliamentary assembly on a promontory of rock in Tórshavn harbour, and their modern government offices occupy the same site to day. Some consider the Icelandic Althing to be the Mother of Parliaments, but the Faroe islands were colonised earlier and must therefore be given precedence.

The situation was entirely different in Shetland, which had been occupied since the remotest prehistoric times and was now the home of an affluent, conservative, cultured Pictish society. The treasure of buried silverware that was discovered in Saint Ninian's Isle gives an intimation of the standard of living, at least of its wealthier members, and of the desperate attempts to save family property. The colonisation of Shetland by the Vikings is thought to have begun before the year 800, and it was on so massive a scale that these islands have remained fundamentally Norse in character ever since.

The first Norse settlement to be unearthed in the British Isles was discovered at Jarlshof, situated beneath Sumburgh Head at the southern tip of Shetland where the airport lies today. Here the Irish bronze-smith of an earlier age had plied his trade, and the broch builders had erected one of their defensive forts beside the shore. What had become of the Picts who had lived in the admirably constructed wheel-houses after the need for defence had passed?

The earliest Norse long-house with its outbuildings, including a smithy and byre erected in about 800, was found to be the home of people whose primary occupation was agriculture. Most surprisingly, they seem to have devoted little time to fishing although they must have arrived by sea, and lived beside a natural harbour where boats could be beached easily. Yet they possessed boats, and even drew sketches of them on stone. Refuting the claim that the Norse colonists were merely peaceful farmers the distinguished scholar F. T. Wainright has written, 'Why should they want boats if not for fishing? The answer may lie in the several camp fires which were found to the north of the farmstead and which may have been lit by boat crews returning from the south, a suggestion supported by the discovery of an Irish-Scottish metal pin in the ash of one of the fires.' This ideally situated base on the route to gold-bearing Ireland grew ever-larger and more prosperous as the years passed, its crops and animals provisioning a race of seamen who evidently had more lucrative objectives in mind than catching fish.

The second Norse settlement to be discovered in Shetland has been unearthed at Underhoull, on the northernmost island of Unst. As at Jarlshof, it occupies a site where earlier peoples had lived. The Norse homestead at Underhoull is much smaller than those of Jarlshof. The site does not reveal what became of its former occupants, and the fate of the previous inhabitants of these islands remains something of a mystery. Some might have fled, others been murdered. They could have been carried off into slavery, or housed as thralls of their new masters in humbler dwellings than those they vacated. Orkney has contributed to the tantalising evidence on this subject. Here, too, the Scandinavians colonised in such large numbers that the ancient Pictish society was overwhelmed and its language, institutions and culture obliterated.

At Buckquoy on the northern mainland of Orkney there is a site that had been occupied by Picts since the seventh century, in three successive homes before a Norse farm was placed right on top of the final one. This building was as different as could be from the Norse long-house. It was designed in the architectural style called figure-of-eight, somewhat resembling the shape of a recumbent human torso and head. It contained separated rooms, and roof supports that consisted of protruding piers reminiscent of those that gave their name to the wheel-houses of an earlier age. One of the spindle-whorls found here had been marked with an ogam inscription, and a white pebble came to light, painted overall with small circles like a decorated Easter-egg. A few household articles had been left behind, bone pins, a bone comb and spoon, some plain pottery and iron knife blades.

Perhaps their owners fled in time with more precious possessions. The Picts of Orkney could see the mountains of the Scottish mainland across the Pentland Firth, and it may be that many of them made a timely escape to the relative safety of those hills. Kenneth Mac Alpin, King of the Scots, did the same in 843, when he set out to establish a kingdom of Picts and Scots in what remained of the heartland of the two peoples.

Not far from Buckquoy lies the tidal island called the Brough of Birsay. On it stood a Celtic monastery where the fragments of a stone picture have been found, showing a procession of three warriors holding spears and square shields. The leader's is carved with a more elaborate device than the shields of the men who follow him, and above their heads are carved the Pictish symbols of an eagle, the curious beast described as a swimming elephant, the crescent with a V-shaped rod superimposed on it, and a mirror. This memorial is unique in having stood beside a triple grave. Nowhere else in Pictland has a portrait identified by the symbols been found, associated with a particular burial.

Whatever happened to the families of these important personages, the monks seem to have left the Brough in a hurry. About two miles away, an elaborate wooden box was recovered from a bog, of a design that dates it to around the year 800. The box contained the tools of a woodworker, and it is a fair guess that it was dropped by one of the brethren during their flight from Viking marauders. Yet,

Ring of stones at Callanish, Isle of Lewis
Prehistoric home interior, preserved at Skara Brae, Orkney

Broch of Mousa, Shetland

Norse homesteads at Jarlshof, Shetland

Iona abbey

Kildalton Cross, circa 800 AD, Islay

Tobermory, Mull

Duart Castle, Mull

paradoxically, the Norsemen who settled on the Brough built their long-houses on the slope above the sanctuary area, as though respecting this sacred site despite their propensity for looting such places and murdering their occupants.

There is clearer evidence of a violent takeover from North Uist. Here is another island, like Orkney, whose fertility had attracted the colonist from the earliest times, and on a flat, sandy peninsula called the Udal, a Norse settlement has been discovered. Its previous Pictish inhabitants used the same kind of figure-of-eight architecture as at Buckquoy, and the obliteration of their old way of life is commemorated by the rectangular buildings planted on top of three of their cellular homes. A small Norse fort contributes to the evidence that the change of ownership on the Udal was sudden and violent. As at Jarlshof, the Udal settlement grew in size through the tenth and eleventh centuries until it contained some six buildings, forming the establishment of a major magnate.

Such were the winter bases from which the Norsemen sailed to loot the wealth of the Irish monasteries. The temptation to sail south between seed-time and harvest must have been very great, because news would have spread fast that Ireland was an orchard whose fruit was ripe for picking. So far from uniting in the face of a common danger, its tribal inhabitants were all too apt to invoke the help of well-armed foreigners in their inter-clan disputes.

Examples of what occurred may be selected at random from the succinct records of their chroniclers. '881. The oratory of Ciaran was broken into by foreigners and its full of property taken out of it.' Such places were used in those days as the equivalent of a bank vault. After the Norse kingdom of Dublin had been established, the annalist recorded in the year 949: 'Godfrey son of Sitric, with the foreigners of Dublin, plundered Kells, Donoughpatrick, Ardbraccan, Dulane, Castlekeeran, and other churches in like manner: but it was out of Kells they were all plundered. They carried upwards of three thousand persons with them into captivity, besides gold, silver, raiment, and various wealth and goods of every description.' This was the heyday of Viking power.

The number of captives can be explained by the slave trade – a highly profitable Viking enterprise. A few decades before those three thousand people were carried off from Ireland, a diplomat from Baghdad witnessed the sale of slaves on the Volga and described what he saw in Arabic. The entrepreneurs in this case were no doubt

Vikings, since he called them Rus. 'They arrive from their distant lands and lay their ships along the banks of the Atul, which is a great river, and there they build big wooden houses on its shores. Ten or twenty of them may live together in one house, and each of them has a couch of his own where he sits and diverts himself with the pretty slave-girls whom he has brought along to offer for sale. He will make love with one of them in the presence of his comrades, sometimes this develops into a communal orgy and, if a customer should turn up to buy a girl, the Rus will not let her go until he has finished with her.'

The eastern Vikings were reported to acquire their slaves by raids on the Slavs, but there is no direct evidence that young girls from the Scottish islands also found themselves involved in communal orgies on the Volga. The most famous of them to have been carried off from the Gaelic world is Sunniva, who was taken from Ireland to Norway with other young girls to add to the comforts of home. She persuaded her companions to commit suicide with her soon after their arrival, and became the patron saint of north Norway.

It would be as absurd to suppose that the Scottish islands were exempt from similar practices as that Jarlshof was the home of peaceful farmers throughout the Viking age. An Irish annalist recorded that a certain Norseman named Ragnald took up his residence in Orkney in about the middle of the ninth century, and that his two sons went on an expedition to Spain and Africa. Presumably Ragnald's sons were not the first to have used these settled islands as a base for long-distance commercial enterprises, just as the traffic that the Baghdad diplomat described must have been well-established by the time of his visit to the Volga.

One of the most far-flung practices of the Vikings was the burial of a slave-woman with her dead master. The Arab account relates: 'She was plied with drink, went to each household in turn, and there had sexual intercourse with its headman who said, "Tell your master that I did this out of love for him."' Finally she was taken into the ship for a final orgy of booze and sex beside his corpse before she was strangled, the ship was set on fire, and a mound heaped over the ashes.

The only example of such ritual human sacrifice so far discovered in the British Isles occurred in the Isle of Man. Here another Gaelic society had been overwhelmed early in the Viking age. The annalist recorded the first raid in 798, four years after the initial attack on

24

Iona. It was perhaps fifty years later that a burial mound was raised over the corpse of some Viking leader and, above him, the body of a woman, face downwards, whose skull had been shattered from behind by a heavy blow. She was between twenty and thirty years old, and was accompanied by oxen, horses, sheep and dogs.

This was not a ship burial, but among the western isles Man is particularly rich in such burials, as might be expected of such a suitable launching-pad for assaults on Ireland. One site contained a thirty-five-foot clinker-built boat filled with fine Viking jewellery, placed directly over the graves of Celtic Christians. A ship burial of the same period has also been uncovered on Colonsay.

The island of Colonsay at the wide mouth of the Firth of Lorn, not far from Iona, had been an integral part of Kenneth Mac Alpin's kingdom. Whatever may have happened to the kindred of Lorn who inhabited it, or their foundation of Kiloran, the island became a base for the last leg of the journey to Ireland when the Vikings arrived. Here a Norse warrior took his rest in his boat, accompanied by his horse, weapons and ornaments together with a pair of bronze scales and their balance and weights. These items prove that he had not lost his pagan beliefs, since Christian burials never contained grave goods. Yet two crosses were incised on stone slabs forming part of the sepulchre, as though he or those who interred him were not sure which form of religion's magic would prove the more effective.

Arran has yielded a ship burial resembling that of Colonsay, though there is nothing left on the ground for the visitor to inspect today. So has Canna, where there had been a nunnery of the Celtic Church. On its little neighbouring isle of Sanday there were no less than three, and although they had been rifled they were found to contain such homely objects as glass beads and a comb.

These raise a question of the identity of womenfolk of the Norse settlers. Generally the Vikings took women for sport, sale or thralldom, since they had brought their wives with them from the beginning. Although surprisingly few pagan graves have been found, considering the number of incomers who must have died in the islands from about the year 800, about as many contain the corpses of women as of men. Interred with the women were the bronze brooches of tortoise-shape that they wore on each shoulder. They also possessed a third brooch that varied in design, and could be worn anywhere on their costume. A particularly beautiful one comes from a Viking grave at Westness in Orkney. It was made of silver and gold, fastened by a long pin, and must have been about a hundred years old when it was buried with its last owner. The grave goods of the consorts of these women – their swords, axes, spear-heads and shield bosses – reveal their way of life unmistakably.

Such chance grave finds and settlement sites cannot give an accurate picture of the distribution and density of the Norse colonisation. For this information we have to turn to the island place-names. In Shetland and Orkney they became almost entirely Norse, while four out of five place-names in Lewis today are of Norse origin, compared to one in three on Islay and one out of eight on Arran. Lewis is the most northerly isle in which the Gaelic language supplanted Norwegian after the end of the Viking age, all the more remarkable because Gaelic could not have taken deep root there before it. Professor Magne Oftedal has written of the modern tongue: 'Lewis intonation bears a striking resemblance to the tonal pattern of my own south-western Norwegian.' Similarly, a study of the old Norse tongue of Orkney and Shetland has revealed that the great majority of settlers in those islands came from the coastal areas of south-west Norway.

In Skye the Trotternish peninsula which extends westwards towards Lewis across the Minch possesses a ratio of two Norse settlement names to one Gaelic one, and the Norse names mark the better sites. Here the foundation of Kilmoluag had been established in the time of the Celtic Church. Today the car ferry sails from a port called Uig, a Gaelic modification of the term Vik.

Gradually the Norse settlers became acquainted with the religion of the older inhabitants, and at first they simply added the Christian magic to their beliefs, as the Colonsay ship burial bears witness. In Denmark a smith's mould has been discovered which was used impartially to manufacture both Thor's hammer and the cross of Christ as amulets. It was a sad loss to archaeology when the Scandinavians decided to pin their faith exclusively on the Christian message, and ceased to bury their grave goods with the dead, even as a precaution.

What the Vikings failed to learn from their subject islanders was the art of literacy. They continued to use their runic script, though only one runic inscription has been found in the Outer Hebrides, on the isle of Barra. It was carved on a slab decorated with interlace and a cross on its reverse side. Iona possesses a runic inscription on a slab decorated with a double-ribbon cross interlaced with a square ring. It reads: 'Kali son of Ölvir laid this stone over his brother Fugl.' The spelling conventions date it to the late tenth or early eleventh century.

This is a century earlier than the largest collection of runic graffiti that survives in the Scottish islands, or anywhere else in the world. They were scratched on the interior walls of Maes Howe in Orkney, after Vikings had broken into the neolithic tomb. Characteristically they expresss an almost exclusive preoccupation with loot, though there is also a charming reference to 'Ingebjorg the fair widow. Many a haughty woman has stooped to walk in here.' A great deal of skaldic verse devoted to the same themes was handed down by oral tradition from this age, to be committed to vellum when the Scandinavians took to writing after the end of the Viking age.

Of all the Scottish islands, Orkney alone possesses a saga of its own, composed in Iceland in the thirteenth century. It relates how Earl Sigurd accompanied Sitric of Dublin to fight the High King of Ireland at Clontarf in the spring of 1013. 'There was no man who would bear the raven-standard and the Earl bore it himself and fell there, while King Sitric fled. King Brian fell in the hour of victory.'

By the time of Sigurd's death, over two centuries after the Norse settlement, it may be that intermarriage had become general between Norse and native islanders as it had among the top people. Sigurd's mother was the daughter of an Irish King, while he himself had married a daughter of Malcolm II, King of Scots. His son Earl Thorfinn owed allegiance to distant Norwegian kings who came and went, asserting a tenuous authority. But he was more than half Gaelic in blood and he probably spent a great deal more of his time at the court of his grandfather, the King of Scots, than at that of the Norwegian sovereign. Thorfinn was, indeed, heir to the crown, since Malcolm had no sons and Thorfinn was the son of his elder daughter. Yet he made no claim to the throne when Malcolm died in 1034 and his junior grandson Duncan succeeded as King. Only when Duncan brought an army north, claiming tribute from him, did Earl Thorfinn cross the Pentland Firth and chase him to his death.

Macbeth then succeeded according to the old law of tanistry, which gave the crown to the senior collateral relative, and still Thorfinn made no protest. On the contrary, he and King Macbeth appear to have lived in amity throughout their long reigns and it is even probable that they made a pilgrimage to Rome together.

Ironically, in standing aloof from the perils of kingship, Thorfinn avoided the fate which finally befell Macbeth.

He spent his last years in Birsay, where he built himself a palace, and also a church which the saga called 'a splendid minster'. It used to be assumed that both were situated on the Brough, although the little chapel there could scarcely be described as a splendid minster, and it is particularly unworthy of islands with such a magnificent building tradition. As for the remains identified as a palace, they might have been used for any domestic purpose. Today, increasing numbers of people are inclining to the theory advanced by R. G. Lamb that the ruins on the Brough of Birsay are those of a Norse monastery that replaced the earlier Pictish one, while the true minster and palace await excavation on the mainland opposite, where local tradition has always placed them.

How long had the islanders been Christians by the time Thorfinn's minster was built? According to the saga, the Norwegian King Olaf Tryggvason sailed to Orkney in 995, soon after he had been converted himself, and announced to Earl Sigurd: 'It is my wish that you should be baptised, and all under you. Otherwise you will die here at once, and I shall carry fire and sword through the islands.' Sigurd consented, possibly because he and his people had been Christians for considerably longer than King Olaf. Once again, the value of the saga account is that it reflects the spirit of the age in describing King Olaf's methods of proselytisation. Some scholars, pointing to the evidence of the Brough of Birsay in particular, believe that the interval of paganism was a brief one, but no doubt this varied greatly from island to island.

Thorfinn the Mighty's long life ended in 1064, and relative peace reigned in the isles until King Magnus of Norway appeared in Orkney in 1098, on his way to reduce them to his obedience. He was a murderous thug of the traditional sort. He carried off the grandsons of Earl Thorfinn and left his own son Sigurd as his deputy in Orkney. He plundered Lewis, the Uists, Skye, Mull and Tiree, and after devastating Islay, he made the Isle of Man his base for an attack on the Welsh.

Magnus concluded the first known agreement between a Scottish and Norwegian king, defining their territories in a manner that acknowledged formally the Norse conquest of the isles. In order to include the Mull of Kintyre as an island according to the wording of the treaty, he had himself carried across the isthmus between east and west Loch Tarbert in a skiff with its rudder set. His career ended violently in Ireland in 1103.

The grandsons of Thorfinn, Magnus and Haakon, were left in joint control of their earldom until the cousins quarrelled. In 1117 Haakon murdered Magnus on the isle of Egilsay, where a church still stands, dedicated to his memory. It possesses the northernmost example that survives of the round tower of Ireland, Orkney's most conspicuous landmark from the sea. There had been little evidence of sanctity in the life of Magnus, but people who made pilgrimages to his tomb began to announce miracles, and twenty years after his death, now seen as a martyrdom, his nephew Earl Rognvald laid the foundations of a more impressive memorial than the church of Egilsay.

Thus there came into being the cathedral of Saint Magnus at Kirkwall, the most magnificent structure ever raised in any of the Atlantic islands. Masons of the Durham school were brought to contribute their skill, and by mid-century the new choir and transepts soared above the little port.

The piety of Earl Rognvald, commemorated so gloriously in stone, also inspired him to go on a crusade in the company of William, first Bishop of Orkney. The saga account of their adventures gives no impression that they were burdened by religious motives. Although it was written after Rognvald had been canonised, it describes the expedition as Viking piracy of the traditional kind, in which they harried Spain, collected booty, and were not restrained by the Bishop from taking their captives to the nearest slave market when they reached the Mediterranean. In the Holy Land they found no infidels to fight, and so they returned home happily with their swag. Perhaps it helped to finance the building of the cathedral.

Rognvald was murdered by his relatives in 1158 and was declared a Saint in Rome thirty-four years later. The Bishop who promoted his cause was Bjarni the poet. His home on the island of Wyre is possibly the earliest stone castle that has survived in Scotland, built by his father Kolbein Hruga and known as Cubbie Roo's castle today. From its well-tended walls the tower of Saint Magnus, Egilsay, can be seen to the north and the spire of Saint Magnus, Kirkwall, to the south. Bjarni could gaze on both, but his imagination was also fired by the legends of the Jomsvikings, and the lay he composed about them is the sole substantial contribution which the Scottish islands made to the Norse literature of that age.

Across the water from his home he could also see the isle of Gairsay, where lived a companion of Saint Rognvald named Sweyn. He too preserved the spirit of the Viking age. On one occasion he seized a merchant ship belonging to monks of the Scilly Isles and plundered it. Nowhere between those southern isles and Gairsay was safe from his thieving hands, as he set out on his annual raiding expeditions. Rognvald warned him to give it up, but he would not, until be perished in Ireland. By this time his sainted friend was dead. As Sweyn faced his own end, he declared with the utmost confidence: 'Let all men know that I belong to the bodyguard of Earl Rognvald, and now my trust is in him where he stands with God.'

Such were the people who left such a vigorous, distinctive and enduring influence in the Scottish islands.

4

Lordship of the Isles

At the end of the Viking age the western isles found themselves between the gravitational pull of two powerful magnets. To the north of the Butt of Lewis lay the Orkney and Shetland islands which belonged to the Orkney earldom. The Orkney earls advanced a claim to the Hebrides on several occasions at the height of their power during the eleventh century. To the south of these lay the Isle of Man, whose ruler was invested with the title of King, although he was subordinate to the Norwegian sovereign. He was the recognised ruler of all the northern Scottish islands as far as Lewis, whatever the Orkney Earls might claim, and when the great King Godfrey fought his way to the throne of Man in 1079 he enforced his title to them effectively. He is remembered in Manx tradition as King Orry, and he spent much of his time in Islay, where he may have been the first to entrench himself on the site of Dunyveg castle.

Seen from Norway, the Hebrides appeared as the southern isles, or Sudreys. When the Norse diocese of Orry's kingdom was established in about 1100, the term became corrupted, so that it is now known as the bishopric of Sodor and Man.

King Orry's son Olaf ruled Man effectively for about forty years, but took a viper into the bosom of his family when he permitted one of his daughters to marry Somerled of Argyll. His name appears respectable enough, Norse for summer-sailor. But he possessed a Gaelic pedigree that can be established with reasonable certainty to the beginning of the ninth century, and in outline to the far-off days before the establishment of the kingdom of Dalriada in Scotland in about the year 500. Somerled set out to recover the islands of this kingdom from the rule of Man by force of arms, and by the time of his death he had restored Mull and Islay, as well as many smaller isles of the Sudreys, to Gaelic control. His descendants were Clan Dougall and Clan Donald.

The house of Somerled set about the restoration of Iona, which had remained a place of pilgrimage and interment throughout the Viking age. King Somerled himself built the mortuary chapel which is still to be seen there, dedicated to Columba's cousin and contemporary, Saint Oran. A little later the church of Saint Ronan was erected. Somerled's son Ranald (or Reginald) built the Romanesque abbey church that is still used by the Iona Community, and the Augustinian nunnery, now a well-tended ruin. He invited monks of the order of Saint Benedict to occupy the new premises and the last Columban Abbot, Cellach, became the first Benedictine one. Cellach petitioned the Pope to take his abbey under the direct protection of the Holy See, to which Innocent III agreed in 1203.

The achievement of King Somerled had a curious consequence. The two largest Hebridean islands, Lewis and Skye, had been Pictish in the days of the Celtic Church. Now they remained once again outside the Gaelic sphere of influence, detached pendicles of the kingdom of the Sudreys and Man. King Orry had established a Council that met on the Tynwald Hill of Man, consisting of thirty-two leading men of the islands, of whom sixteen came from the Hebrides. When only Lewis and Skye remained within his kingdom the number was reduced to twenty-four members, still the number in the Isle of Man's House of Keys today. At the time, it was designed to include representatives of the two islands in the north.

During the final years of Norwegian sovereignty over the Hebrides, a younger son of the King of Man called Leod received Lewis, Harris and Skye as his inheritance. He made his home on the rock of Dunvegan, where his curtain wall, surmounted by later battlements, is still to be seen. He bequeathed this property, together with Harris, to his son Tormod, a name that was to become altered to Norman. His other son Thorkil, which became Torcuil in Gaelic, received Lewis.

In the lifetime of Leod the King of Scots approached Haakon IV of Norway with an offer to purchase the Hebrides, but the great King Haakon had no intention of selling off the islands. On the contrary, he added Iceland, Greenland and the Faroe islands to his empire. The most powerful man in the western isles at this time was Ewen, the descendant of Somerled and representative of the senior branch of Clan Dougall. In 1248 Haakon invited Ewen to visit him in his capital of Bergen, and there invested him with the formal title of King. It was a shrewd gesture, in as much as Ewen owed allegiance to the King of Scots for his possessions on the mainland, and in the event of a war between the two monarchs he would be torn by a conflict of loyalties. Such an outcome became increasingly likely when the Scots took to invading the Sudreys. In 1262 they made an assault on Skye, 'sacked villages, desecrated churches, and . . . in a wanton fury raised children on the point of their spears and shook them until they fell to the ground.' So says the Saga of Haakon.

Haakon was an old man by the time he decided that he must mount an expedition to his Scottish islands and demonstrate his authority. He summoned Ewen to his support, but Ewen resigned his island kingdom into Haakon's hands rather than fight against the King of Scots. It was the most honourable response he could have made. Haakon sailed south, taking his fleet through the narrows between Skye and the mainland which have been called Kyleakin ever since, the Straits of Haakon. He called at Islay where the junior branch of Somerled's descendants lived in the castle of Dunyveg, the Clan Donald. These showed equal reluctance to join him, but since they did not possess any mainland territories for which they owed allegiance to the Scottish King, Haakon threatened to ravage Islay unless they performed their duty. Reluctantly they submitted.

Haakon led his ships round the Mull of Kintyre and anchored in the harbour of Lamlash off Arran before continuing as far as the Cumbraes. There was an inconclusive skirmish on the coast of Ayrshire before bad weather compelled the Norwegians to lift anchor and make for home. Their ships were battered by a storm and King Haakon died at Kirkwall after they had reached the haven of Orkney. He had come too late in time and too late in the year. But even if the weather had favoured him he could not have held the western isles when Ewen of Clan Dougall stood aside and the MacDonalds were lukewarm in their support.

The Scots followed up their advantage in 1264 by ravaging the isles and killing Haakon's supporters. Two years later the sovereignty of them all, even the Isle of Man, was ceded to the Scottish Crown. Alexander III, King of Scots, placated the Norwegian King by the gift of his daughter in marriage. Twenty years later this had momentous consequences when Alexander fell to his death on a stormy night as he rode along the cliffs of Kinghorn beside the Forth. He left no son, and the baby daughter of the King of Norway and his wife was the sole heir by direct descent to the Scottish Crown.

Europe north of the fifty-fifth parallel consists of Scotland and Scandinavia, in the maritime world of the Atlantic islands. Briefly, the Scottish islands enjoyed the prospect that they might be drawn back into their natural orbit when the baby Margaret, the Maid of Norway, was recognised as Queen of Scots. In 1290, when she was considered to be old enough, she took ship to her kingdom, only to die in Orkney as her ancestor King Haakon had done. The consequence was Edward I of England's attempt to add Scotland to his empire, and Scotland's long war of independence.

Apart from all the other upheavals it caused, there were the consequences of the rival claims of Bruce and Balliol to the Scottish Crown. The MacDougalls supported the Balliol faction, as did the great patriot William Wallace until his capture and death. But Angus MacDonald of Islay was among the staunchest supporters of Bruce, and brought his clansmen to fight with him on the field of Bannockburn. After the victory of King Robert in 1314, the MacDougalls' lands were forfeited and the MacDonalds received their island of Mull with all its surrounding satellites. The MacDougalls did recover their mainland lordship when their Chief married a granddaughter of Robert Bruce. But the descendants of King Ewen, who had been described as 'the most prominent Highlander in Scotland in his day', passed out of the history of the western isles. It was the junior branch of Clan Donald who took their place. In 1354 MacDonald of Islay was styled 'Dominus Insulorum' – Lord of the Isles – for the first time in any document that has survived.

The casualty of the war of independence was the Isle of Man, not least because its inhabitants showed no enthusiasm for Scottish rule. This must have been one of the most miserable periods of their history as they were invaded by the English, Irish and Scots in turn, until all hope of establishing Scottish sovereignty was abandoned a few years after Robert Bruce's death.

The Hebrides, by contrast, embarked on a period of semi-autonomous rule that may well have been the happiest in their troubled history. This was the era of the Hundred Years' War between England and France, followed by the Wars of the Roses in England. The kingdom of Scotland relapsed repeatedly into anarchy and strife during the same centuries. Relatively immune from the miseries that afflicted such large areas of Europe during this age, the islanders developed the gifts they had received from their parent country of Ireland to lay the foundations of their own Gaelic civilisation.

Among the bearers of these gifts was the bardic dynasty whose name MacMhuirich became corrupted in the Hebrides to Currie. The first of this name is supposed to have been Muireadhach Albanach, Murach the Scot, of the Irish bardic family of O'Daly. One of his poems was addressed to an Earl of Lennox who died in 1217.

Murach's finest composition is judged to be his elegy for his dead wife, while another is of particular interest because it was evidently composed in the Adriatic while he was on a crusade. His descendants were to become the bards and historians to the Lords of the Isles.

The first Beaton probably reached Islay in the time of Angus MacDonald who fought at Bannockburn, as a member of his Irish wife's household. This family brought a knowledge of medicine in addition to their literary enthusiasms, and Patrick Beaton, the earliest in Scottish record, became chief physician to King Robert Bruce. None of their surviving medical manuscripts can be dated to before 1400, but their contents extend back to the texts of Hippocrates and include the chief scientific authorities, Greek, Arabic and European, of the intervening centuries, with enlightened commentaries in Gaelic. In the course of time, separate branches of the Beatons settled in Mull and Skye, and by the early seventeenth century they were reported on the mainland to have been performing successful operations 'time out of mind'.

The archivists to the Lords of the Isles were the MacPhees or MacDuffies. The earliest of their name on record was Lector of Iona in 1164, the year of King Somerled's death, and later they became owners of the isle of Colonsay. Pathetically few of the muniments in their charge have survived. There is no more than a single Gaelic charter of 1408, a long, sophisticated document that could only have been one of many. The signatures of MacDonald and his witnesses are the earliest secular autographs of their kind in Scottish records. Another charter of 1415 in Latin attests the use of both languages for administrative purposes at this time.

A Council of the Isles met on an island in Loch Finlaggan in the north of Islay. Little more than the foundations of its complex of buildings can be seen there today, most of them buried under rank grass. This is the more regrettable because the palace of Finlaggan is a notable example of a form of building especially characteristic of the western mainland and islands in this age – the unfortified mansion. This palace did stand on an island, but the surrounding water was no substitute for stout walls since a horse could trot through its shallows in a matter of minutes. Nothing could demonstrate the prosperity and stability of the islands in the days of the Lordship better than this defenceless structure, built at a time when massive castles were the norm in other parts of the country.

Sixteen Hebridean representatives had attended the assembly in

Man. Here on Islay, 'Fourteen persons sat down in the Council Isle, and discerned, decreed and gave suits forth upon all debatable matters according to the laws made by Reginald Mac Somerled, called in his time King of the Occident Isles.' So Donald Monro, Archdeacon of the Isles, wrote in 1549. In such a literate society these laws must have been committed to paper, though no trace of them remains. The treaty under which the isles passed to the Scottish crown stated that 'the men of the said islands, as well the lesser as greater, shall be subject to the laws and customs of the realm of Scotland', but it appears that they enjoyed a high degree of autonomy. Different islands had families of hereditary brieves or judges, from whose verdicts people could apparently appeal to the Council.

This included the Abbot of Iona among its members. From the fourteenth century until the Reformation this office was monopolised by the Mackinnons of Mull, descended from Finguine, who is presumed to have been of the Founder's kin. One of Iona's monuments commemorates five generations of this family. It displays Gilbride Mackinnon, wearing a pointed bascinet, chain-mail on his chest and shoulders, a claymore at his belt, carrying a shield on which is depicted a galley. Below the ship an otter pursues a salmon. This sculpture was carved in the second half of the fourteenth century when Gilbride's great-grandson was Abbot, and its inscription names the intervening generations.

Craftsmanship in stone is another of the arts that flowered under the patronage of the Lords of the Isles, in a form that is unique to the region. There are surviving examples of it on the Council's isle of Islay as well as elsewhere, though the most interesting concentration of these sculptures is preserved on Iona, the greater number now assembled under cover in the abbey buildings.

The earliest portrait of a member of the house of Somerled was erected on the little isle of Texa off the parish of Kildalton in Islay, until it was removed from there in the present century. It depicts Ranald, the eldest son of John the Good, a person of some significance in the Hebridean story for he is the progenitor of the MacDonalds of Clanranald. His father had made a second marriage to a daughter of Robert II, the first Stewart King of Scots, and their son Donald succeeded as Lord of the Isles while his elder brother, Ranald, had to be content with a lesser inheritance. However, this included the huge castle of Tioram in Moidart in which he died, as well as some of the western isles.

Donald, Lord of the Isles by virtue of his royal descent, made a fateful marriage to the heiress of the earldom of Ross. This vast property, comprising much of the northern Highlands, also contained lands in Aberdeenshire. Here Donald's first cousin James Stewart, Earl of Mar, held sway, a man described as 'a leader of caterans' or freebooters. His father, who had died five years earlier, was the rogue remembered as the Wolf of Badenoch, the desecrator of Elgin cathedral. These semi-royals were reducing the mainland of Scotland to a state of anarchy while the King of Scots, James I, was a prisoner of the English. It would have been well for the Lord of the Isles, as the outcome was to prove, if he had kept clear of their squabbles and remained in his comparatively peaceful island world.

When he appeared with his Gaelic host to assert his legitimate title to the eastern properties of his wife's earldom, the English-speaking Lowlanders rose against them, and Stewart of Mar placed himself at their head while the very burgesses of Aberdeen rallied to him in a panic. So was fought the bloody and inconclusive battle of what became known as the Red Harlaw. A tall monument still dominates the field in which it took place, while two poems remind us of a fatal element in the conflict. One is the traditional ballad in which local people told the tale of carnage in their Aberdonian speech: the other is the elegant poem in which the MacMhuirich composed his incitement to battle in classical Gaelic. MacLeod of Dunvegan was in the company of the Lord of the Isles, and while he was away his bard in Skye composed another poem, expressing the anxiety of those who awaited his return.

> I sleep not night or day,
> While I do not see from this beach in the north
> The good ship with its white sail,
> The ship of the man by whom foes are routed.

The battle of Harlaw in 1411 achieved no apparent result, yet it proved to be a portent for the future. In the Gaelic society of the islands such families as the MacDonalds of Islay and the MacLeods of Skye were bound by ties of marriage. It was otherwise in the earldom of Ross, where Donald of the Isles was asserting a feudal authority, and where the most influential Gaelic kindred, the Mackenzies, were opposed to him. Ten years after the battle of Harlaw he took a step which appears to have been designed to remedy this.

For the first time, a Mackenzie was appointed Abbot of Iona when a vacancy occurred.

Even if the motive was a political one, it was to prove a blessing to the abbey. Abbot Dominic Mackenzie held his post for nearly forty-five years, after the Mackinnons had neglected the fabric of the church and embezzled its revenues for the benefit of their families. Abbot Dominic employed the man who is commemorated in the Latin inscription, 'Donald O Brolchain did this work,' to carry out much-needed repairs as well as handsome embellishments. It is fitting that Mackenzie's effigy still lies beneath those words, in the choir.

Donald of the Isles visited his captive King in London, where he was esteemed as a most cultured man. It is his signature that appears on the Gaelic charter, and he who was responsible for the appointment of the reforming Abbot. But he had married a wife with the ring of the Nibelungs and their descendants inherited the fatal gold. The lure of the Earldom of Ross lost them the Lordship of the Isles in the reign of their grandson John.

He lived through a period of turmoil in which English dynasties fell like skittles in the Wars of the Roses, and the fate of the royal house of Stewart frequently hung in the balance. Again and again the King died, leaving only a solitary child as his heir, and his relatives scrambled for perquisites and power during his minority. One of the most unscrupulous of these was James, 9th Earl of Douglas, the tycoon of the Border country. While James III was still a youth Douglas came to John of the Isles, bearing a proposal from England. Douglas and MacDonald, the greatest men of the English-speaking and Gaelic-speaking regions of the realm, would divide the old Scotland, north of the narrow waist formed by the Clyde and the Forth, between them. In return for recognising the ancient claim of the English King that he was Lord Paramount of Scotland, they would be invested by him in their authority.

In effect, this would have given John of the Isles the birthright which his family had failed, in their opinion, to obtain from the Stewarts. It would have turned Gaelic Scotland, with its islands, into a principality like Wales. The Lord of the Isles accepted these terms in a treaty that he signed in 1462 at Ardtornish, a castle whose ruins stand by the shore to the east of Loch Aline, where the ferry from Mull reaches Morvern. Immediately afterwards he assumed regal powers in the north, and even began to collect the King's rents. But the Black Douglas did not prosper in the south, the English made a truce with the Scottish government, and James III grew to manhood while John of the Isles was left in treasonable isolation.

In the circumstances John escaped lightly. Forfeited for treason in 1475, he was restored to his island Lordship, and created a Peer by virtue of this office. Possessing no legitimate heir, the succession passed to his natural son, Angus. But he lost his mainland territories with the Earldom of Ross, and it was Angus who set out to recover the power of the ring, assisted by his cousin, Alasdair of Lochalsh.

The popular support Angus received suggests that the measures taken by central government to extend its authority over the Gaelic islands and Highlands engendered a secessionist movement which John of the Isles could neither direct nor suppress. The strength of feeling nourishing the movement was expressed in Gaelic prose and verse when Angus was murdered in Inverness in 1490 by Diarmaid O Cairbre, his Irish harper. In the eyes of the King he was a dangerous trouble-maker, and his own father had fought against him in the sea-battle of the Sound of Mull that gave its name to Bloody Bay near Tobermory. But the Gaelic annals commemorated him as 'MacDonald of Scotland, the young lord, the best man of his contemporaries in Ireland or Scotland'.

The Dean of Knoydart addressed a poem to the severed head of the harper, executed for his crime, in which he went so far as to describe Angus as the Hebridean King.

> By thee was destroyed the King of Islay,
> A man who dispensed wine and silver,
> Whose locks were fresh and crisp,
> Thou head of Diarmaid O Cairbre.

> Islay's King of festive goblets,
> Who raised his friends to honour;
> Woe to him who wounded his bright white skin,
> Thou head of Diarmaid O Cairbre.

The bard to the Lord of the Isles himself, Giolla Coluim, paid tribute to the qualities of the dead heir.

> No wonder I am so deeply afflicted
> At the death of Margaret's son;
> When I remember the goodness of the man
> I cannot bear to look upon a Prince.

As a matter of fact this Prince was one of the most attractive and talented of all the Stewart sovereigns, James IV, and he is the only one on record as having learned the Gaelic language. Yet it is difficult to approve the step he took next. When Alasdair of Lochalsh continued the depredations in which he had engaged in company with the dead Angus, the King made John of the Isles responsible for his nephew's behaviour and stripped him of his Lordship. In 1493 he left Islay forever, to spend the remainder of his days a pensioner at the Stewart court. The Hebrides were deprived of their ancient source of law and government without any effective alternative authority being planted in its place.

But the Hebridean resistance movement continued after the dissolution of the Lordship of the Isles, with a persistence that still astonishes, while island society relapsed gradually into chaos, all the more so after James IV was killed on the field of Flodden and succeeded by another minor as King. As usual, it is a contemporary Gaelic poem that brings home to us the islanders' sense of loss.

It is no joy without Clan Donald,
It is no strength to be without them,
The best race in the round world;
To them belongs every goodly man.

A race the best for service and shelter,
A race the best for valour of hand;
Ill I deem the shortness of her skein
By whom their thread was spun.

In the van of Clan Donald
Learning was commanded,
And in their rear were
Service and honour and self-respect.

For sorrow and for sadness
I have forsaken wisdom and learning.
On their account I have forsaken all things.
It is no joy without Clan Donald.

5

Campbell Takeover

The abolition of the Lordship of the Isles created a power vacuum, and it was the Campbells who stepped forward to fill it. Originally this family had been of little consequence compared with the house of Somerled. But one of their number had supported Robert Bruce and married his sister, and then another had married the grand-daughter of a Stewart King and been created Lord Campbell in 1445. Colin, the son of this pair, married the Stewart heiress of Lorne and became Earl of Argyll in 1457. He also received a commission of Lieutenancy that invested him with vice-regal powers. The Campbells were among the earliest Gaelic families to offer themselves as trusty servants of the Crown, and to be rewarded with its offices.

Their stronghold was the castle of Inischonaill, whose ruins can still be seen on a little island in Loch Awe. But in 1473 Colin of Argyll moved his headquarters to Inveraray on Loch Fyne, and Inischonaill became a sinister Campbell prison. In it the first Earl of Argyll kept a very special captive, Donald Dubh MacDonald, the disinherited heir to the Lordship of the Isles. Donald was the son of Angus, murdered by his harper in Inverness, but he was also the grandson of the Earl of Argyll, whose daughter Angus had married. It is not clear whether she was a consenting party to the incarceration of her baby son.

Colin of Argyll died in the year after the forfeiture of the Lordship of the Isles, leaving his son Archibald, the 2nd Earl, to exploit the situation. He obtained a new commission of Lieutenancy that gave him sweeping powers in the Isles, and he was quick to place his cousin John Campbell in Iona in succession to the last Mackinnon Abbot. He also petitioned the Pope to recognise his seat as the Bishopric of the Isles, which augmented Campbell authority in them still further.

Donald Dubh was nineteen years old before a party of MacDon-alds succeeded in rescuing him from his prison. In 1503 they made their way stealthily from Glencoe to Loch Awe, rowed across the water in the dark, stormed Inischonaill and carried the youth to safety. His freedom lasted for three years, until he was recaptured and imprisoned this time in Edinburgh castle. But once he had been seen, he was recognised throughout the Hebrides as rightful Chief of Clan Donald, and the resistance movement was continued by others in his name.

However, it was not until forty years after he had made his first escape from captivity that Donald Dubh was able to break out of Edinburgh in 1543. Throughout the islands and the Gaelic west people thronged to his support, Macleans of Duart and Mackinnons from Mull, MacQuarrie of the isle of Ulva, MacLeods from Lewis and Skye, MacDonalds of Clanranald and the mainland. In retrospect it appears an astonishing gesture on the part of men generally accused of preferring the anarchy which the abolition of the Lordship had engendered in the region. Once more the Council of the Isles was convened at Finlaggan in 1545, and to it came every island Chief of any account.

This was the last serious attempt to revive the Lordship as an instrument of Hebridean local government, and it expired when Donald Dubh died of a fever in Ireland while he was on a recruiting campaign. In the sixty years of his life he had enjoyed less than five years of freedom and none of the happiness of family life. James of Dunyveg was chosen to succeed him after his death and wrote to the Privy Council of Ireland, informing it of his election as Lord of the Isles. But lack of support led him prudently to drop his claim and return to his allegiance. As for the unfortunate Donald Dubh, he received in death what he had been denied in life, the funeral due to a Lord of the Isles.

James of Dunyveg received equal honour at his death. He and his brother were performing military service in Ireland in 1565 when Angus was killed and James taken prisoner by O'Neill. Both Queen Elizabeth of England and Mary of Scotland wrote to O'Neill demanding his release, a remarkable instance of agreement, especially as it was endorsed by the judgement which the Gaelic annalist pronounced on the MacDonald Chief. 'His peer was not to be found at that time among the Clan Donald of Ireland or Scotland, and his own people would not have deemed it too much to give his weight in gold for his ransom, if he could have been ransomed.' But neither two Queens nor the love of his people could save James MacDonald of Islay from his fate.

The chief activity of the Argyll family during this period seems to have consisted in planting Campbell wives in the homes of leading Hebrideans. James of Islay was married to one of them, Hector Maclean of Duart to another. When Angus MacDonald, the heir to Dunyveg, married Maclean of Duart's daughter, his son consequently possessed two Campbell grandmothers. What part, if any, these ladies played in island politics is beyond divination. Suffice to say that Angus embarked on a quarrel with his brother-in-law, Lachlan, the 13th Chief of Duart, which led to the loss of both their properties to the Campbells.

The quarrel erupted over their disputed ownership of the long peninsula of western Islay known as the Rinns. At its northern end lies the tiny Nave (or Holy) island, at its southern one the inlet of Portnahaven with its entrance protected by a rocky islet. Between these extremities, the cliffs of the Rinns face the open Atlantic, a treasury of wrecks. The peninsula is joined to the remainder of Islay only by a narrow plain between the shallow sea inlets of Lochindaal and Loch Gruinart, so that the Rinns comprise almost a separate island, larger than Coll or Tiree and scarcely less fertile. This was a desirable property, yet it is unlikely that its ownership would have given rise to armed conflict if the Lord of the Isles had still been exercising his jurisdiction at nearby Finlaggan.

The guilty party appears to have been Sir Lachlan of Duart, for all that he was evidently a man of some culture. His father Hector had granted the lands of Pennycross in Mull to Andrew Beaton in 1572 'together with the supreme and principal office of surgeon' in his territories. The only visible souvenir of his family's presence here today is the cross that his son Malcolm erected by the shore of Loch Scridain, inscribed with the date 1582 and his own and his son's initials. About a decade after it had been placed there, Sir Lachlan made the medical services at his disposal available to his Campbell relatives. He wrote a letter in Gaelic which Dr John Bannerman has translated as follows: 'A thousand greetings from Lachlan Maclean to his personal physician, namely Malcolm Beaton: and he asks you, for his own sake and that of his son, the Laird of Coll, to respond in the matter of going to the daughter of Argyll's daughter, and to do her all the good you can. That is enough, but my best wishes to Stewart of Appin's daughter and all her offspring.' He concludes by signing himself: 'I am Lachlan Maclean', *Misi Lochlaoinn Mac Giolla Eoin*.

The impression conveyed by this solicitous letter is unfortunately a deceptive one. Lachlan's father had died leaving his estate in debt. The power of the Macleans had expanded as that of the MacDonalds diminished, matched by an extravagant lifestyle in their splendid castle on the Black Height, and rather than retrench, Sir Lachlan set out to increase the means of supporting it. The methods he used have earned for him the epithet of a 'ruffianly megalomaniac' from the Hebridean scholar Dr John Lorne Campbell. One of his ploys was to seize the church lands of Mull, adopting the Protestant religion for the purpose. Another was to lay claim to the Rinns of Islay.

He invited his brother-in-law Angus MacDonald to visit him in order to discuss the question of ownership. When his guest arrived, he was thrown into the dungeon, and released only after he had signed away his title to the Rinns.

This occurred in 1586, and it was not long before Angus of Islay invited Sir Lachlan to pay a return visit to Dunyveg. In his simplicity, MacDonald does not seem to have reflected that the Chief of Duart would only have walked into such an obvious trap if he had devised a means of using it to his advantage. So it proved when he was imprisoned in his turn, and the Earl of Argyll immediately obtained a royal commission to intervene in the quarrel. In obedience to this warrant Angus delivered Sir Lachlan to Argyll, who first conducted him home to Duart, then to the King. James VI lectured him severely, though he did not descend to any ruling on the ownership of the Rinns. Sir Lachlan was then allowed to return home.

Archibald the Grim, 7th Earl of Argyll, was the most evil of all the Campbell Chiefs. He had succeeded only two years earlier, so that he had not yet found the time to hound the MacGregors to their doom in the lands that were to be erected into the Campbell earldom of Breadalbane. But although he was young in crime, he soon displayed a flair in selecting his associates. Henceforth, every move of his reveals that he had decided to use Maclean as his tool for the destruction of the house of Islay, rather than the other way round, for the MacDonalds presented the more formidable target as well as the richer prize. It would be relatively simple to mop up the extravagant and insolvent Macleans, as the outcome was to prove.

The sense of security with which Sir Lachlan returned to Mull expressed itself in no uncertain manner. When a Spanish galleon of the Armada was wrecked in Tobermory bay in 1588, Maclean enlisted its sailors as his mercenaries and launched them against the MacDonalds to right and left. At the end of that year he was brought to trial in Edinburgh, charged with crimes that would have brought anyone to the scaffold in ordinary circumstances. It was proved that he had 'burnt with fire the lands of Canna, Rum, Eigg and the isle of Muck, and here plundered the same: that he slew and cruelly murdered Hector son of John of Canna and Fair David his brother, with a great number of wives, bairns and poor labourers of the ground, about eight or nine score of souls. Whoever escaped the fire was not spared by his bloody sword'.

The supreme enormity was that he had employed foreigners to commit these atrocities in the small isles. Yet he was enabled to escape from his prison in Edinburgh, and after he had done so he forfeited nothing more than his bail.

The royal authority was vested in Archibald the Grim, and he ought to have used it to arrest Lachlan of Duart and bring him back to face justice. Instead, he used his commission to bring a charge against Angus of Islay that he had failed to hand over some Maclean hostages, taken when Sir Lachlan had visited Dunyveg. Argyll represented the dispute between the island Chiefs to James VI in such terms that the King actually bestowed MacDonald lands on the man who had been ravaging them. This was the traditional method of setting the Gaels at one another's throats, employed by successive Stewart regimes.

The astonishment of Angus of Islay may be imagined, and also his sense of relief when Campbell of Cawdor castle, a junior cousin of the Earl of Argyll, made friendly overtures to him. Campbell offered to purchase some lands in the isle of Gigha, which lies between Islay and the Mull of Kintyre. No doubt this helped to defray the expenses when Angus was commanded to travel to Edinburgh with Lachlan of Duart in 1591, to face the King. One of them had escaped from trial on the gravest of capital charges, the other was accused at the most of a misdemeanour, yet both were imprisoned on their arrival as though their crimes were equal. They were released only upon finding security.

Campbell of Cawdor appeared once more, like a guardian angel, and undertook to stand surety for Angus, whose two sons were taken as hostages. The same had occurred to Angus's father and he had benefited by it, not only in his education but in what he had learned of the mysteries of Scottish government. It appeared that

Angus's son and heir might prove even more fortunate when the susceptible King took a fancy to the boy and bestowed upon him a knighthood.

If Angus returned to Dunyveg with a sense of relief, it was short-lived. Two years later he found himself accused of treason on grounds that were by no means clear to him. When his property was forfeited he tried to save the lands by renouncing all his rights in them in favour of his son, Sir James, to whom the King had shown such favour. In 1596 he took the additional step of presenting himself without any summons before the King in Council, and submitting himself to the royal will. But while Lachlan of Duart went scot-free after all his crimes, there was no possible way in which the Mac-Donald Chief could find justice in Edinburgh.

Sir Lachlan invaded Islay in 1598, and a bloody battle was fought beside the sands of Gruinart bay, that favourite estuary of migrating geese that borders the Rinns. Sir James MacDonald marched to bar his passage there, and was left for dead after he had been struck by an arrow. But he recovered. It was his uncle, Sir Lachlan, who perished within sight of the peninsula he had coveted for so long.

The death of this ruffian ought to have freed the MacDonald inheritance from further danger. But Sir James, in whom it was now vested, was evidently aware that it was still at risk. There was no son to whom he could convey the property as a precaution, since he was not yet married. His solution was a proposal that the Mull of Kintyre, the most desirable of the MacDonald territories, should be conveyed to the Crown while a royal garrison should occupy Dunyveg castle. But his father, Angus of Islay, had sealed his fate in transferring the title-deeds of Clan Donald to him, as surely as if he had handed Sir James the Koh-i-noor diamond.

It took the Campbells a year or two to plot the next move, and during this interval the Thane of Cawdor made his third appearance, bringing his sister to Sir James for a wife, an addition to his two Campbell grandmothers. Whatever this contributed to the im-broglio, Angus of Islay was fed with suspicions that his son was plotting against him with his Campbell relatives and arrested Sir James, handing him over to Campbell of Auchinbreack, who passed him on to Archibald the Grim. This occurred in 1603, the year in which Elizabeth of England died and James VI left Scotland to occupy her throne. He prided himself on possessing the wisdom and statecraft of Solomon. 'Here I sit,' he boasted after he had reached

London, 'and govern Scotland with my pen, which my predecessors could not do by the sword.'

While Solomon was on his way to the new Jerusalem, allegations against Sir James MacDonald were submitted to the Scottish Privy Council and in 1604 he was committed to Blackness castle, the time-dishonoured royal hostelry for Highland Chiefs. He was removed from here to Edinburgh in the following year, when he wrote a letter in Gaelic that the late Professor Angus Matheson published in translation. It is perhaps deliberately enigmatic, warning his friends not to make any attempt to rescue him.

'A greeting to you, friends and kinsmen. I have heard that you have come to Falkirk: and know that I am as satisfied with you as though I had need of you. But on account of all the information I have received, I do not purpose to do anything but remain as I am. And therefore I ask you to return home without delay and do not come nearer this town than the length you have come, and maintain strict secrecy lest any person whatsoever obtain information that you are in these parts. No more. But do not come to Stirling on your return lest anyone should obtain information that you are in these parts. Tell Donald to come here tonight and send my clothes back to me from the Blackness . . . .' It is the kind of letter a man would write when he knows he is the chosen victim of the mafia.

No sooner was Sir James locked in his Edinburgh prison than Archibald the Grim proposed himself as Crown tenant of the Mull of Kintyre, received the isle of Jura in addition, and instantly set about evicting their inhabitants to make room for Campbells. No offence had been alleged against them, nor had their proprietor been convicted of any crime. He had merely been hi-jacked. But in 1607 Sir James made a desperate attempt to escape, was recaptured, convicted of treason, condemned to death and had all his property forfeited. Well might he have reflected on the administration of justice in Edinburgh, which had allowed his uncle Sir Lachlan to go free, except for forfeiting his bail, after committing the most heinous crimes.

When Angus of Islay learned of the appalling consequences of his simplicity, he made an attempt to reach the ear of the King in London, presumably hoping that he might succeed in convincing him of the true state of affairs. He wrote, 'Beseeching your Majesty for the cause of God to respect my age and poor estate, and to let me know your Highness's own mind signed with your Majesty's hand.' But if he supposed that he could plant any misgivings in the smug mind of King James about the misuse of his authority behind his back, Angus was to be disappointed. Archibald the Grim continued to dominate the Scottish Privy Council, as he laid his plans for the final assault.

In 1612, while Sir James MacDonald still lay in prison under sentence of death, his father sold his remaining rights in the heritage of Clan Donald to Campbell of Cawdor for the paltry sum of 6000 merks.

His younger son Angus Òg now prepared to defend his family's last foothold in what remained of the kingdom of Somerled, the strong castle of Dunyveg. His brother James wrote to him from his prison, begging him to abandon such a futile and fatal undertaking, but his Campbell relatives incited him to continue, warning him that if he did not hold out the entire Clan Donald might be ruined. Their advice prevailed until a battery of artillery was launched against Dunyveg in 1615, the castle was captured and its gallant defender taken prisoner. Angus of Islay had died miserably in the previous year, and now that Sir James was the Chief a warrant was issued for his execution. Again he broke out of prison and this time he made his escape, but they hanged his brother Angus Òg in Edinburgh in his place.

It was the signal for Archibald the Grim to move. Such was his power that he was able to employ government troops to scourge the MacDonald lands, though to his vexation he found himself compelled to pay £7000 for the privilege in due course. Sir James attempted a return to lead the resistance of his people to what had become a campaign of naked genocide. But he was compelled to flee to Antrim in Ireland, where his family also possessed lands. Argyll pursued him there, until he finally made his escape to Spain.

Once the MacDonald lands were securely in Campbell hands, it was as though the death sentence passed on Sir James had been no more than a mere hoax. He found it safe to visit London in 1620, where James VI was graciously pleased to grant him a pension, followed by a royal pardon. But there was no question of restoring his property to him, nor was he ever permitted to return to his native land.

Sir James possessed children, and his wife was no less than Campbell of Cawdor's daughter. Yet after his death in London his widow was reduced to petitioning for their maintenance, the final reference to the heirs of the last MacDonald to have been brought up in the stately home of his ancestors on Islay, before they disappeared from history without trace.

Archibald the Grim consolidated his grip on Kintyre, but the ancient seat of the Lordship of the Isles eluded him. The open enemy of the MacDonalds was passed at the winning post by the apparent friend as Campbell of Cawdor moved in to take possession. He did not even hold Islay as a vassal of his Clan Chief, but as a fief of the Crown. Ever prompt to make the first move, Cawdor obtained his royal charter in 1614, the year before Dunyveg was surrendered. So Judas became the disciple of King James rather than of the Earl of Argyll, which was appropriate enough.

In the islands there lived a junior descendant of Somerled named John MacDonald, remembered as Iain Lom the bard. Perhaps his kinsfolk were comforted a little when he lashed the house of Campbell with the most venomous and astringent tongue of that age.

The sharp stroke of short pens
Protects the Campbell Chief,
He who is as eloquent as a parrot in his talk.
You filched from us by trickery
Verdant, lovely Islay
And Kintyre with its green plains.

6

MacLeod Mini-Kingdom

The territories of the sons of Leod, Tormod and Torcuil, centred on the north Minch. The descendants of Torcuil possessed Lewis, and later established themselves also on the isle of Raasay. The branch of Tormod were known as the MacLeods of Harris, although they lived across the water from there in their castle of Dunvegan on Skye. Other branches were settled in Assynt and Gairloch on the Scottish mainland. Here they were backed by mountains through which no roads penetrated, so that their nearest neighbours were the islanders across the Minch in the days when the most convenient means of travel was by sea.

Lewis-Harris and Skye, Scotland's two largest islands, had remained within the kingdom of Man after those further south had been conquered by King Somerled. Consequently they had remained more distinctively Norse, although today they are bastions of the Gaelic language. As late as 1304 an Earl of Ross described them as the 'foreign isles', despite the fact that they had passed to the Scottish Crown with all the western isles in 1266.

A unique souvenir of the MacLeods' Norse past is the Fairy Flag of Dunvegan. It is a piece of silk of Syrian origin, that has been dated to at least as early as the eleventh century. Probably it was a sacred relic brought back by Vikings from the Middle East, and there are plausible grounds for identifying it as the sacred talisman that they carried into battle, calling it Land Ravager. King Orry of Man took part in an unsuccessful invasion of England with the King of Norway in 1066, when Land Ravager may have come into his possession, to be handed on as an heirloom to Leod.

The gradual integration of the inhabitants of the MacLeod islands into the world of Gaelic culture can be glimpsed at a popular level in their fireside entertainments. From the thirteenth century the ballad craze swept through Europe, a retelling of folk legends in sung verse. The Norse themes were those of Sigurd the Dragon Slayer and other heroes of Norse mythology. Traces of them remain in the folklore of the northern isles, but with the Gaelic language it was the Ossianic heroes who supplanted them in the MacLeod islands. The leader of these was Finn, or Fingal, the father of Ossian.

He was supposed to have lived in the time of Saint Patrick in the fifth century, though this does not prevent him from fighting King Magnus of Norway in the eleventh, so timeless is oral tradition. The ballad makers were generally anonymous, and their verses were often sung to a chain-dance, as they still are in the Faroe islands to this day.

Among all the ballads of Europe, the Gaelic ones are notable for the antiquity and seriousness of their themes. In no other is there any equivalent of the conversations in which Ossian the son of Finn discusses the relative merits of Christian and pagan standards of behaviour with Saint Patrick. While the Lords of the Isles savoured the classical metres of the MacMhuirich bards, this more popular form of poetry was carrying their culture to the Butt of Lewis.

The MacLeod Chiefs themselves stood at the fountain-head. They attended the Council of the Isles at Finlaggan in Islay with their peers. After the Lords of the Isles had become Earls of Ross, Torcuil of Lewis obtained a charter in 1433, by which he held his island not from the Crown, but 'for homage and service' to MacDonald in his capacity as Earl. This helps to explain the loyalty of the MacLeods of Lewis to the Chiefs of Clan Donald.

The attitude of the MacLeods of Harris to the Lordship was more ambivalent, and there is a likely reason for this. The lords of Dunvegan claimed ownership of two large areas of Skye, the peninsula of Trotternish that points towards Lewis in the north, and that of Sleat, opposite to where a King had once granted them the lands of Glenelg. Whatever their original titles to Trotternish and Sleat, these were not recognised by MacDonald. In 1469 John of the Isles bestowed Sleat on his brother Hugh. The Chiefs of Harris and Lewis both witnessed the charter, evidently accepting the grant, however resentfully, and it received royal confirmation after John had been forfeited and the Lordship of the Isles abolished.

The King judged the Trotternish peninsula to be MacDonald property also, but in this case he bestowed it on Torcuil, the 8th Chief of Lewis, in 1498 with the offices of hereditary Baillie, explaining that 'the office and the estates came lawfully into the King's hands by reason of the forfeiture of John, Lord of the Isles'.

There is no apparent reason why MacLeod of Harris did not receive the disputed prize. He was an outstanding Chief named Alasdair Crotach, who succeeded his father in 1480 and preserved his patrimony through the hazardous years that followed the breakdown of law and order in the Hebrides. He is commemorated by the Fairy Tower that he built at Dunvegan, no doubt so called because the Fairy Flag was housed in it.

But Alasdair Crotach's most precious contribution to Hebridean architecture is his rebuilding of the church of Rodel in Harris. There is no finer ecclesiastical building in the Hebrides outside Iona, whose abbey it resembles in many of its details. Rodel is unique in possessing transepts and a west tower, perched on a rock above the nave. But its most arresting feature is the memorial which he designed for himself, and in which he was interred at his death.

His recumbent figure lies in armour under an arch on which the twelve apostles are depicted. A panel beneath them displays the heraldic symbols of his house; a castle on the left and a galley on the right. It is curious that the three legs of Man are not included. Another part of the panel displays a deer hunt and, beside this, a weighing of sins and virtues. This is particularly interesting in that it resembles a carving on one of the capitals of Iona abbey.

What we see here is material evidence of the same Gaelic influence from the southern Hebrides that manifests itself in literature, and

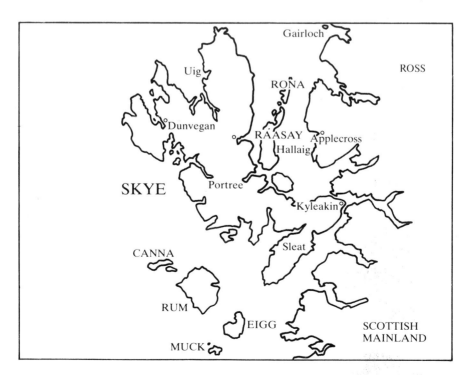

further examples in stone are also to be found in Lewis. Here stood a church on the narrow neck of the Eye peninsula which the MacLeods are thought to have rebuilt in the fourteenth century and embellished later. The art of the Iona stonemasons reached Lewis in time to preserve what is thought to be the effigy of the MacLeod of Lewis who died in 1498, and here it remains inside the ruin, placed upright against a wall. On the opposite wall there is a memorial whose inscription relates that it commemorates MacLeod's daughter Margaret, widow of the Mackinnon who died in 1503. These sculptures, like others in Rodel church, show as much of the cultural influence that stemmed from the Lordship of the Isles as has escaped the blight of Calvinism.

Before Alasdair Crotach built his Fairy Tower at Dunvegan, the MacLeods of Lewis had already contributed one of the most arresting features of the Hebridean landscape, the castle of Brochel on Raasay. Even as a much decayed ruin it looks fantastic, perched on its pinnacle of sheer rock beside the shore. Once it rose three storeys high in an eccentric shape governed by the contours of the rock, and then it must have resembled one of Arthur Rackham's fairy-tale illustrations. On the landward side the castle cliff was unscalable, and even its sole entrance facing the shore was almost impregnable.

Brochel castle overlooked the Sound between Raasay and the Applecross peninsula which most boats would have preferred to the more dangerous waters of the Minch as they journeyed to north and south. But Raasay and the barren isle Rona to its north became a resort of displaced persons, 'broken men' as they were termed, who lived by piracy. Many a boat may have chosen to risk the dangers of the Minch rather than face those of the Sound of Raasay. When Archdeacon Monro published his description of the isles in 1549 he mentioned that Rona was still a base for thieves and plunderers, and there is no need to doubt that MacLeod of Raasay would have welcomed such men among his supporters. The same was going on in most parts of Scotland at this time, especially in court circles.

The first MacLeod to take up his residence in Brochel was called Calum Garbh, Lusty Malcolm, and his line was called after him Mac Gille Chaluim, for he was a younger son of Calum the 9th Chief of Lewis. Unlike so many island potentates after the Lordship was abolished, he was secure in the possession of a royal charter of 1511 for the 'free barony and lordship of Lewis', as well as his title to Trotternish and lands in Assynt. It was in 1518 that he established the line of Mac Gille Chaluim, the MacLeods of Raasay and Rona, with additional properties in Trotternish, Vaternish and Assynt.

In the year 1540 Ruaridh, the 10th MacLeod of Lewis, sat in his castle of Stornoway, his younger brother Calum Garbh in the tower of Brochel by the Sound of Raasay, and the comparatively elderly Alasdair Crotach in Dunvegan. Here they received tidings that James V, King of Scots, had embarked on an expedition to the islands with a fleet of twelve ships containing an army of over 1500 men and artillery. Sailing round the north coast, he dropped anchor to summon the Chief of the great Clan Mackay to his presence and took him captive as soon as he arrived.

In Lewis, Ruaridh came aboard the King's ship with his family to pay his respects and suffered the same fate. The MacDonalds of Glengarry and Clanranald were added to the bag. There is no evidence that James V came to Brochel to seize Calum Garbh, which is surprising in view of the long record of piracy in the Sound of Raasay. Nor is it certain what happened to Alasdair Crotach. But it seems that he was left at large after meeting the King, while one of his sons was taken hostage. All the captives were incarcerated in the prison at Dunbarton.

Such was the latest move to replace the administration of the dismantled Lordship with effective royal authority. The prime cause of the breakdown of order in the interval has been described by the historian of the MacLeods, Dr Isobel Grant. 'One of the most disastrous features of the Government policy was the granting of charters for the same land to more than one Chief. Sometimes it may have been due to inefficiency, in other cases . . . it was probably a deliberate attempt to encourage one clan to destroy another.'

Ruaridh of Lewis was soon released from Dunbarton, and in 1541 he was granted a fresh charter to his properties. Yet this did not save him from his downfall, which resembled that of the last Lord of the Isles in several curious ways. Both men were dragged down by domestic misfortune and both displayed a remarkable ineptitude. But Ruaridh, unlike John of the Isles, never committed treason or any other capital crime, and people are not usually expropriated and their heirs disinherited on grounds of incompetence. In fact the ruin of MacLeod of Lewis was occasioned by the same kind of person as that of MacDonald of Islay, a man with the skill and contacts that enabled him to manipulate the government machinery of Edinburgh to embezzle his property.

Ruaridh entered into a fatal marriage with Janet, daughter of Kenneth Mackenzie of Kintail, who bore a son not to him but to the Morrison Brieve of Lewis. So he affirmed in a notorial instrument dated 1566 just before his death, when a man is most likely to speak the truth. His evidence has survived because it reached the charter room of Dunvegan before the Mackenzies could carry off the muniments of Lewis.

After providing Ruaridh with a bogus heir, Janet eloped with another man so that he would be unable to beget a legitimate one. Ruaridh divorced her and entered into a most promising union with Barbara Stewart, a member of the royal house. He named their son Torcuil as he had done in the case of Janet's son, presumably before he discovered that her child was not his own. So now there were two rival heirs to Lewis; one supported by the Mackenzies, the other by the sovereign.

He had grown to manhood by the time Queen Mary returned to Scotland to begin her personal reign. 'Torcuil MacLeod, We greet you well,' she wrote to him in 1563. 'We are informed that some of the Isles are desirous to have you allied to them by marriage, and because you have the honour to be of the Stewart blood, we thought it expedient to give you advertisement that it is our will and pleasure that you ally yourself with no party in marriage without our advice.' Torcuil the bastard would not have stood a chance against a true heir with such backing, but in the same year in which Mary wrote to him the latter was drowned in the treacherous seas that surround his island. It could be said that, in the last resort, Ruaridh of Lewis was not brought down by the Edinburgh mafia or by his own stupidity, but by bad luck

Meanwhile the other Torcuil was behaving in a way that might have inspired Shakespeare in his delineation of Edmund the Bastard in *King Lear*. He assaulted Ruaridh's castle in the bay of Stornoway, captured the man whose son he claimed to be, and kept him a prisoner for four years in various mountain hideouts. Although his violent behaviour in the isles was already a subject of censure by the Scottish Privy Council, this body nevertheless took his part when he carried his demoralised 'father' to Edinburgh in 1572.

By this time Queen Mary had been deposed, two successive Regents had been murdered, and the Earl of Mar was acting in the name of the five-year-old James VI. Ruaridh was compelled to resign all the properties to which he held such apparently unassailable titles, and received a new charter to them that named the Mackenzie bastard as his 'son and heir apparent'. The most significant stipulation in this document provided that if Torcuil should fail to leave a male heir, the succession would pass to the nearest claimant 'bearing the arms and name of MacLeod'. In other words, there was at least the proviso that the Chiefship and its patrimony were not up for grabs by anyone having designs on an heiress.

Ruaridh repudiated this charter in a solemn deed as soon as he had returned home. He argued in his defence that he had been coerced into recognising Torcuil 'by evil handling, captivity, fear of my life, peril, hunger and cold and manifest compulsion'. Once again an essential document in this case found its way in time to the safety of Dunvegan.

Then Ruaridh took a third wife, a daughter of Maclean of Duart, and when she bore him a son he was named Torcuil once again. A second son was christened Tormod. But his enemies were busy in the capital, where they succeeded in inducing the latest Regent, the Earl of Morton, to summon Ruaridh and compel him to accept the claims of the bogus heir once more. This time the bastard was awarded the property of Coigach on the mainland for his maintenance. Again Ruaridh formally rejected the arrangement, on the grounds of coercion, as soon as he reached home.

The bastard, Torcuil, stormed Ruaridh's castle on its rock in the bay of Stornoway, seized its muniments, and handed them to the Mackenzies of Kintail. Thus stripped of all his titles of ownership, the Chief of Lewis was summoned to Edinburgh, not as the victim of these disorders, but as the culprit. When he failed to appear on a charge of persecuting his heir and other crimes, he was put to the horn. Two years later he was carried a prisoner to the capital, and forced to recognise the bastard as his heir for the third time.

This was hard on his legitimate sons, who had grown to manhood by the time the long-lived Ruaridh died in about 1595. In the following year James VI issued a proclamation summoning his subjects for military service, and Torcuil the true heir responded at once, as did Torcuil the bogus one. In the event they were not called upon to act, but the true heir strengthened his position by marrying a sister of MacLeod of Dunvegan who stood high in the King's favour.

The bastard resorted to a measure that had served him well in the past. He sailed to Stornoway and invited his far younger rival to take wine with him aboard his boat. Torcuil arrived with seven companions, they were all bound, their ship sailed across the Minch to Kintail, and there Mackenzie murdered the lot of them. The latter had already kidnapped Torcuil's younger brother Tormod from his school in Perth, though he had not taken his life. For these crimes the Laird of Kintail was never indicted, let alone brought to justice.

By this time the King had proved himself to be an effective ruler for many years, yet the young heirs to Lewis were being treated in very much the same way as the Islay heir. In this case it was the Mackenzies who were being permitted to commit virtually any crime in their assault on the property of Hebrideans, whereas further south it was the Campbells. Both were doing so with every assistance from the organs of government, which raises the question of the King's complicity. James VI enunciated his attitude in no uncertain terms: 'As for the Highlanders, I shortly comprehend them all in two sorts of people: the one that dwelleth in our mainland that are barbarous, and yet mixed with some show of civility: the other that dwelleth in the Isles and are all utterly barbarous.'

James was, in fact, motivated by a somewhat lunatic racial prejudice against the Gaels. He was also a victim of the delusion that peaty Lewis was extremely fertile, and this perhaps helped him to decide that the solution to the problem of ownership was to exterminate all its inhabitants and settle Lowlanders in their place.

It was enacted that everyone who claimed to own land in the Highlands and Islands should produce their title-deeds on 15 May 1598 before the Scottish Privy Council. These could not possibly have been unaware that the charters of the MacLeods of Lewis had been stolen. Nevertheless their property passed into the King's hands for want of evidence of title, and he bestowed it on twelve Lowland speculators known as the Fife Adventurers, who were invited to conquer Lewis for themselves, but forbidden to lease any land to a Gael after they had done so. Among the Adventurers was the young Stewart Duke of Lennox, a cousin and intimate favourite of the King's. With over 500 troops they sailed for Stornoway towards the end of 1598, captured its castle, and settled down for their first winter in what they assumed mistakenly to be the island of El Dorado.

As for its rightful owner, old Ruaridh had recently died, his elder son had been murdered, and his younger one, now the legitimate MacLeod of Lewis, was in the clutches of the Mackenzies. It was a

repetition of the tragedy of Donald Dubh Macdonald. The Mackenzies were extremely vexed to see others in possession of a prize that
they had been planning with such care to obtain for themselves, and
they devised a stratagem to unseat the Fife Adventurers. They let
loose the captive Tormod MacLeod, to whom the menaced islanders
rallied as soon as their Chief appeared in their midst. Invading the
camp of the Adventurers, they seized the leaders and held them
prisoners for eight months, releasing them only when they had
promised to leave and never return.

James VI responded to this set-back by appointing its instigator a
Privy Councillor. But still Mackenzie of Kintail was cheated of his
prize. After the King had harangued Parliament about the beastliness
of islanders, he gave the Duke of Lennox a fresh commission, and
another to the head of the Gordon family, the Marquess of Huntly,
whose resources might suffice to extirpate the Hebrideans. Then
Queen Elizabeth of England died, and James was distracted from
this preoccupation while he travelled south to assume her crown.

Tormod MacLeod of Lewis followed him, in the common yet
mistaken belief that the King was a victim of evil council in Edinburgh, and would respond to the true facts with justice. Tormod
submitted that he was the legitimate heir to Lewis, that Mackenzie
of Kintail had murdered his elder brother and was in wrongful
possession of his family charters, for want of which his patrimony
had been sequestered. For his pains, Tormod was sent to Edinburgh
where he was imprisoned for ten years without trial. His tragic life
continued to be a repetition of Donald Dubh's.

When King James learned that the islanders had succeeded in
beating off a second invasion, he was moved to new heights of anger.
But Huntly assured his sovereign, on receiving another commission
to return to the assault, that he would 'put an end to that service by
extirpating of the barbarous people of the Isles within a year'. That
was the kind of talk the King liked to hear about his Gaelic subjects,
though his Privy Council in Scotland were to prove strangely squeam-
ish. They ventured to protest: 'Anent the Lieutenancy, they think
it likewise unreasonable that the King's power should be put in the
hands of a subject to conquer lands for himself.' Especially someone
other than Privy Councillor Mackenzie.

James remained adamant, writing to Huntly in 1607 to remind
him that his task was 'the extirpating of the barbarous people in
those bounds . . . and also that the said Marquess, before the

expiring of the year, shall plant those Isles with civil people'. That meant Lowlanders, James warned Huntly, not Gaels from the mainland, either 'Badenoch or Lochaber men.' But Huntly made the mistake of haggling over the feu duties, the King responded by attacking him for his Catholic convictions, and the Adventurers chose this impasse to cut their losses, selling their interest in Lewis to Mackenzie of Kintail.

An element of luck helped to sway events at this crucial juncture. Torcuil, the bastard son of Janet Mackenzie and Brieve Morrison, died in 1609. In his life he had performed vital services to her family, and in return they had saved him from a hanging. He did as much in death, by leaving only a solitary daughter as his heir. She was married to her uncle, Mackenzie's brother, and the family concocted a title to Lewis from their kit of bogus descent, stolen charters and purchase from the Adventurers. Of course it could not have been valid, even if the bastard had been the legitimate son of Ruaridh of Lewis. More than one royal charter stipulated that his Chiefship should descend to a MacLeod of the male line, so that if the true heir in his Edinburgh prison were to be excluded, this would merely pass the title to the branch of Raasay.

But such niceties had rarely detained the judicature in Edinburgh where the rights of Hebrideans were concerned, and least of all in the reign of James VI. Mackenzie obtained the latest commission for the conquest of Lewis in 1611, and two years later the last of Ruaridh's family to resist was hanged in Edinburgh, only a short while before Angus Òg, the last MacDonald to attempt to defend Dunyveg in Islay, suffered the same fate.

Tormod the MacLeod heir remained a prisoner in Edinburgh, unlike Sir James of Islay, who had just made a timely escape. The Mackenzies gave an allowance to the gaoler of the Tolbooth for Tormod's maintenance, on so mean a scale that Tormod petitioned for the money to be paid to himself, 'To the effect that he may use the same, as by a sparing diet he may reserve some part thereof to buy him clothes.' By 1615 the Mackenzies felt sufficiently secure in the possession of his properties to permit his release. He went into exile in Holland, and here the heir to the MacLeods of Lewis simply disappeared from knowledge, just as the heir to the MacDonalds of Islay did at about the same time.

But there is a difference between the two stories. While the house of Torcuil had been disinherited in Lewis, it retained possession of

Raasay, and the house of Tormod avoided every pitfall during this perilous age. The MacDonalds of Islay had lost all.

In Dunvegan, the MacLeods of Harris were thus in a position to defend the Gaelic culture which James VI was so determined to destroy, and they were to prove noble champions of it. The hero of this achievement was the greatest of the MacLeod chiefs, known in his own lifetime and ever after as Ruaridh Mór.

Ruaridh Mór sailed close to the wind on many occasions but always succeeded in extricating himself from trouble. One such occasion was his journey to Ireland to assist the patriot O'Donnell in his resistance to the Elizabethan conquest, at a time when James VI was waiting anxiously to inherit the English Queen's throne. The King did not take kindly to any of his Scottish subjects who compromised his reputation in London like this. But Ruaridh Mór returned safely from a successful expedition, bringing with him a superb memento. It is a wooden mazer, believed to have belonged originally to a tenth-century Irish king, still preserved in Dunvegan Castle. It had been enclosed in a silver casing with an inscription bearing the date 1493, and there is no reason to doubt the tradition that it was a token of appreciation from O'Donnell.

Ruaridh Mór incurred even greater disfavour when he quarrelled with MacDonald of Sleat, fell foul of the central government, and was declared a rebel and saw his property forfeited in 1601. The Fife Adventurers were already in Lewis, and Skye now lay open to a similar enterprise. But Ruaridh Mór invited MacDonald of Sleat to a feast of reconciliation in Dunvegan, and by standing together the two Chiefs achieved what those of Duart and Dunyveg had failed to achieve in similar circumstances, because they could not combine in the face of a common danger. The memento of this occasion is the pibroch that Donald Mór MacCrimmon composed in its honour, known as *Failte nan Leòdach*, Welcome of the MacLeods.

Ruaridh Mór evidently possessed a personal magnetism sufficient even to reconcile him to James VI despite his past record, and in spite of the fact that he was a barbarous Hebridean. At any rate he fared better than many others at this time in his personal relations with the King. He may have met his sovereign first when he visited London to pay his respects in 1603. On this occasion the souvenir he brought home with him was an enormous sideboard, richly carved, that is still to be seen in the dining room of Dunvegan. It must have been difficult to manhandle up the narrow steps of the water-gate, unless it was somehow winched over the battlements.

The next emergency occurred in 1608, when the lands of Ruaridh Mór and MacDonald of Sleat, on which greedy eyes had been fixed ever since the forfeiture of 1601, were granted to the Fife Adventurers. Another expedition to the isles was mounted, this time under the command of a semi-royal Stewart called Lord Ochiltree. Accompanied by the Bishop of the Isles, he sailed to Mull, where he summoned all the Hebridean Chiefs to attend him in the castle of Aros. Ruaridh Mór absented himself, but sent his brother. If he suspected another kidnapping operation, his guess was correct.

The Chiefs were lured aboard a ship on the pretext that they were to hear a sermon from the Bishop, carried to the mainland and imprisoned. Some were confined in Blackness castle, but Ruaridh's brother was taken to the Tolbooth in Edinburgh where Tormod MacLeod of Lewis was languishing on short commons. While he was still there the Chiefs of Duart and Clanranald, Dunyveg and Sleat were released in order to attend a solemn gathering on Iona. Here Ruaridh Mór ventured to join them, and so did other potentates, Mackinnon, MacQuarrie and Maclean. Here they all signed what became known as the Statutes of Iona in 1609.

Their most significant provisions were those designed to eradicate the Gaelic civilisation of the islands. Bards were to be placed in the stocks and then driven from the country, a measure that struck at the popular culture of the Gael. The indigenous literature and learning could still be fostered by the Chiefs, but these were required to send their eldest sons to school in the Lowlands, and it would be only a matter of time before the leaders of island society would be transformed by this means into anglicised aliens.

Religion was pressed into serving the same end. In islands that had taken no part in the Calvinist Reformation and remained almost entirely Catholic in their faith, the Chiefs were ordered to support a Protestant Ministry. In 1616 the Scottish Privy Council stated the purpose of this without ambiguity. Schools were to be established in every parish for instruction in the 'true religion', so that the 'English tongue be universally planted and the Irish language . . . be abolished and removed'. The Lowland language and religion were to effect their conquest in close alliance.

After signing these Statutes, Ruaridh Mór took a calculated risk. He appeared in person before the Privy Council in Edinburgh to protest his obedience to the King and ask for the release of his brother. His reward was not only his brother's freedom but also a fresh charter to his lands. Dunvegan was erected into a barony, and it was provided that the Chiefship and its properties should descend in the male line. The royal charter of the MacLeods of Lewis had contained the same stipulation, yet the Mackenzies had just succeeded in expropriating them through the claims of a bogus heiress while they kept the true heir a prisoner in the Tolbooth. Ruaridh Mór could assess the worth of his new charter accordingly, and the importance of maintaining a direct link with the sovereign in London, behind the back of his royal Council in Edinburgh.

To the unconcealed consternation of its members, they learned too late that he had sped to England as soon as his business with them was transacted. On other occasions they had managed to reach the royal ears with their slanders in time, and their victims had been posted back to them as captives. On this occasion Ruaridh Mór had been knighted by James VI before a word of warning reached the King from his assiduous Councillors in the north. Ruaridh returned home as Sir Roderick, bringing with him a silver communion cup inscribed with his initials and the date of his triumph, 1613. It remains in the charge of the Minister of Duirinish, the local parish on Skye.

Evidently Ruaridh Mór had a liking for cups. He had his family's ancient drinking horn embellished with engraved silverwork, so that it became known as Ruaridh Mór's horn although it dates from long before his birth. To this day, every MacLeod Chief drains it at a single draught on his succession, as a proof of his capacity.

Ruaridh had inherited his castle home just as his ancestor Alasdair Crotach had left it, with the old keep on one side of the curtain wall, the fairy tower on the other, and sundry smaller buildings between them. Ruaridh demolished these and built the great hall in their place. In the nineteenth century this was lengthened to join it to the keep, and divided into a dining room and a library. The original work was completed in 1623, when a kinswoman of the Chief was growing up in Harris, the poet Mary MacLeod. In her later years she alluded to the hospitality of Ruaridh Mór in one of her poems.

In his great house I have been joyful,
Dancing merrily on a wide floor,
The fiddle playing to put me to sleep,
The pipe music to wake me in the morning.
Carry my greeting to Dunvegan.

Another visitor who received a warm reception in the new hall, although he had not come in search of entertainment, was Father Paul O'Neill. Of the two years he spent in the Hebridean mission before he abandoned it in 1626, all but four months were spent in Skye. For Ruaridh was a devout Catholic, and had no mind to foist Calvinism or the English language on his people, even though he wisely did not advertise the fact in either Edinburgh or London. Instead, he supported the old religion and culture to the best of his abilities.

The MacMhuirichs had lost their patrons in Islay and were threatened by the recent enactments of Iona. But they too could enjoy the festivities of Dunvegan, which Niall MacMhuirich described in his poetry in 1613, long before Mary MacLeod did so. Dunvegan consequently witnessed the transition from the old classical forms of poetry, with their intricate metres, to utterances in the everyday language of the present. This development began at about the time when the English Elizabethan poets broke a silence of 150 years that had lasted since the death of Chaucer in 1400. In the Hebrides there was no such vacuum. No radical language change occurred as between Chaucer and Shakespeare's time. But the poetry of Mary MacLeod, like that of her contemporary Iain Lom, the MacDonald bard, lifted their art to an unprecedented level of excellence in the idioms of modern speech. Her poems possess a further value, in that they preserve the all-too-rare comments of a woman on her society in the age of Ruaridh Mór.

It was this flowering of the cultural life of the islands that the Lowland government was setting out to destroy, without even attempting to discover what it contained. Lowlanders had no conception that the Hebrides possessed at the time of the Reformation more medical manuscripts in the Gaelic language than Scotland possessed in Latin. In fact, Scotland was probably the only country in Europe where vernacular writings on scientific subjects actually outnumbered those in Latin, and it is largely due to Ruaridh Mór that the Lowlanders did not succeed in leaving posterity to share their ignorance.

Mary MacLeod was too young to have composed an elegy at the death of Ruaridh Mór in 1626, but there were plenty of others to commemorate the passing of the patron of their arts. The most famous of them is Donald Mór MacCrimmon's son, Patrick. Mary knew his music well and recalled it in these words.

At the ocean's sound my mood is forlorn.
There was a time when this was not what I was accustomed to hear,
But the great shrill-voiced pipe, surpassing all other music
When Patrick's fingers aroused it.

Ruaridh Mór was not the first of his family to have nurtured the art of the MacCrimmons. Pipers of this family are on record long before he was born, and Alasdair Crotach is believed to have patronised one of them a century earlier. But Donald Mór MacCrimmon is credited with the invention of the forms of theme and variation that are defined today as piobaireachd, or pibroch, although originally this term simply meant piping. His descendants continued to expand them as composers, exponents and teachers until the nineteenth century in Skye, and the magician who awoke these sounds in Prospero's island was Ruaridh Mór.

At his death Patrick Mór MacCrimmon composed his pibroch lament for the MacLeod Chief, but he also wrote a song to his own words that expressed his grief with such heartfelt simplicity that it has earned a continuing place in the modern repertoire.

Give me my bagpipe and I will go home.
There is grief within me, seeing what has happened.
Give me my bagpipe, anguished as I am
Over Ruaridh Mór, over Ruaridh Mór.

A Gaelic chronicle of the time stated succinctly: 'death of Ruaridh MacLeod, the best Gael in Scottish Gaeldom of his time.' A MacMhuirich added later, 'The death of MacLeod of Harris was greatly deplored among the Gaels of that time.' As for Mary MacLeod, she never lost an opportunity to refer in her poems to 'Ruaridh the powerful, proud and wise'. She liked to emphasise his strength, as though she understood what a bulwark he had been to her heritage.

One of Ruaridh's daughters was married to Iain Garbh, the Chief of Raasay. This junior branch of the house of Lewis had survived largely by avoiding any involvement in the misfortunes of that island. Calum son of Gille Chaluim was rewarded for his discretion with a charter he obtained from James VI in favour of his heir in the nick of time, before everyone in his position was required to produce his title deeds in Edinburgh.

Calum of Raasay was also a poet, and he is the first member of his family whose thoughts and feelings we can share. No more than five verses of his composition survive, and their sentiments are remarkable for a man who had been so much more fortunate than many of his relatives. They express a melancholy disenchantment with the world such as his poor cousin Tormod might have felt, held without charge or trial in the Tolbooth of Edinburgh.

His son Calum, the 4th Chief of Raasay, showed similar discretion when he accepted the feudal superiority of Mackenzie of Kintail after his conquest of Lewis, instead of asserting a title that would have been incontestable in a court of law, if that of his cousin Tormod was disallowed.

But tension between the two clans continued, and it erupted when Murdo, the son and heir of Mackenzie of Gairloch, sailed into the bay of Raasay. Calum happened to be at Clachan to witness it, and boarded the galley with a party of his men, intending to take him prisoner and exchange him for a MacLeod whom the Mackenzies had seized in Gairloch. Murdo Mackenzie dived overboard and attempted to swim across the straits to Skye, but was pursued by a boat whose crew battered him to death in the water with their oars. Meanwhile Calum of Raasay was killed in the galley before the surviving Mackenzies succeeded in hoisting sail and fleeing home to Gairloch.

Tragically, it was Ruaridh Mór's son-in-law Iain Garbh of Raasay who provided one of the most memorable themes for poetry during this century. His name might be translated Lusty John, and he was remembered as handsome, strong and athletic. In 1671 he sailed with sixteen of his kinsmen to Lewis to attend the baptism of a child of the Mackenzies who had now advanced to the rank of Earls of Seaforth. On the return journey his boat foundered in a storm and all aboard were drowned.

The eloquence with which Iain Garbh's death was mourned reveals the affection in which he was held. Mary MacLeod composed for him one of her most beautiful elegies, in which she recalled his patronage of music as well as his prowess.

You were a big courageous man, well-built and strong,
From elbow to fist, from head to foot,
O Son of Mary, what an affliction to me that you are lost in the field of seals.
You were a hunter of geese, with a hand that did not err nor injure,
That dispensed gold freely for the maintenance of music.

65

Iain Garbh's own sister lamented his untimely death in two poems of heartbreak, one of such outstanding excellence that it has been sung from that day to this. Patrick Mór MacCrimmon also commemorated it in a pibroch that is still performed regularly. Iain Garbh was the last of his family to live in the fairy-tale castle of Brochel and it has since crumbled into ruin. But its final inhabitant lives on in Gaelic song as a fairy-tale prince.

Mary MacLeod's portrait of him was obviously drawn with sincere admiration, but it could not contain the personal affection she felt for Ruaridh Mór's third son Tormod, also known as Norman. His father settled him on the fertile island of Bernera in the Sound of Harris where the remains of his home are still to be seen, with its view of the tower of Rodel church and the hills of Skye across the Minch.

Norman's contract of fosterage has survived, drawn up in Gaelic in 1614 when he was about five years old. Like the unique Gaelic charter, the sole Gaelic letter written by Sir Lachlan Maclean of Duart, and the only Gaelic letter that has been preserved from the pen of Sir James MacDonald of Islay, this contract reveals a great deal more than its contents. All of these documents are entirely functional, so there would not be one of them unless there had once been hundreds. They serve as a reminder that the Hebrideans shared the fate of the Mayas whose records were destroyed deliberately by the Spanish conquistadors.

Norman of Bernera was only slightly older than Mary the poet, who may have met him first in her youth when she crossed over from Rodel in Harris, her birthplace, to act as a nurse at Dunvegan. Later he performed gallant services on behalf of Charles II during his exile, for which he received a knighthood after the Restoration in 1660. Consequently Mary's most celebrated address to him must have been composed after this date, since it gives him his title. It recalls his father's as well, whom she could not mention without saying that he had 'excelled in wisdom every one of Scotland's knights'.

Mary was in exile when she composed this praise poem, known as a *Luinneag* or Lilt, and sung to an air of great beauty. The reason for her expulsion and her movements during her absence from the MacLeod country have been subjects of much speculation. She begins, at least, with a fairly precise indication of her location and mood.

I sit on the mound, forlorn and perplexed;
I gaze towards Islay and marvel the while.
Time was when I did not think, before my circumstances altered,
That I should come here to look at Jura and Scarba.

Although Mary spent much of her life at Dunvegan, Sir Norman gave her a house at Bernera near to his own. Its outlines can still be traced under the soil. He was a notable patron of the Gaelic intelligentsia, who repaid his support with tributes to his learning. When he died in 1705 he received two contrasting obituaries, representing the old poetry and the new. Cathal MacMhuirich composed an elegy in the classical bardic form, while Mary uttered her last tribute to his memory before following him to the grave.

She had lived to a great age, long enough to witness the arrival at Dunvegan of Scotland's last minstrel. His name was Roderick or Ruaridh Morison, and he belonged to a family of the gentry of Lewis that had provided the hereditary judges of an earlier age in that island. One of them had also supplied Janet Mackenzie's bastard, the bogus heir through whom her family claimed the MacLeod inheritance. Ruaridh Morison was born in about 1656, and he is thought to have been blinded by smallpox while he was attending school in Inverness. This led him to take up the study of music, especially that of the clarsach, or little harp. Travelling about the country, he gradually attained recognition as its finest exponent and became known as *An Clarsair Dall*, the Blind Harper. In 1681 the Chief of MacLeod happened to be visiting Edinburgh while Morison was there, and invited him to Skye where he was established in a home close to Dunvegan.

The man who took this inspired step was known as Iain Breac, Freckled John, and he was the 18th Chief, grandson of Ruaridh Mór. He is the first of his line whose features we can examine, in the portrait that hangs in Dunvegan. But more illuminating by far is the picture of his social world that the Blind Harper brought to life so graphically with sightless eyes.

There had been others besides Mary MacLeod to add their brush-strokes to the canvas before Blind Ruaidh arrived; MacMhuirichs and O'Mhuireaghsains of the classical school, bards from Mull of the new dispensation. Other musicians played at Dunvegan before his harp was heard in the hall of Ruaridh Mór; MacCrimmon pipers, and the fiddler whom Mary mentioned and the Blind Harper named. For Iain Breac was the last Gaelic Chief to maintain in his household the full establishment of piper, harper, poet and fool. In adding Morison to his retinue he helped to preserve the output of the last man on record in Scotland who practised the four skills, able to sing poetry of his own composition to his own melody, accompanied on the clarsach by himself. Indeed, he is the only artist with these qualifications whose work has survived.

His accompaniments on the harp are lost except for the tributes to their excellence. Of the melodies that remain, his editor William Matheson will not allow that more than four are likely to be of his own composition, rather than borrowings from a common store. 'Gaelic-speaking musicians such as the Blind Harper, familiar with older indigenous traditions of Gaelic song, may have contributed something to this themselves; though not a great deal, if the notation in our earliest collections of music – some of it transmitted from the harpers by the fiddlers – is any guide.' But the content of his poetry is altogether fresh and original, giving a graphic, intimate picture of people, in stark contrast to the old formal portraits composed of conventional compliments. Also, he spoke about himself as candidly as Byron did, so that we become acquainted with the singer as well as his song.

The Blind Harper lived to see the sunset of this long summer at Dunvegan, as did Mary MacLeod. After the death of Iain Breac in 1693, patronage of the arts declined, though Sir Norman still lived in Bernera to give a welcome to their exponents. As for the next MacLeod Chief, he would have gladdened the heart of James VI as he moved into the English-speaking world of the Lowlands and there aped its fashions. Ruaridh Dall composed a poem of savage power in which he contrasted the silence and gloom that had descended on Dunvegan with the antics of its proprietor in a distant city. He depicted MacLeod flinging aside the clothes he had worn yesterday because they had ceased to be fashionable, and mortgaging his property to pay the cost of replacing them with a still more extravagant costume. 'A higher rent will be charged for my land,' Morison predicted.

The music and song that Dunvegan had fostered throughout the seventeenth century passed, in William Matheson's words, 'From the hall of the Chief to the firesides of the people.' So it came about that the poverty-stricken peasantry of a later age, who were even denied any education in their own language in the present century, retained a refinement of mind and taste that can only be explained by the fact that they were the custodians of such a rich, aristocratic culture. They could not rescue all of Mary MacLeod's poetry by oral tradition alone, nor save it from a certain degree of corruption. But they did a great deal better than their Chiefs, whose archives contain not a line of the greatest poet their family ever produced.

In her tribute to Sir Norman of Bernera, at his death in 1705, she commented:

> This MacLeod who is our Chief
> Is not a little grieved;
> No wonder, for he has lost his rudder.

In fact the golden age of poetry and music in Dunvegan was at an end. It is sufficiently remarkable that it occurred at all during a century in which Islay, their natural centre, was ravaged by the Campbells and all the Hebridean islands were afflicted by the persecution of central government and the strife engendered by insecurity.

7

Mull Changes Hands

Since the beginning of historical records the destiny of the islanders had been dominated by distant political events over which they had no control. This occurred again during the rebellion against Charles I. Hebrideans owed little to any Stewart King, but in such a conservative society there were those who would have been influenced by traditional feelings of loyalty to the Chief of Chiefs. The most immediate sanction was the decree of their own Chief, and the paramount power in Mull was that of Maclean of Duart.

The revolt against King Charles had been initiated by Lowland Calvinists, repudiating his high church policies. When they formed the army of the Covenant, the Earl of Argyll stepped forward as its leader, a man whom the islanders watched as mice watch a cat. Once the Campbell Chief had taken the field in opposition to the royal authority, the Hebrideans had a motive of their own for supporting the King. If they were Catholics or Episcopalians whose religion was threatened by the Calvinists, they possessed a double motive. Fear of the Campbells exercised a powerful influence in Mull, whose inhabitants must have heard of their atrocities in Islay, and whose best hope of escaping a similar fate lay in a royalist victory.

The influence of religious beliefs on political attitudes in Mull was complicated by a circumstance as common throughout Scotland as in the islands. Many families were divided among themselves by differing faiths. Catholic missionaries had been moving through the Hebrides, reconciling some to the Church of Rome, being repulsed by others. In Mull, the Maclaines of Lochbuie were received into the Roman Church while Hector Maclean of Duart, son of the Protestant Sir Lachlan who had perished in Islay, would have none of it. Since these two potentates of Lochbuie and Duart were also contesting the chiefship of Clan Maclean, religion and politics became entangled even at a local level.

In these times there must have been many islanders who no longer knew what to believe, or what it was safe to believe. Their predicament is well illustrated by an episode that occurred on the little island of Eigg to the north, though it might equally have happened in Mull. When the missionary priest, Father Cornelius Ward, came to Eigg in 1625, he was the first to have been seen on the island since the Reformation. The people of Eigg were supposed to receive their religious instruction from the Protestant minister Neil Mackinnon in Skye, but his parish of Sleat and Strath was already too large for the care of one man. Father Ward soon reconciled Eigg's population of nearly 200 to the Faith.

When the Reverend Mackinnon learned of this, he came by night with a party of soldiers to seize the priest, but the people were also armed, and they induced Mackinnon to sail back to Skye without his prey. Then the Catholic MacDonald of Clanranald, to whom Eigg belonged, bought off Mackinnon by offering him the tithes of a third of the island of Eigg, on condition that he left the Catholics there in peace. Mackinnon was wise to agree. He had difficulties enough to face in Skye, where Ruaridh Mór of Dunvegan had gone over to Rome, and was giving all the succour he could to those who shared his beliefs.

While Maclean of Duart shared the Campbell Chief's opposition to the religion of Rome, he was surrounded by Catholics, not only

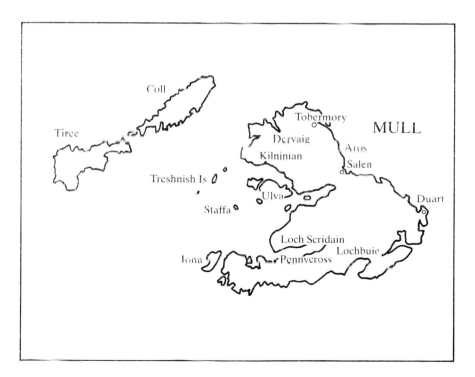

in other islands but even among fellow-clansmen on Mull. And what Maclean shared with these was a fear and hatred of the Campbells and their leader. He was the son of Archibald the Grim, only eighteen years old when he had accompanied his father on the brutal expedition of 1615 which devastated Kintyre and Islay. He inherited the earldom and the chiefship in 1638 on his father's death, just as the great rebellion erupted.

Naturally it was the Catholic MacDonalds who provided the most active opposition to the Covenanters, and especially those who had been disinherited in Islay. They found a gallant leader in the young giant Alasdair MacDonald, the son of left-handed Coll, Mac Colla Ciotach, known to Lowlanders as Colkitto. Whether or not the Protestant Sir Hector Maclean of Duart would have supported him was not put to the test because at this point he died. Campbell of Argyll threatened his successor Sir Lachlan that unless he joined the Covenanters Campbell would ruin him, but the new Maclean Chief refused to be intimidated.

Argyll had made himself the most powerful man in the British Isles by the time Montrose arrived with a royal commission in 1644 to lead the Hebridean consortium commanded by Colkitto and supplied with money and men by Maclean of Duart, while he failed to pay his dues to the revolutionary regime. In a succession of lightning victories they utterly destroyed the power of Argyll. Iain Lom, the MacDonald bard, witnessed the rout of Inverlochy beneath Ben Nevis in 1645, and exulted over the Campbell corpses.

> Ruin take you if I pity your plight,
> Listening to the distress of your children
> Lamenting the company that was on the battlefield,
> The wailing of the women of Argyll.

But their Chief was buying up Maclean's debts, and after Montrose had been defeated and Colkitto killed in action, Argyll had amassed an account for £30,000 against him. When Sir Lachlan travelled to Edinburgh to contest this claim, Argyll secured his arrest and imprisonment. The extravagance of his Maclean forbears had caught up with him, compounded by the unlucky outcome of the civil war. He signed away his castles of Duart and Aros and a bond for £30,000 in addition, as the price of his release.

Sir Lachlan was a dying, ruined man, yet Argyll had not finished with him. He bought in the debts that Sir Lachlan had incurred on the King's behalf, secured on the lands of Mull, and when Maclean died in 1649, soon after the execution of Charles I, he presented a bill for £70,000 to his heir. But his victim, young Hector, died at Inverkeithing in 1651, fighting for Charles II, and now it was a mere child who was left to face the rapacious Campbell Chief. His guardians did succeed in raising £22,000 for him, yet Argyll obtained a decree against the estate for £85,000 in 1659.

During the interval Argyll had been prominent among those who offered young Charles II the Scottish Crown on condition that he accepted the National Covenant of the Calvinists. Charles never forgave those who had tried to impose their beliefs upon him in this way, and, moreover, lectured him about the sins of his mother and father. Nor did he ever return to Scotland after he had accompanied the army of the Covenant to England, to be defeated by Cromwell. Although Argyll stood aside from the regime of Cromwell, and travelled expectantly to London after the restoration of Charles II in 1660, it was to discover that the King had not forgotten the humiliation to which he had been subjected ten years earlier. Argyll was executed on a charge of treason.

The Macleans might have expected to be compensated for their loyalty both to Charles II, in whose cause their Chief had been killed, and to his royal father on whose behalf they had incurred such heavy losses. But gratitude was not among the virtues of the royal Stewarts, least of all to their Hebridean subjects, and Charles II restored all the ill-gotten gains of the Campbells to the son of the man who had done more than any other to ruin his royal father. By this act he helped to seal the fate of his own dynasty, but more immediately he destroyed that of Duart.

Sir Allan, the 18th Chief, visited King Charles in London, in a desperate attempt to save his clan's property. But like so many islanders before him, he sought grace at a graceless face and so returned to die, leaving a four-year-old son to face the final ruin of his house.

In 1674 Argyll obtained a commission of fire and sword, and invaded Mull with 2000 men. It was a repetition of what had occurred in Islay sixty years earlier. Duart and Aros castles were occupied, and when an appeal was made to the King on behalf of the Macleans, he decided in favour of Argyll in 1680. His victims made a last stand in the Treshnish isles, but they surrendered a year later when Argyll obtained a fresh commission against them.

There were accounts of 'wanton barbarity committed upon the property of the unresisting inhabitants', and these may be measured against one particular case, that of John Beaton. He was the senior representative of the distinguished family of Pennycross, and he had moved from his home beside Loch Scridain to the manse of Kilninian, where he was the Episcopal Minister. Here he kept his priceless Gaelic library, and since the national church was an episcopal one at the time, both he and his property ought to have been safe from annoyance on any grounds. Yet he sent a petition to the Scottish Privy Council in 1683 which reveals that he was as vulnerable as the humblest of his parishioners. He submitted that he was destitute 'through the general devastations and herships [plunderings] committed by the Campbells in Mull, there being taken from him at one time thirty-eight great cows and eighty sheep, thirty-six goats and all his plenishing, household furniture and victuals.'

In comparing all this wealth with the average requirements of a manse and glebe, it must be remembered that the Beatons were among the most considerable families of Mull, and John Beaton their senior representative. He continued: 'The petitioner had no security within his own house, either for his person or goods, but the house itself was broke up, spoiled and robbed of all that was therein, in high contempt of his Majesty's authority and laws and of the petitioner's sacred function. Neither durst the petitioner ever complain hitherto of these injuries and oppressions for fear to be treated with more severe cruelties.' That was the end of part of the Beaton library, as he was to disclose later. Indeed it is a great marvel that any part of this collection escaped the fate of the muniments of the Lordship and the records of Iona.

But the greatest wonder of all is that the Campbells were still on the rampage in Mull so late as this. For King Charles had failed to win the Earl of Argyll at the expense of his loyal supporters, and in 1681 he was indicted for treason and condemned to forfeiture and death. He escaped from Edinburgh castle before the sentence could be carried out and took refuge in Holland. Yet there was still a Campbell from the mainland in occupation at Duart castle a year later.

Even when Argyll returned to take part in the Monmouth rebellion against James VII after he had succeeded to the throne in 1685, and was executed for his pains, this brought no relief to the Macleans of Mull. Whether or not the Reverend John Beaton received any redress for his losses, he was soon menaced again after Calvinism had triumphed in the Revolution of 1688. Episcopalians then shared the fate of Catholics, so that Beaton was obliged to leave Kilninian. He retired to Ireland, taking what was left of his library with him, and nothing more might ever have been heard of either had not a Welsh scholar from Oxford, Edward Lhuyd, travelled in search of him.

Lhuyd was the second Keeper of the Ashmolean Museum, who visited the Highlands in pursuit of his Celtic studies in 1699. He travelled through Mull, and passed the former home of the Beatons beside Loch Scridain on his way to Iona. After his return to the mainland he wrote to a colleague about the people he had met. 'They are nothing so barbarous as the Lowlanders and English commonly represent them; but are for what I could find a very hospitable and civil people.' He attributed this hostile Lowland attitude largely to their ignorance, especially of the Gaelic language. Lhuyd himself was bilingual in English and Welsh, and had also learned Gaelic. But he confessed his limitations to another corres pondent. 'In the Highlands we found people everywhere civil enough; and had doubtless sped better as to our enquiries, had we the language more perfect.'

Early in 1700 he traced John Beaton to Coleraine in Ireland, and there wrote a description of the ousted Minister's manuscript collection in his native Welsh. He asked Beaton to answer a questionnaire about Gaelic history, folklore and linguistic matters, and he circulated this also among other scholars. It was a task that any of Scotland's four universities might have been expected to undertake, rather than a scholar from Oxford.

Among those who replied to the questionnaire was the Reverend John Maclean, Beaton's successor in the parish of Kilninian. He told Lhuyd about another learned family of the name of Morison, whose languages were Latin and Gaelic but not English, and who had been supported by the Macleans of Duart. But they had lost this patronage 'by reason of the controversy betwixt them and the family of Argyll', a singular understatement.

A large number of Edward Lhuyd's own papers perished subsequently in a fire, and the very existence of a Beaton library remained legendary until Dr John Lorne Campbell traced their scattered remains, with the help of other scholars, in a feat of detective work that the Oxford University Press published in 1963.

Of all the lost literature of the Hebrides, this is the only collection whose contents and whose fate have been explored in such detail.

John Beaton left a poem on the Revolution of 1688 and the persecution of Episcopalian Ministers which followed, while his successor at Kilninian gave moving expression to his people's awareness that they were the victims of a long-matured policy of genocide. John Beaton himself had been banished, the last fully-qualified practitioner of the ancient Gaelic-learned orders. And now that poetry was the only form of self-expression left, Mull produced a choir of bards, notably the Reverend John Maclean.

Poetry memorised and handed down by oral tradition cannot be destroyed by ransacking a library, and the islanders became ever more retentive in their memories, and more devoted to their last remaining literary asset. The outburst of poetry in the seventeenth century, fostered in Dunvegan after the downfall of Dunyveg and Duart, expanded in the eloquence of the eighteenth, musical airs taking the place of pen and ink. Perhaps John Maclean could not foresee this as he lamented the fate of his language.

> Gaelic obtained respect and was valued everywhere:
> A widely-spoken, vigorous, sweet and melodious tongue,
> A strong, polished, beautiful and accurate language.
> In the court of kings for a thousand years and more
> It held first place, before the speech of the English raised its head.
> Every philosopher and poet, every physician, genealogist and religious teacher,
> Craftsmen, and story-teller too . . . wrote in Gaelic.

Colm Ó Baoill published these poems of the Mull bards with his translations in 1979.

Maclean recalled that its speakers had once been the civilisers of Europe. He exaggerated the part that Iona had played in this, but he was right in recalling the early English King who had visited Iona and invited its monks to establish the monastery of Lindisfarne, where they taught his people to read and write.

> It was Gaelic that Patrick spoke in Ireland of the kings,
> As did that gentle prophet Saint Columba in Iona.
> The learning of the refined French, whose fashion every land has followed,
> Derived its roots from Iona of the exiles.
> It was the teacher of every land and language.
> Norsemen and English sent their kinsfolk and children there.
> Now it has gone from us completely, for shame and alas.

That proved to be an over-pessimistic forecast, and it is still not quite true of Mull today, though very nearly.

The Campbell takeover at least saved the islanders from the consequences of involvement with the Jacobites after the Revolution of 1688. The 19th Chief of Maclean joined James VII in his exile, while the Earl of Argyll came home at the elbow of William of Orange and was created a Duke. His successors planned a new structure of landholding in Mull, designed to release the cultivator from 'the tyranny of tacksmen', the middle order of leaseholders who were for the most part members of the Maclean gentry. Their tenants-at-will had to perform personal services for them which were often ill-defined and arbitrary. Now they were offered nineteen-year leases, paying rents directly to the Argyll estate that would be adjusted to their means.

The Duke entrusted the task of recommending his plan to Duncan Forbes of Culloden, one of the ablest lawyers and most humane men of his age. But after Forbes had visited Mull to attempt this he had to report, 'To my very great surprise, every creature from the highest to the lowest seemed to undervalue the leases proposed.' It is no wonder that the native tacksmen did so. The abolition of the archaic system of sub-infeudation struck at the economic roots of their social order. Nor is it surprising that John Maclean, the Minister, joined the confederacy of those who opposed it, since he was a member of this class. What is so interesting is that ordinary folk did not welcome it wholeheartedly as a release from servitude. From that day to this there has been argument over whether the tacksmen were oppressors, living idly on the labours of their peasantry, or assets to their communities, providing little oases of culture and succour, all the more precious after the great landlords had become absentees.

Duncan Forbes wrote severely about John Maclean, the aristocratic Minister of Kilninian, but it is doubtful whether he could have had the slightest conception of the value of this man to his parishioners. Forbes brought them the new religion which the authorities in Edinburgh ordered to be taught entirely in English, and with the explicit purpose of eradicating Gaelic. Maclean, on the contrary, composed excellent poetry in Gaelic which proclaims his opposition to this policy. From at least as early as 1723 he was concerning himself with the composition of what was to become the first published *Galick and English Vocabulary*, a venture that reached fruition in 1741.

The Minister of Kilninian fought valiantly for schools in his island. There was no man better qualified by his position and principles to face the prejudices of Edinburgh officials. After the school at Torleish had been closed by those who suspected (not without reason) that there was a connection between Gaelic and Popery, Maclean protested in 1728 that Torleish school 'was the most successful in all that island, yea equalled all the other three in Mull and Coll, and that Torleish is the only fit place for a school'. In the same year he appealed for a school in his parish, using the subtle argument that there were Catholics infiltrating there. 'Four gentlemen of some note who lately apostatized do reside in it, and priests and other Traffickers to Popery do frequent that place.'

Maclean had his way. His authority was based on the power of his poetry, his learning, his religious orthodoxy and his social position in the Clan hierarchy. After the failure of the Jacobite uprising of 1745 he sat with the Presbytery of Mull in Aros, where Maclean Chiefs had laid down the law in former times, to judge the Reverend Duncan MacPherson for his part in 'the late wicked and unnatural rebellion'. It was not only the Duke of Argyll who had helped to keep the islanders clear of this disaster, but also such as John Maclean, a man who looked to the future without sacrificing the heritage of the past.

Among the laymen of the Clan were others who clung to the old values under the new order. For instance, there was Donald Maclean of Brolas by the shore of Loch Scridain, who had fought for the Jacobites in 1715, without suffering more than wounds from which he recovered. When he died in 1725 he was buried on the little isle of Inch Kenneth with its ancient chapel. One of the poems translated by Colm Ó Baoill said of him:

> In a tomb in the Inch lies the prudent man
> Who had great courage and the respect of the Duke.
> You were gentle and kind and liberal to poets,
> And your bearing was ever fine and masterly.

His son Allan inherited the baronetcy that went with the Chiefship after his predecessor had died in Rome in 1750, but he lived the life of a professional soldier, for there was no patrimony to support his titles. But he was esteemed as his father had been, and when he sailed for Jamaica with the rank of Captain in 1757, a bard identified all his clansmen with the grief of his family. His home was a modest contrast to the castle of Duart in which his ancestors had held court. When Johnson and Boswell visited Sir Allan Maclean on Inch Kenneth, Boswell found himself sharing a bed with another of his guests.

This was Donald Maclean, son of the Laird of the neighbouring island of Coll, another family that helps to illustrate a society in transition. The 4th Chieftain of Coll had been a bard who composed both in Gaelic and in Latin until his death in about 1560. His successor Lachlan was a gallant soldier, celebrated in local verse, who was drowned accidentally in 1687. Lachlan's grandson Hector, thirteenth of Coll, maintained the last harper to a Maclean chieftain in his home. He also used his best endeavours to keep his clansmen out of the rebellion of 1745, and received a royal charter to his property so that he was not a vassal of the Duke of Argyll.

The attitude of such people to the Campbells tended to be ambivalent. Hector of Coll supported not only a harper in his household, but two successive Campbell wives. Yet when two farms on Coll which belonged to the Duke were advertised to be let, a Maclean wrote that he and his brother were prepared to 'go to the length of their tether rather than let a Campbell into Coll'. Argyll owned the nearby isle of Tiree, and here one of his agents reported to him that, 'the small tenants of Tiree are disaffected to the family . . . and much incited by their chieftains of the Maclean gentry'. It is hard to determine whether their prejudices were nourished by a memory of past wrongs or influenced by the fact that Campbell tacksmen tended to be absentees.

What is certain is that the 1st Duke of Argyll's plan to expropriate the Maclean gentry was not carried out. Aros was in the hands of Duncan Campbell when he entertained Thomas Pennant there in 1772, and Duart castle was garrisoned by government troops. But Pennant observed that the Macleans still retained about half of the island. What is more, they still controlled the organ of the Church to a considerable degree. John Maclean, the poet-Minister of Kilninian, died in 1756 and was succeeded by his son Alexander. When Alexander followed his father to the grave in 1765, the parish elders rejected the nominee proposed by the Duke of Argyll and called another Gaelic scholar to their charge.

In 1764 the parishes of such men received a visit from Dr John Walker. He was one of the trustees of the estates annexed after the failure of the 1745 rising, and he had been sent by the Edinburgh authorities to report on the situation in Mull.

He commented severely on the order that Ministers in the island should preach in English. 'It is very doubtful if this measure really promotes the end it is designed to answer.' In other words, this regulation was intended specifically to destroy the language by means of religion. 'When a Minister confines his public instruction to a dozen or twenty persons, which are sometimes all that understand an English sermon in a parish that contains two thousand; instead of conciliating, [this] rather irritates the people.'

The policy was abandoned, not because it was wrong, but because it was unsuccessful. In 1767 its author, the Society for the Propagation of Christian Knowledge (SPCK), at last published the New Testament in Scottish Gaelic. Ever since the Reformation, the Bible in their own vernacular had been the first book that most people throughout Europe learned to read. At last the Protestant Hebrideans were to enjoy the same privilege.

In 1770 a man who had risen to the rank of Field Marshal in the profession of arms succeeded as the 5th Duke of Argyll. Instead of retiring to a life of idle luxury in his fine new castle of Inveraray, he turned his exceptional talents to the improvement of his estates. He became President of the Highland and Agricultural Society, and when the British Fisheries Society developed from it, Argyll became its Governor in 1786.

In the following year he paid a visit to Tobermory to confirm the advice he had received that it was 'a proper place for establishing a village and port'. In the following decade he was devoting himself to the erection of a storehouse and custom-house there, a breastwork along the shore and an inn. By the 1790s Tobermory could boast its wrights and carpenters, shoemakers and tailors, boatmen and sailors. It was unfortunate that the herring shoals deserted their fishing grounds towards the end of the century, in the periodical cycle that was little understood in those days. Such attempts to encourage the fishing industry were also hamstrung by a duty on salt that prevented catches from being preserved so that they could be marketed at a distance. But the enchanting little port of Tobermory remains to this day a memorial to the enlightened efforts of the 5th Duke to add to the prosperity of his island.

The Macleans of Coll vied with him in their activities. Two Campbell wives had failed to provide Hector with an heir, even with a harper to encourage them with sweet music. So his island passed at his death in 1754 to his brother Hugh. He also bequeathed a modern dwelling house as a more commodious home than the old family castle of Breachachadh, though today the castle has been restored for habitation while the mansion is a ruin. Johnson was a guest in it in 1773 and remarked, 'There was nothing becoming a Chief about it: it was a mere tradesmen's box.' But Hugh Maclean had been a merchant and presumably did not mind that.

In it he maintained Neil Rankin, believed to have been the last of his family of hereditary pipers to the Maclean chiefs, and the manner in which he discharged his inherited responsibilities to the inhabitants of Coll earned this tribute from Dr Johnson. 'Their chieftain, for whom they have the greatest affection, governs them with great equity and mildness, and lives amongst them in this remote island, like a master of a family consisting of above a thousand people.' He subsidised the development of linen manufacture in his island, and provided accommodation for a spinning school there.

But it was his son Donald, with whom Boswell was so embarrassed to share a bed in his Chief's house on Inch Kenneth, who excited the greatest admiration of the visitors. 'He has begun a road capable of a wheel-carriage,' Johnson recorded, 'what no islander perhaps ever thought on.' The Doctor described him as, 'A noble animal. He is as complete an islander as the mind can figure. He is a farmer, a sailor, a hunter, a fisher.' Boswell praised him equally. 'He has been a good deal in England, studying farming, and was resolved to improve the value of his father's lands, without oppressing his tenants or losing the ancient Highland fashions.'

Soon after Johnson and Boswell had left, young Donald of Coll was drowned in the waters between Inch Kenneth and Ulva, a tragic loss to his community. But his brother, Alexander, who succeeded their father as the 15th Chieftain of Coll in 1790, did his best to follow his example. His most enduring achievement was the foundation of the village of Dervaig on their lands in Mull. Unlike Tobermory it was not a port, but a well-planned rural centre. Alexander also recruited his clansmen as a Lieutenant Colonel of the Breadalbane Fencibles, an employment outlet for the rising population of young men.

This increase in the numbers of islanders, and the need to find means of their support other than the old, primitive forms of subsistence agriculture, had become a principal preoccupation of the age. Among the most enlightened pioneers in the search for solutions were the proprietors of Islay.

8

New Order in Islay

Neither the Mackenzie takeover in Lewis nor the dispossession of the Macleans in Mull had been half so traumatic an experience as the Campbell conquest of Islay. This island had been the most closely linked with the Gaelic culture and Catholic religion of Ireland, and for centuries its inhabitants had disseminated the distinctive architecture and sculpture, poetry and music, laws and social practices of the Hebrides. The physical shock when their leaders were expelled, their most prominent buildings defaced, their land ravaged and their religion insulted, must have been accompanied by a profound spiritual demoralisation.

Their miseries intensified over the years. Sir John Campbell of Cawdor was still fighting for his property four years after he had obtained his charter to Islay in 1614. 'The rebels has spoiled mightily the land, that the poor tenants is almost undone,' someone reported, meaning by rebels the previous occupants. Argyll carried away the seat and table at which the Lord of the Isles had sat in the Council at Finlaggan, as well as the bells of Iona, and henceforth it was as though a curse hung over the island. Sir John's conversion to Rome brought no more relief to his Catholic islanders than Archibald the Grim's did to those of Kintyre.

Two years later Sir John gave Islay as a wedding present to his son, who was pronounced insane in 1639. He had already produced a baby heir, in whose name the estate was managed, but he died as a youth leaving another minor as heir. During these changes of ownership the great rebellion against King Charles was in progress, but although they diminished Islay's involvement, still the island failed to recover its prosperity. A flotsam of administrators from the mainland bungled its affairs, few possessing any local knowledge or caring about anything except what money they could squeeze from the inhabitants. Campbells of the owner's kin received tacks of land and either could not or would not pay the rents they owed.

After the Restoration in 1660, Sir Hugh Campbell succeeded as Thane of Cawdor, and remained in possession of his island estate for longer than any of his predecessors. He took an interest in its management as well as in its sporting amenities. He built himself a home overlooking Lochindaal, the central block of the present Islay House. Yet in the year after his death in 1716 one of his managers wrote that he 'was grieved to find this place in so very dismal a condition, these that were rich and had great flocks having lost more than the half and the small tenants are next to beggery'. Bad weather and animal diseases had made their contribution to the curse, until this agent 'thought it impossible Islay could have been brought to such a low pass'.

It was exorcised when the island was sold to Daniel Campbell of Shawfield. An astute businessman, he obtained it at a bargain price, but considering the price at which the house of Cawdor had acquired it in the first place, they had little right to complain. The author of that invaluable study, *Islay: Biography of an Island*, Dr Margaret Storrie, remarked that this sale was probably the best thing that any of the Campbells of Cawdor ever did for Islay.

Daniel Campbell was fifty-five years old when he became proprietor, yet he lived to run his estate for another 27 years. He was succeeded by two grandsons in turn, and their total period of management was 90 years. Between them they turned the stricken

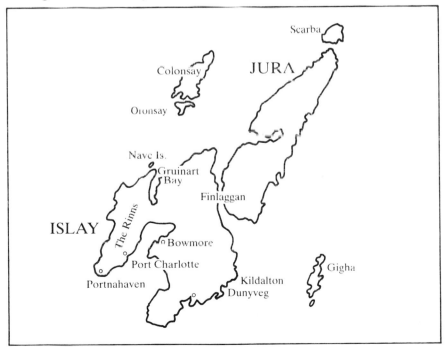

island into 'the most improved of the large Hebrides, and the leader and model of the other isles'. The author of those words was James MacDonald, born in the Outer Hebrides in 1777, when Daniel Campbell's grandson, Walter, succeeded to his office. MacDonald became the companion of the Chieftain of Clanranald, and author of a book on the Hebrides that was hailed as the most authoritative of its time. The Campbells could not have received their accolade from a more expert or impartial quarter. In Islay, the Furies had been transformed into the Eumenides.

Daniel Campbell of Shawfield does not seem to have encountered anything resembling the concerted opposition of the Macleans in Mull when he set out to modernise the agricultural structure of the island, for the old order of MacDonald gentry had already been swept away in the seventeenth century. It was the more recently arrived families of Campbell tacksmen who now began to emigrate in large numbers across the Atlantic, and they appear to have left without resentment, for a land that promised better prospects than Islay did at that time.

The transformation of this island occurred gradually, avoiding the sudden upheavals that were to cause such distress in other parts of the Highlands and Hebrides. The object was to create rational farm units, developed on a basis of long leases, without the presence of subtenants, cottars and squatters who worked the land on a communal basis. In the end only a few regions, such as the Oa peninsula, continued to be occupied by joint townships of crofters into the age of the clearances, with the same unhappy consequences as occurred elsewhere. For the rest, Daniel Campbell was determined to find other employment for those who merely encumbered the land, deriving a precarious subsistence from it which exposed them to starvation in bad seasons.

His most significant innovation was the growing of flax, to be spun into yarn and manufactured into linen, a process that involved both men and women at different stages. But his most important legacy was the fortune he left, derived from the international trading business he had created and his skill as a financier. It was inherited by his grandson, the second Daniel, when he was only sixteen, and he might well have been tempted to squander it on his pleasures or to buy himself a peerage in the corrupt world of politics. But his grandfather's ultimate achievement was to have reared a family who regarded their inheritance as a sacred trust.

The younger Daniel stated as much in moving words recounted by Dr Storrie. 'Upon his death, strongly impressed with the same ideas, I have endeavoured to follow his plans with ardour and attention. Agriculture and the flax husbandry in particular have been my favourite objects. Manufacturers have been brought, public markets for the sale of yarn have been instituted, and large quantities of yarn sold . . . I have assiduously pursued my plan of the improvement of that island.'

Indeed, he could not have displayed a more total sense of vocation if he had been in holy orders. Daniel the Younger succeeded a few years after the failure of the 1745 uprising had been followed by the forfeiture of Jacobite estates. These were administered by the Trustees of Annexed Estates for the promotion of the Protestant religion, English language, schools, agriculture and industries of the Highlands and Islands. Daniel bombarded the Trustees with proposals for the building of roads, bridges, harbours, fishing stations and schools. He undertook to pay from his own pocket an equivalent of any sums that he was granted. Such was his record that the trustees paid him in the end an exceptional compliment.

'They have a gentleman to deal with who for activity and public spirit may be safely trusted with the management of the sum promised by them, without the least doubt of his being a faithful Steward for the good of the public as well as for his own. Without such a person there would be no safety in giving away a considerable sum to be employed at a distance from our inspection.'

Daniel was only just over thirty years old when, in 1767, he established the first regular boat service in the Hebrides, between Islay and Kintyre, opening his island to commerce with the mainland. Immediately afterwards he began the building of Bowmore, an early and beautifully planned design for urban living that can still be seen, more or less as he created it, with its famous distillery beside the quay. Its distinctive round church dominates the broad main street that runs down to the water, its side roads branching off on a geometric plan. The neat houses were for farm workers, linen weavers and fishermen, their ancient attachment to the land recognised by the granting of sufficient land with each for potatoes, oats, flax and cattle pasture.

When the Welsh naturalist, Thomas Pennant, visited Islay in 1772, he did not omit to mention the people who still lived in the old rural squalor. 'Their habitations were scenes of misery, made of loose stones; without chimneys, without doors, excepting the faggot opposed to the wind at one or other of the apertures, permitting the smoke to escape through the other in order to prevent the pains of suffocation.' But Pennant was eloquent in praise of the steps that were being taken to provide a better life, to which people could be lured gradually, rather than being evicted summarily from their old surroundings.

Pennant noted that the population had risen to between 7000 and 8000, about double today's, and also that 'few as yet have migrated', at a time when there was a mass exodus from other islands. Whatever the reason, these people could see the evidence that they might find a livelihood in their own island, even if they were encouraged to leave the land. Pennant stated that 700 men were employed in mining for lead and in fishing, but he was critical that there was not more weaving. 'Much flax is raised here, and about £2000 worth sold out of the island in yarn, which might better be manufactured on the spot to give employment to the poor natives.'

He arrived too early to witness the establishment of another enterprise, one that flourishes to this day and has brought worldwide renown to the name of Bowmore. Its distillery is the second oldest in the island, but it was not founded until about 1779. By a curious whim of the goddess Fortuna, Islay became the only place in Scotland where no excise officer operated from the Union with England in 1707 until 1823. The expertise that this helped to engender in the island was matched by its other assets. The soil is suitable for growing barley, the peat for drying the malt, the burns and rivers co-operative in their quality and in their periods of spate for making their essential contribution to the Water of Life, *Uisge Beatha*. Islay enjoys a cool, moist climate whose sea breezes assist the process of maturing.

The younger Daniel was particularly concerned to lure the islanders into fishing from sailing boats, rather than merely catching fish by rod and line from the shore. He wrote in 1766, 'The shores of this island abound with most kinds of fish known in the Scotch seas. There are several rivers abounding with salmon, and in Lochindaal . . . great quantities of herrings have been taken. There are cod banks on every side of the island, most of which were of late discovered by fishing vessels from Liverpool and other parts of England.' He wished to convert this occupation from a part-time activity into a full-time one. But it was one of the many projects that he was not able to implement before he died at the age of forty.

Loch Coruisk with Cuillin mountains beyond, Skye
Tarskavaig in Sleat, looking towards Cuillin mountains, Skye

Dunvegan Castle, Skye

Portnahaven, Islay

Laphroaig distillery, Islay
Harbour at Bowmore, Islay, overlooked by its round church

Scything above the Sound of Raasay

Bringing in the sheep, Raasay

Stornoway, Lewis
Rodel Church, Harris

Tarbert pier, Harris
Spinning at home, Harris

His grandfather had added flanking wings to the original home of the Cawdors, to house his large family. The younger Daniel built an extension to the front, and also the first of the two circular staircases which spiral upwards from its two ends. Yet he died a bachelor, and his younger brother had died unmarried a year before him.

Consequently it was his second brother Walter who inherited Islay so unexpectedly in 1777 and remained its owner for 39 years, far longer than either of his predecessors. A man who had made his career as an advocate, with no expectation of succeeding to the estate, could scarcely have been expected to adopt the mantle of Elijah at a moment's notice. Yet this is what he did, and he was continuing to implement his grandfather's schemes for the improvement of Islay at a time when the senior descendant of King Somerled, Clanranald, was squandering those resources of the MacDonalds in the Outer Hebrides which had escaped the Campbell conquest, living a life of debauchery in London and Paris.

Walter did not possess financial assets such as his brother had inherited, for the younger Daniel had poured their grandfather's fortune into his improvements. But Walter disposed of the family's original estate of Shawfield and also their lands in the neighbouring isle of Jura, so that he could concentrate his assets and attentions on Islay.

His stewardship was the subject of widespread and unqualified admiration. James Anderson, in his *Account of the Hebrides*, published in 1785, contrasted Islay with islands that had been 'hitherto so entirely neglected', and described what could be achieved 'under the care of a judicious proprietor who has studied to augment his own revenue by promoting the prosperity of his people'.

James MacDonald from North Uist witnessed the continuing process two decades later, and likewise used this example as a stick with which to beat other landlords. 'Walter Campbell,' he wrote, 'has within a period of 34 years tripled the rents, and the intrinsic value of his fine island; and what is peculiarly gratifying to mention, he has bettered the situation of his tenants beyond description, and at the same time *doubled their numbers*. Most of the other great proprietors are at present non-residents, and spend very little of their time upon their estates.' In increasing numbers, these proprietors were evicting whole populations and handing their lands to Lowland sheep farmers able to pay higher rents than the crofting natives could afford.

MacDonald described Walter as spending 'among a tenantry who love and respect him a very large portion of the rents which they pay. He plants trees, and they grow where it was supposed none could thrive. He encloses, drains and embanks, and has shut out the sea from several hundred acres of fine land'. He encouraged others by his example to improve waste ground for agricultural purposes. 'Green crops are generally introduced – lime stone is burned for manure with peat fuel, even by small tenants who pay no more than eight to ten pounds of rent; and enclosures, roads and draining give the soil an air of sheltered richness and comfort rarely witnessed on this side of Scotland.'

Walter's regime was exceptional in this age for preserving the old cattle husbandry at a time when it was increasingly the fashion to turn the land over to sheep. The beasts were sent to the mainland market by way of the narrow sound between Port Askaig and the isle of Jura, and here he built a new pier, and a road from Port Askaig to the narrow waist of the island in which Islay House stood. He constructed another to Portnahaven at the southern end of the Rinns, and substantial piers at Bowmore, Feolin and Lagg. MacDonald described him as employing a hundred labourers all the year round on such improvements.

As for other forms of non-agricultural livelihood, flax was still grown to be spun into yarn and woven into linen cloth, though mining for lead ceased. The distilleries were developed and fishing encouraged. Circumstances resembled those of today, in that although there were more job opportunities than ever before, the population was rising constantly, outstripping the number of employment openings. But in the more mobile society that the Campbells had created in Islay, people were able to move within the island or to emigrate in search of work without the forced removals that were occurring elsewhere. They lived in a crucible of change in which the ratio was shifting gradually away from almost total dependence on a pastoral and agricultural economy.

The most notable contribution that Walter did not make to this process was the planting of any more villages. This was left to the grandson who succeeded him at his death in 1816.

Walter and his elder brother had both known their grandfather the Great Daniel of Shawfield. Walter Frederick who followed him was far removed in time from that powerful influence. But his mother was Lady Charlotte Campbell, daughter of the improving Duke of

Argyll who had built Tobermory in Mull, and this was the grand-father whose example he followed most conspicuously. On the west side of Lochindaal he built Port Charlotte where there was already a malt mill, as a centre for fishing and distilling. On the east side of the island he created what was to become Islay's principal port of entry and named it Port Ellen after his wife. Her father was the Earl of Wemyss, after whom he named Port Wemyss, a village designed on a semi-circular plan to provide an incentive for people from the rural areas of the Rinns to take up fishing. He built a church and manse at Portnahaven, whose fishing boats were described in 1825 as 'probably the finest on the west coast of Scotland'.

But Walter Frederick's programme of urbanisation could not contain the population rise, which peaked at over 15,000 in 1831. He transformed the pattern of landholdings more completely than any of his predecessors. But although he reduced the number of people dependent on agriculture, it did not fall below sixty per cent and increasing sub-division of the land took place in certain areas. The products of Lowland factories, producing cotton and wool, undermined Islay's linen industry. The fisheries could not compensate sufficiently.

Walter Frederick was reduced to the expedient of clearing townships that still operated the archaic run-rig system, but he did so far more sparingly and humanely than the proprietors of many of the other islands. In the case of those who were unwilling to leave, although he could see no future prospect for them in their island, he wrote that he would have been 'very glad to have got those people to emigrate, and would have advanced a moderate sum of money'.

When the potato blight hit the Hebrides in the 1840s, Islay's economy was better armed to withstand the shock than that of any other island. But unfortunately this prompted Walter's representative in Edinburgh to inform the Treasury that the island would not require any of the government relief which was being offered. 'Although severe privation must inevitably be caused by the failure of the potato crop in that island, the measures taken or intended by Mr Campbell's order will suffice, without Government interference of any kind, to prevent any absolute destitution.' This took no account of the fact that Walter Frederick was pouring out money in relief while he was receiving no rents from his distressed tenantry.

In 1847 there occurred a financial crisis throughout Britain which led to widespread foreclosure on debtors. Campbell of Islay was declared a bankrupt and his island seized by his creditors. While he went abroad to live on a pension provided by his friends, Islay was administered for the next five years by a firm of lawyers. It is a sad end to the story of the worthiest landowners in all the islands during this formative age. But they bequeathed one more priceless gift to Gaeldom, Walter Frederick's son John, *Iain Òg Ile* as he is remembered. His lifelong labour to rescue the oral traditions and poetry of his race laid the foundations of modern Gaelic folklore studies, enshrined in such publications as *Popular Tales of the West Highlands*. Fittingly, his monument overlooks the house of Islay that he did not inherit.

The new bosses embarked on a policy of eviction that had reduced the population to 12,334 by the time Islay was sold in 1852. An association was formed which proposed that 3000 purchasers should be allowed to buy the island in separate lots of 50 acres. But although this would have raised £700,000, it was disposed of instead to James Morrison for £451,000.

Yet Islay proved fortunate once more. Morrison was a wealthy merchant as Daniel of Shawfield had been: he did not come with the object of trying to make money out of the island. And from that day to this there has been continuity of ownership by a single family, although portions of the island have been sold to others. When James Morrison's grandson married the niece of *Iain Òg Ile*, this continuity gained a new dimension. The present proprietor, Lord Margadale, is a descendant of the Great Daniel Campbell who first began the moulding of Islay's unique character.

9

The Raasay Experience

The story of this island is an instructive contrast to that of Islay. Here the MacLeod patriarchs continued to preside over a tradition-based society until they were toppled at the same time as the Campbells of Shawfield, and in similar circumstances. They dominated the lives of far fewer people. The population of Raasay did not rise above 400 until the second half of the eighteenth century, less than a tenth of Islay's. Raasay is smaller than the Rinns of Islay, over which Macleans and MacDonalds had fought so disastrously in an earlier age, and less fertile. But it is the differing experiences of the inhabitants, not their relative numbers, that are significant.

The Skye physician Martin Martin commented in about 1695 on the attitude of the Raasay islanders to their MacLeod Chief. 'They have as great a veneration for him as any subjects can have for their King.' This was the same tribal feeling as the people of Mull and Coll entertained for their Maclean Chiefs, and quite different from any good opinion that Campbells might earn in Islay or Mull by their benevolence. Evidently loyalty retained its binding force in Raasay when the Jacobite uprising of 1745 occurred. MacLeod of Raasay was able to muster no less than 100 men from the small population of his island in the Stewart cause.

His decision to do so appears rather eccentric. Many Hebrideans were motivated in their support for Prince Charles by the fact that he shared their persecuted Catholic faith, but the people of Raasay were Protestants. Some were influenced by the climate of opinion among their more powerful neighbours, but the two most prominent men in Skye, MacLeod of Dunvegan and Sir Alexander MacDonald of Sleat, both sided with the Hanoverian government as soon as the Prince had landed. The Raasay Chief's initiative was chivalrous and his clansmen followed him gallantly, but the consequences for their homes and families were catastrophic.

The battle of Culloden was fought in April 1746. Prince Charles fled to the Outer Hebrides, and when he could not find safety there or a ship to carry him to France, Flora MacDonald conducted him to Skye disguised as her servant. Paradoxically, he seems to have been least at risk among Hanoverians, since these would not betray him and were not suspected of harbouring him. The Flora MacDonald's step-father, who gave her a pass to travel from Uist to Skye with her servant, was a Hanoverian officer who must have known perfectly well what he was doing. Flora took the Prince to the very home of the Hanoverian MacDonald of Sleat, where his wife was entertaining government soldiers when they arrived. Nevertheless, she organised his escape. The fatality for Raasay was that they decided to dispatch Prince Charles to this Jacobite island.

He was taken there by Captain Malcolm MacLeod, a young nephew of the Raasay Chief who had fought bravely at Culloden and escaped from the field. The Prince skulked for the first two nights of July in a small hut on the island. Then Malcolm decided that this was too dangerous an asylum for him and rowed him back across the sound to Skye before returning to care for his own family. Soon he was caught by Hanoverian MacLeods from Skye, searching for the Prince, and carried off to London among all the other prisoners.

Dreadful things were going on in Raasay during his absence. The men chiefly responsible for the systematic devastation of the island were Lowland Scots of the names of Dalrymple, Hay and Scott. But the most despicable was the commander of the sloop of war in which Captain Malcolm MacLeod had been incarcerated, whom he described as 'that cruel, barbarous man, John Ferguson of Aberdeen-shire', after witnessing his treatment of the Jacobite captives aboard his ship.

It was not only the homes of the humbler folk that were destroyed, together with their livestock and their boats. The Chief had conveyed his estate to his son before he joined the uprising, so that he was exempt from forfeiture, but his house was demolished and all its contents looted. While many atrocities must have gone unrecorded, one witness testified that the marauding soldiers 'ravished a poor girl that was blind, and most unmercifully lashed with cords two men, one of which soon after died.' The terror lasted until September, when Prince Charles finally succeeded in making his escape. By then, according to the testimony of a certain Donald MacLeod, 'the whole island of Raasay had been plundered and pillaged to the utmost degree, every house and hut being levelled with the ground; and there was not left in the whole island a four-footed beast, a hen or a chicken.'

Captain Malcolm returned from London to a stricken land. He was released under the general amnesty of 1747, together with Flora MacDonald, who chose him as her escort on the long journey home. The house beside Clachan bay was rebuilt, and in it the son of the Jacobite Chief entertained Johnson and Boswell when they paid their visit in 1773. What is more, Captain Malcolm, by this time a living legend, rowed them across the sound, as he had rowed the Prince over twenty-five years earlier. He was 'a gentleman whom I had a great desire to see', wrote Boswell, nor was he disappointed.

Although Malcolm was now sixty-two years of age, he took an oar himself 'and rowed like a hero'. He also sang the visitors Jacobite songs, including the incitement to rise for the Prince, *Tha tighinn fodham éiridh*. The travellers were to discover how the lives of these people revolved to the rhythm of a music of their own. 'As we came to shore, the music of the rowers was succeeded by that of reapers, who were busy at work, and who seemed to shout as much as to sing, while they worked with a bounding vigour.'

The music continued in Raasay House. 'After supper,' Johnson related, 'the ladies sung Erse songs, to which I listened as an English audience to an Italian opera, delighted with the sound of words which I did not understand. I inquired the subjects of the songs, and was told of one that it was a love song, and of another that it was a farewell composed by one of the islanders that was going, in this epidemical fury of emigration, to seek his fortune in America.' Accustomed to provide the entertainment himself, Johnson concealed his surprise that he was invited instead to listen to others. But Boswell gave him away. 'There was such a flow of familiar talk, so much noise and so much singing and dancing, that there was not much opportunity for his majestic conversation. He seemed sensible of this; for when I told him how happy they were at having him there, he said, "Yet we have not been able to entertain them much."'

But although the company was boisterous, the Doctor did not find it hoydenish. 'The family of Raasay consists of the laird, the lady, three sons and ten daughters. For the sons there is a tutor in the house, and the lady is said to be very skilful and diligent in the education of the girls. More gentleness of manners, or a more pleasing appearance of domestic society, is not found in the most polished countries.' As for their host, Boswell declared, 'Raasay has the true spirit of a Chief. He is, without exaggeration, a father to his people.'

Boswell's tour of the island with the energetic Captain Malcolm left him with the impression that prosperity had returned to its inhabitants. There was 'a great plenty of potatoes', wild game, black cattle, sheep and goats in abundance. 'There is a great deal of fish caught in the sea around Raasay: rock cod, haddocks', and trout in the lochs and streams. The Chief had planted woodlands, and was building a wall to enclose the ground for another plantation. 'So far is he from distressing his people,' Boswell observed, 'that in the present rage for emigration, not a man has left his estate.'

The situation was very different in neighbouring Skye. Here the Chief of Dunvegan became known as the Red Man, after the full-length portrait of him in fancy tartan costume that still hangs in the castle. No doubt he wore it in London, where he spent a great deal more of his time than in his island, and where the picture was painted. He held his office during the greater part of the eighteenth century, raising his rents to pay for his extravagance abroad until his tacksmen made concerted plans to emigrate across the Atlantic *en masse*, taking many of their sub-tenants with them. Daniel the younger of Islay must have encountered him in the House of Commons where they both held seats, and one can only wonder what this conscientious youth thought of the degenerate descendant of Leod and King Orry of Man. The Red Man had already begun to rob Dunvegan of its contents before he died, far from home, in the year before Johnson and Boswell made their visit to the castle.

But although Raasay was so much more fortunate in its proprietor, the seeds of future trouble were already sprouting here. The Jacobite Chief had left an excessive number of children, as well as a widow, whom he had married late in life, and for whom provision had to be made. His son had added thirteen children, including ten girls for whom dowries would have to be found.

On the other hand, a lucrative form of employment had been opened to the men. One of the Chief's younger brothers had joined the Dutch army in 1747, at a time when Highlanders were barred from the British service on suspicion that they might be seditious. Ten years later the elder Pitt reversed this rule, and the flood-gates of recruitment were opened in the islands.

When the leading members of this society received military commissions, it was generally on the basis of recruitment among their clansmen, their rank depending on the numbers they enlisted. After the son of Dr Johnson's host in Raasay had succeeded to the

Chiefship, he received the rank of Lieutenant Colonel in circumstances that received this comment in a letter of 1798. 'You will be surprised when I associate war and Rissy MacLeod together, but 'tis a fact that he is now raising a regiment. He signed himself MacLeod of Raasay and Mr Dundas thought a Highland Chieftain was surely entitled to a regiment.' By this time the Napoleonic war was providing almost unlimited scope for a military career, but it was one that could be undermined by the return of peace.

Another source of livelihood to the islands that flourished during almost exactly the same period as military service was the gathering and processing of seaweed. It was discovered that a form of it called kelp could be used for the manufacture of soap and glass, and from about 1750 until the 1820s it became a veritable cornucopia, until the invention of a new process employing a foreign substitute more cheaply destroyed the inflated value of kelp.

In the meantime the colossal profits were reaped solely by the landlords. Under Scots (as opposed to English) law the foreshore and its contents were their property like the land itself. They could pay what they chose to tenants-at-will who gathered kelp for them on threat of eviction. For a time, Lord MacDonald derived an income of £14,000 annually from the kelp of the Outer Hebrides. In all too many cases such revenues passed straight to the mainland and were not used for the kind of productive investment in the islands that distinguished the regime of the Campbells in Islay. It was part of the strength of the economy created on that island that it did not depend on kelp gathering, even at the height of the boom.

Elsewhere, kelp actually proved harmful to other island assets. A chemist named Clarke visited the Hebrides in 1797 and uttered a warning about this. 'The neglect of tillage, which is universally experienced since this discovery was made, is already sensibly felt, and promises to overbalance the good which is derived from it. The lands lie neglected and without manure; and if naked rocks are to succeed corn fields and the labourers desert the pursuit of husbandry to gather seaweed, the profits arising from kelp to individuals will ill repay the loss occasioned to the community at large.' Most serious of all, landlords of the kelp islands welcomed the division of the land into ever-smaller holdings for the rising population, since kelp-gathering was a labour-intensive occupation. Thoughtless of what would become of their tenants or themselves if the kelp market were to collapse, many of these landlords squandered their fortunes and burdened their estates with future settlements as though the bonanza would last forever.

MacLeod of Raasay was not among the kelp profiteers. Ten years before he raised a regiment for the Napoleonic war, he was exploring the prospects of a more permanently productive activity. The opening was presented to him when the Duke of Argyll became Governor of the new British Fisheries Society, and sent him a questionnaire in 1787. MacLeod replied enthusiastically.

'There is a part of my property (an island called Rona) which is allowed by the best judges to be one of the most advantageous places on this coast for a fishing station. It is surrounded with numbers of banks which are daily discovered by the country people who came to fish from the mainland, which makes me think there is an in-exhaustible fund of them about the island. It is likewise supplied with the best harbours at every creek, both for large vessels and small boats.' He estimated that the cost 'is £16 to a boat fitted with cod and ling nets with four men, £26 to a boat fitted with cod, ling and herring nets with four to five men.' MacLeod had recently inherited an estate burdened by debt as well as those ten sisters, and could not finance such an enterprise. So he suggested that it should be subsidised by government.

Only a few years later the local Minister testified that his parishioners were well qualified for the undertaking. 'The men of Raasay are excellent fishers and excellent seamen . . . they are more expert in fishing, and appear to be fonder of a seafaring life than most of their neighbours.' Writing in the *Statistical Account of Scotland* that was published in the 1790s, the Minister put his finger on the fatal obstacle to his enterprise. 'Were the encouragements to the fishing greater, which might be effected by the removal of those difficulties and obstacles which at present stand in the way of that useful and beneficial branch of business, in consequence of the rigour of the salt laws, much good and great profit would thereby accrue not only to this parish, but to the whole country around.'

If the fish were to be marketed, they must first be preserved in salt, which was rendered impossible by the high duty that had been imposed on salt since early in the eighteenth century. The chorus of complaint echoed from every corner of the Hebrides. In 1797 Maclean of Coll's brother wrote: 'A slight alteration in the excise laws respecting the article of salt would produce a very rapid change in favour of the Highlanders. For want of this necessary article some hundreds of them, during the present years, will be compelled to manure their lands with the fish they have taken. If they were permitted to manufacture it themselves, all Europe might be supplied from these islands, with the fish they would be able to cure.' MacLean was speaking on behalf of the inhabitants of Rum, who were more dependent than most on fishing for their livelihood.

But just as the younger Daniel Campbell of Islay watched vessels from Liverpool fishing off his island and MacLeod of Raasay reported the mainland boats that scooped the wealth of his surrounding seas, so the people of Rum were deprived of their essential form of livelihood until they were all driven to emigrate.

How did it happen that advice so consistent was ignored, especially when it had the great Duke, Field Marshal Argyll, to promote it? The answer lies, to a large extent, in the character and career of Mr Dundas, who gave Rissy MacLeod a regiment because he was a Highland chieftain. Henry Dundas, later created Viscount Melville, ran Scotland as one huge rotten borough and boasted openly of the fact.

One of the means by which he extended his influence in Gaelic Scotland was the restoration of forfeited estates to the former Jacobites. The responsibilities of the Trustees of Annexed Estates were terminated in the islands, together with their support for such schemes of improvement as Campbell of Islay had proposed throughout his stewardship. The mediaeval system of landownership was reimposed, to buttress the support of Scotland's pernicious dictator in the Parliament of Westminster. In 1806 Lord Melville became the last man in Britain to suffer the public disgrace of impeachment, for misappropriating public money, But by then the opportunity was lost to transform the feudal vassals in large areas of Gaeldom into Crown tenants with long leases, and to develop their fisheries.

In the Outer Hebrides John MacCodrum the bard was receiving a pension from his landlord the MacDonald Chief, and the kelp boom was keeping his increasingly crowded neighbours busy as the eighteenth century drew to a close. It is all the more significant that he should have advised them to emigrate, and that he should have referred to his benefactor in such terms as he used. 'It's better for you to leave of your own free will than to be ordered about like serfs.'

In Raasay there is no record of any emigration before 1803,

although by this time the population had risen to over 900. Ten years later a visitor to the island described a continuing prosperity. 'Such parts as are capable of tillage bear an aspect of thriving and judicious cultivation, which evinces that the worthy proprietor has not confined his spirit of improvement to the mansion itself and its pleasure grounds.' By this time the house in which Boswell and Johnson stayed, still visible from the rear, had been enlarged by wings at either end. And here, at a time when the music of the MacCrimmons had sunk to a faint echo in Dunvegan, it rose to its final crescendo in the hall of a Hebridean Chief.

John Mackay, born in Raasay in 1767, received instruction from the MacCrimmons in Skye just in time before their finest living exponent sailed to America. Mackay went on to win the prize donated by the Highland Society of London. As piper to MacLeod of Raasay he taught his son Angus, who was to become the first piper to Queen Victoria. It was this son who published in 1838 *A Collection of Ancient Piobaireachd or Highland Pipe Music* which, together with his manuscript collection, comprise the most valuable single source for one of the most distinctive arts of the Hebrides.

At this time the art and repertoire of the Rankins, pipers to the Macleans of Duart and Coll, vanished entirely. By maintaining the traditional culture of the Hebrides for so much longer than many others in their position, the MacLeods of Raasay had preserved a treasure as precious and unique as the Beaton library.

They did it just in time before disaster struck the islands. The ending of the Napoleonic war had caused a decline in recruitment. The kelp industry collapsed. The price of black cattle fell below the level that enabled crofters to buy meal from the mainland after paying their rent. The fisheries had not been developed scientifically, and the herring disappeared in accordance with their seasonal cycle. A succession of catastrophic summers wrecked the harvests. The ever-rising population of Raasay was forced to scratch a living in barren areas not previously cultivated. In 1841 a traveller observed: 'A few huts were here and there discernible among the crags, while small green patches, varying from the size of an ordinary grave to that of a dining-room carpet, betrayed at least an attempt at cultivation.'

The last Chief was compelled by his financial difficulties to adopt the conventional remedy. His father had already introduced sheep, and in 1836 he cleared the glens of Oskaig and Balachuirn to let as sheep farms. Both of the leaseholders were MacLeods, not incomers. A few years later the Chief cleared lands in the Hallaig and Screapadal areas on the east side of the island for the same purpose. But it did not save him from bankruptcy in 1843. Raasay was sold by auction in London for 35,000 guineas while its former owner sailed away to Tasmania with his family. This price bore almost exactly the same relationship to the number of the island's inhabitants as the sum paid for Islay nine years later.

It must have been a traumatic experience when the apex of their society vanished from their midst after so many centuries, and a stranger who could not understand their language arrived to fill his place. It was also during this interregnum that they were struck by the added disaster of the potato blight.

The island was purchased by George Rainy, who had made his fortune in Demerara, from the sugar plantations of the West Indies. He was a son of the Minister of Creich, member of an estimable, talented family. His brother, Dr Harry Rainy, became Professor of Forensic Medicine at Glasgow University, and the Professor's son was the first Moderator of the General Assembly of the United Free Church. Although not a Gael himself, the new proprietor of Raasay had been brought up among Gaelic people and possessed them among his relatives. Also, he shared the religious convictions of the islanders. There were well over a thousand of these when he took up residence in the home of their Chief beside Clachan bay in 1846, and it was not long before he was pouring out money for their relief.

Famine struck Ireland at this time on a scale so appalling that the plight of the Scottish Gaels, equally dependent on the potato, was a relatively minor emergency. But it was real enough to those who faced it in the Hebrides, and the establishment of a Central Board for the Relief of Destitution in the Highlands and Islands of Scotland acknowledged this fact. After the Board had ceased to provide funds in 1850, Sir John M'Neill headed a Royal Commission to investigate the disaster that had occurred. Consequently the first five years of George Rainy's residence in Raasay were described by three different witnesses: the owner, the Destitution Board and the M'Neill Commission.

In 1851 Rainy submitted a detailed memorandum to the Commission in which he told of 'the apathetic state of the greater part of the people'. He found them enervated by dependence on charity, apt to marry early and produce children for whom they could not provide, sinking into 'apathy and indifference, losing all energy and spirit of enterprise'. Paradoxically, he did not attribute this to their precarious yearly tenancies as the Campbell administrations of Mull and Islay had done, but argued against longer leases.

Rainy resided in Raasay and provided employment in enlarging his mansion. His attitude to the islanders was based on personal observation, not the reports of factors, and despite his criticisms it was a favourable one. 'Taking them as a whole, they are peaceable, orderly, and singularly patient in enduring hardships and privations.' According to the independent evidence of the Destitution Board in 1849 they were certainly orderly, while their inertia was due simply to lack of opportunity. This was proved by their response to public works, for which Rainy contributed three times as much as the Board, a great deal more than the entire rental of Raasay.

One of the forms of employment designed to provide relief was the building of roads, about which the Board's representative had this to say. 'I was much struck with the workmanlike habits and performance of the men employed at piece-work on this road; and the proprietor – who at the time of my urging this co-operation upon him, had felt timidity and hesitation in undertaking works with people not workmen, and the responsibility of supporting those who had hitherto made no effort to support themselves – now, at the completion, assures me that the abilities and inclinations of the people were adverse in the extreme to work at the commencement; but after six months' experience they worked willingly, indeed, keenly.' Perhaps this was because they had food in their bellies. It was discovered elsewhere that starving people proved apathetic when invited to do heavy work.

What is so surprising is that all these well-meaning people still neglected the solution of fishing. There was a particular circumstance that ought to have directed their minds to it. The rise in population had driven people into the least fertile northern areas; and while the number of people fell in favour of sheep in the best lands of Raasay, they became crammed instead on rocky Rona and the little isle of Fladda. Raasay contained 987 inhabitants in 1841, Rona 110 and Fladda 29. By 1851 Raasay contained 834, Rona 115 and Fladda 47. This trend continued in the ensuing decade, and might have led anyone to wonder how people could be supporting themselves among those barren northern rocks except by fishing.

But by now George Rainy had adopted the prescribed cure – as in the days when a patient was bled, whatever his disease – and turned to rearing sheep. He embarked on it with more humanity than many other island proprietors, trying to persuade people to emigrate so that their lands could be leased to sheep farmers. In 1850 he handed three farms to Royston Mackenzie, who took up his residence at Suisnish where the ferry from Skye berths today, south of Clachan.

In the following year an emigration agent visited Raasay, while Rainy offered financial assistance to anyone who chose to settle in Australia. It was important to Mackenzie that his sheep-walks should be cleared of people, which this voluntary exodus could not achieve because it was not systematic. So in 1854 Rainy decided to oblige Mackenzie by exercising his feudal right to evict his tenants-at-will. By 1861 the population had sunk to 387, less than half the number of the island's inhabitants ten years earlier. On the other hand, Rona now supported (or failed to support) no less than 147 people.

If Rainy's object had been to improve the condition of the islanders by culling the population in order to prevent overcrowding, he had achieved the precise opposite. The residue of them were now concentrated as never before in the barren north, while the more fertile south was given over to sheep. Such was the state of affairs when George Rainy died in 1863 and was succeeded by his eighteen-year-old son.

This lad's attitude was truly remarkable. We may believe the Free Church Minister who came to Raasay four years later, when he said of the younger Rainy, 'He removed none, and was not at all disposed to do so, and during the short time he possessed the property, did everything in his power for the comfort of the people.' From London he frustrated the attempts of Royston Mackenzie to enlarge his property at the expense of others, despite the financial inducements he was offered. But within ten years young Rainy died, and his island and its inhabitants were put on the market again.

There is something peculiarly shocking about the behaviour of the next purchaser. He was a Gael named George Mackay and he belonged to the north of Scotland. Yet he forced up the rents of poverty-stricken people in order to enhance the value of his asset, then sold it again within a space of three years. The Free Church Minister, Angus Galbraith, described his exactions in detail and commented that Mackay's chief aim 'appears to have been to make a pecuniary gain by the purchase'.

He sold to an Englishman named William Armitage, in whom the islanders found the natural roles of the two men reversed. From his home in London, Armitage wrote in 1875 to Professor John Stuart Blackie, the champion of the Gaels, after he had completed his purchase. He enclosed a donation towards the endowment of a Celtic chair, such as still did not exist in any of Scotland's four universities. 'If the Celtic chair which you propose establishing facilitates the acquisition of the Gaelic as it is spoken now, it will be a boon to all who have the comfort and welfare of the people at heart.'

Armitage's attitude to Raasay was equally enlightened, according to Angus Galbraith. 'He spoke repeatedly to me of the injustice of having all the good land devoted to sheep, and all the worthless land given to poor people.' It was now in his power to rectify this, yet he spent only one summer in Raasay, then sold the island after eighteen months. Why?

By this time the sheep had largely destroyed the residual fertility of lands once broken in for cultivation by intensive labour, but they were acquiring a new, inflated value as sporting estates. Sheep were cleared from them to make way for deer. Armitage sold Raasay to another Englishman named Edward Wood, an industrial magnate in search of just such a pleasure-ground, and according to the Reverend Angus Galbraith he paid 'a fancy price' for it. Armitage's attitude to Raasay may appear more attractive than that of Mackay the previous owner. Yet he too was prepared to make a profit at the expense of its inhabitants when the temptation was offered to him, despite the sympathy he expressed for them.

It was this conversion of huge areas of their homeland to the service of sport that provoked the Gaels, more than anything else, to take the offensive. Hitherto they had reacted in a relatively passive way when they were cleared from their best lands to see these placed in the hands of strangers. They had little option, since the penalty was summary eviction if they showed the least insubordination. But now, at scattered points, there were men, and women too, who were prepared to resort to violence as a means of drawing attention to their predicament. The most dramatic conflict with the law occurred in 1882 at Braes in Skye, across the water from Raasay House in which the Wood family had settled so happily. It caused a national sensation.

The Prime Minister at this time was William Gladstone, a Scot related to Principal Rainy. With commendable speed he appointed a Royal Commission under the chairmanship of Lord Napier to tour the Highlands and Islands and report on the situation. It arrived in Raasay in May 1883, just over a year after the battle of Braes, as it came to be called. As in Rainy's time, conditions in the island were to be commented upon by the proprietor and by an external team of investigators. But on this occasion the opinions of the islanders were to be heard as well.

By now the house in which Johnson and Boswell had stayed was enlarged prodigiously, until it had almost assumed the proportions of a palace. Up in the north of the island, beyond a narrow neck of land defended by a stone rampart, lived the natives, crowded on the barren peninsula and on Rona and Fladda beyond. In the context of a hundred years ago the situation might be compared to that of Florida today, where prosperous magnates have their mansions at a distance from the Everglades, where the original Seminole inhabitants live. The principal difference is that the natives of Raasay, unlike the Seminoles, were not yet a protected species.

James Ross, a solicitor in Inverness who acted as Wood's factor, described to the commissioners how generously the proprietor cared for them, and was answered by Angus Galbraith the Minister, deputed by the islanders to speak on their behalf. Ross stated that Wood had increased the number of estate workers from 24 to 94 since he came to the island. Galbraith pointed out that no more than half of these belonged to Raasay, and scarcely a quarter were crofters, who comprised most of the native population. Ross could show that his employer had evicted no one, but Galbraith revealed that the crofters had been paying vastly inflated rents, so steeply increased by Mackay, and that they were probably double what they ought to be.

However, the fundamental issue was that of sport, which had brought the Woods to this island, and which was as destructive to the islanders as the potato blight had been forty years earlier. The number of cattle had been reduced from 5000 to 3000 for the sake of the deer, and although the north of the island had been fenced off at its narrow neck, it was absurd to suppose that this protected the cultivated ground of the crofters beyond from animals perfectly capable of swimming round the obstacle.

Then there were the pheasants. Galbraith disclosed that, 'Over two thousand pheasants are reared annually, and these are to be found over all parts of the island. The factor is reported to have said

103

that these are amply fed in the preserves, and consequently have no inducement to wander into the crofters' crops. The fact is, they wander wherever they can get food. He lives in Inverness and does not see the crofters or their crops, but seldom.' As for all the money said by the factor to have been spent in the island, 'It would be interesting to know how much of these thousands was actually paid to crofters for work done. It is well known that large sums are yearly expended on the raising of game, and the payment of gamekeepers.'

But rabbits were the greatest plague of all. 'I have been told by the keepers,' Galbraith submitted, 'that so many as fourteen thousand rabbits have been killed in a season.' He estimated that the island contained about thirty thousand, and they were gradually converting Raasay into a desert. Against these pests the crofters had no effective protection. 'I believe dogs are not allowed, except in a few instances, and if a cat should venture outside the door, a gamekeeper is watching with poison, traps, or gun to destroy it.'

When the commissioners questioned James Ross about the damage done by rabbits to the crofters' crops, he was strangely uncommunicative. A commissioner who was Member of Parliament for Inverness, and himself a landlord, then asked Ross whether crofters were permitted to kill rabbits that strayed on their ground. Ross prevaricated, 'I don't know what Mr Wood's instructions are. He stays here eight or nine months in the year, and keeps almost all these things in his own hands. For instance, he calculates what damage is done by game, and he pays that in money. I know, in several cases, he has paid in money the full amount of damage that they had sustained.'

As usual, the Minister provided more exact information about the damage caused by rabbits and the compensation. 'The Raasay crofters suffer very serious loss. I am aware that three parties received compensation at Martinmas last. Probably the rest did not apply, partly because they did not wish to be troublesome to the proprietor, and partly because they might fear that if the complaint became as general as the loss, they might expose themselves to serious consequences. They are tenants-at-will.'

Paying an inflated rent for their crofts, unable to feed their families adequately because of the depredations of deer, pheasant and rabbits, the young men would leave the island for a season's fishing or to find work on the mainland. But according to Galbraith, the effects of malnutrition were plain to see. 'A medical man of considerable experience, who spent a couple of years in the island lately, on being asked what the prevailing disease in the island was, replied – "the prevailing disease is poverty, and the chief remedy is food."'

According to the factor, the real problem was that Raasay still contained over 700 native inhabitants, superfluous to a sporting estate. One of the commissioners asked him whether he thought they ought all to leave. 'No, I won't go that length. My view is that not less than fifty per cent would meet the requirements. I would not take isolated cases, but by townships, and therefore not injure the natural feelings that exist between them. If you take whole townships, and provide for them when they go out, the natural feeling against emigration would not be so great.'

The native inhabitants desired a different solution. They wished to recover the fertile areas of their homeland, from which they had been evicted, and to restore to cultivation what had become a wilderness for deer, game and rabbits, over which foreign sportsmen roamed. Their spokesman, the Minister, was more modest in his proposals. He suggested that the power of factors should be curtailed, that crofters should be given security of tenure, that the value of their holdings should be assessed by an independent judge, and that damage to crops should be estimated by an outside authority rather than being compensated by the charity of the landlord. When the Crofter Act was passed in 1886, Angus Galbraith was to find that his advocacy had not been in vain.

In that year Edward Wood died in his prime. After her husband's death, Mrs Wood moved with her family out of Raasay House, and in 1912 the estate was sold to a firm of ironmasters, William Baird and Company of Coatbridge near Glasgow. Of all the changes of ownership, this was the most bizarre. The sporting proprietor was succeeded by one who opened a mine at Suisnish, built a tramway, a firing plant and a pier. During the First World War it was profitable to mine for ore here, and in the later years German prisoners were employed. Soon after peace returned, the mine was closed, yet it left one permanent benefit. An attractive complex of houses was built for the company employees at Inverarish. Few of these had been native islanders, but eventually they were able to buy the vacant homes, which comprise the island's one village nucleus today.

The Crofter Acts had protected the cultivators in the lands they still occupied. The lands they had lost during the evictions were not returned to them. In many parts of the Highlands and Islands demobilised ex-servicemen decided to remedy this by raiding and repossessing themselves of territories long abandoned to sheep and deer. Seven families on rocky Rona took this step in May 1921 when they moved to the relatively fertile lands of Fearns and Eyre in the south-west of Raasay, built homes for themselves and prepared to dig the ground that had been cultivated by their forbears long ago. They were sentenced to prison, but like those convicted after the battle of Braes forty years earlier, their demonstration proved effective. In 1922 the Raasay estate was purchased by the Scottish Board of Agriculture, and thus became the first property in Gaeldom to be taken into public ownership since the forfeiture of the Jacobite lands.

Within the lifetime of a Raasayman over eighty years of age, the island had been owned by a MacLeod Chief, a West-Indian sugar planter and his son, a Highland speculator, a London romantic, a sporting industrialist, a firm of ironmasters, and now a government department.

The Board, which became the Scottish Department of Agriculture in due course, leased Raasay House and the sporting rights as William Baird and Company had done, until the mansion was opened as a hotel in 1937. Crofts and grazings were allocated in lands that had been converted into sheep farms and sporting reserves, and grants and subsidies were offered in an attempt to restore the old way of life.

The home farm, however, was often let to an outsider, and in the 1960s the Department began selling off Raasay's most valuable assets to an extraordinary individual, a pathologist who lived in Sussex named Dr Green. For the sum of £4000 he received the mansion of Raasay with its ancillary buildings, the home farm, the neighbouring house of Borodale, the boathouse and estate cottages. During the next five years he purchased more land for £3688, though he did not complete his purchase until 1967. Among these properties was a house with its land which a young islander attempted to buy, in which his uncle had lived as a tenant. Dr Green outbid him in the sale, then left it empty.

Dr Richard Sharpe, the historian of Raasay, has written that 'any account of the period during which Dr Green's ownership of these key properties dominated the island's circumstances is bound to be based largely on hearsay or on newspaper reports'. Why should this be so?

They had been put on the market during a Conservative administration, but the sales were by no means complete when Mr William Ross became Secretary of State for Scotland in a Labour Government, and appointed Professor Robert Grieve chairman of a Highlands and Islands Development Board, established by Act of Parliament in 1965. It was intended to promote the social and economic interests of the people of these regions, and was endowed both with finance and with compulsory powers for the purpose. These would have sufficed to rescue Raasay from Dr Green, but they were not invoked.

He is credited with an expenditure of about £40,000 on Raasay House, which the islanders expected to see reopened as a hotel. But Green paid only one brief visit to Raasay during his eighteen years of ownership, and soon lost interest in anything except long-range obstruction from his home in Sussex. This he exercised with the most devastating effect when an attempt was made to acquire from him one fifth of an acre to build a car ferry terminal at Clachan pier. It had taken long enough to persuade the local authority to provide this essential amenity, and Green's refusal to co-operate could have been met at once with a compulsory purchase order. Yet neither Secretary of State Ross nor Chairman Grieve issued one.

A Conservative government was back in power by the time the Liberal Member of Parliament for the constituency of Inverness, Mr Russell Johnston, raised the matter in the House of Commons. 'The way,' he said, 'in which the islanders have been treated by Dr Green – the man who owns, as a result of successive sales by the Department of Agriculture since 1961, the most significant properties in the key area of the island – and by the authorities, local, regional, and national, which have the responsibility for acting for the public good, is a total, unmitigated, shameful scandal. It has taken seven and a half years to decide on a little ferry to a little island which has suffered, as everyone has agreed and agreed and agreed, depopulation, stagnation and neglect.'

Neither Mr William Ross nor any other Minister of the previous administration was present to offer an explanation. Their successor at the Scottish Office, Mr George Younger, obtained the necessary site for the ferry by compulsory purchase order from Dr Green in 1974, the year after the matter was raised in Parliament, but by then its development was deemed to be too expensive. As a result, the ferry now docks at the pier built originally by William Baird and Company at Suisnish, a few miles south of Clachan.

By this time the fate of Raasay House resembled the fall of the house of Usher: the Raasay story is scarcely less macabre than any invented by Edgar Allan Poe. It was simply left, inadequately locked, a prey to vandals, until its contents were smashed or stolen and even its library vanished. Then, in 1979, the Highlands and Islands Development Board paid Dr Green £135,000 for the shambles of Raasay House and the remaining property that he had acquired in the 1960s for less than £8000. The Board abandoned any notion of restoring the ruined mansion as a hotel, and instead enlarged the smaller house of Borodale nearby for this purpose. But young islanders moved in with the Board's permission and, with the help of hundreds of other eager young people, they tried to repair the damage. They have been running an adventure school here for visitors who have slept on tiers of bunks in the gutted rooms, and manned a boat in the harbour that Dr Green refused as a ferry terminal.

But even this enterprise has been doomed. The later additions to Raasay House are grandiose in appearance, but were shoddily executed. The years of neglect have taken such a toll on this faulty structure that the cost of its restoration has been estimated at £300,000, which the Highland Board declines to provide.

The population has sunk to about 150, a disproportionate number of them elderly or summer visitors. Yet the spirit of the islanders has proved less perishable than Raasay House. The Gillies brothers, descendants of evicted crofters, farm the delicious basin of Bala-chuirn. In the once fertile region of north Raasay, at Arnish, Calum MacLeod does the same beyond the great wall that his grandfather helped to build, to keep the sheep out and the natives in. Calum asked for a road to the crofts of Arnish, and when the local authority failed to provide one, he built it himself.

In 1925, when he was a young man, Calum MacLeod sent a Gaelic essay for a competition run by the Celtic Society of New York, and won a gold medal. Ever since then he has been contributing articles about the traditional life of his island to the Gaelic quarterly *Gairm*, and this precious contribution to Raasay's heritage shows no sign of abating.

In the township of Oskaig, a few miles up the coast from Clachan, the three Maclean brothers were brought up. John became the head of Oban High School, and translator of the Greek classics into Gaelic. Calum was a collector of Gaelic folklore until his untimely death. But Sorley, born in 1911, has eclipsed the other two. His collection of poems called *Dàin do Eimhir*, published in 1943, is comparable to T. S. Eliot's *The Waste Land* as a landmark in the history of Scottish literature. His poems *Hallaig* and *The Woods of Raasay* have cast the same spell over his island as Eliot's *East Coker* and *Little Gidding* have done elsewhere. Comparatively recently, Sorley Maclean published some English translations.

They are still in Hallaig,
Macleans and MacLeods,
all who were there in the time of Mac Gille Chaluim:
the dead have been seen alive.

The men lying on the green
at the end of every house that was,
the girls a wood of birches,
straight their backs, bent their heads.

Between the Leac and Fearns
the road is under mild moss
and the girls in silent bands
go to Clachan as in the beginning.

And return from Clachan,
from Suisnish and the land of the living;
each one young and light-stepping,
without the heartbreak of the tale.

──10──
Lewis

The MacLeods of Raasay were a mere sept of the great Clan Torcuil, which had once owned Lewis. Here they had been dispossessed of Scotland's largest island by the Mackenzies at the end of the sixteenth century. The social upheaval, and the consequence of absentee landlordism, occurred here as early as in Islay.

The Mackenzies established Stornoway as a fishing port soon after they became owners of Lewis in 1610, and it was to grow into the one considerable metropolis of the Hebrides. From the outset it was naturally dominated by members of their clan, and in the eighteenth century its most celebrated citizens were still Mackenzies, Sir Alexander who was the first to cross Canada to the Pacific, and his contemporary Colonel Colin, the soldier-scholar of India.

Even in the rural areas the Mackenzies became paramount, although the name of MacLeod remains the commonest in Lewis to this day. A rent-roll of 1718 reveals that 21 of the long leaseholders, or tacksmen, were Mackenzies, while only three small tacks were still held by MacLeods. Their numbers today reveal that they were not driven out of the island, but merely reduced to subordinate positions in the old country society as well as the new urban one.

This was less ominous for the original inhabitants than the fact that the Mackenzie Chiefs, Earls of Seaforth and owners of their island, were generally absentees. The castle of the MacLeod Chiefs on its rock in Stornoway harbour was allowed to crumble into ruin. The Seaforths owned vast mainland estates and maintained their headquarters at Castle Brahan in the east of Ross-shire. They liked to hunt in Lewis, in the deer forest they created on the peninsula north of Loch Seaforth, consequently known as Park. They also built themselves a residence at Stornoway, called Seaforth Lodge. But they did not fulfil the role of resident patriarchs of a Gaelic island society, leaving Lewis to be managed by their agents.

When the Earl of Seaforth joined the Jacobite uprising of 1715, he was able to raise 3000 men without requiring recruits from Lewis. This was the high-water mark. Despite the failure of that undertaking he rose again in 1719, and this time he suffered attainder and

LONG ISLAND

Butt of Lewis
Ness
Barvas
North Tolsta
Great Bernera
Carloway
Gress
Back
Coll
Loch Roag
Stornoway
Arnish
Eye Peninsula
LEWIS
Park
HARRIS
Taransay
Tarbert
SCALPAY
BERNERA
Leverburgh
Rodel
NORTH UIST
Balivanish
BENBECULA
SOUTH UIST
Garrynamonie
Loch Boisdale
ERISKAY
Castlebay
BARRA
VATERSAY
Barra Head

forfeiture. It appeared that his far-flung estates would remain hence-forth Crown property, their archaic feudal structure transformed into a more modern form of land tenure. But they were returned to him in 1725, though he did not recover his earldom.

His son consequently succeeded to his property, but not to his title, and it was as Lord Fortrose that he occupied a seat in Parliament. This was an expensive privilege, to which his vassals might have been glad to subscribe (though they did not possess a vote) if he had done anything effective for their benefit at Westminster. But he was another member of this London club, like the Red Man of Skye, who merely exploited his island from a distance. His regime in Lewis became a byword for oppression, and there was no improvement after his son had succeeded him in 1761.

The latter's victims adopted the same remedy as others were doing in Skye. In July 1773 the *Edinburgh Evening Courant* reported that 840 emigrants from Lewis had sailed away to Carolina. The Mackenzie Chief was so alarmed when he learned this intelligence in London that he made the long, arduous journey to his island to discover what was wrong. He was faced with a complaint of rack-renting, and a demand that the old rents should be restored, the increase of the past three years refunded, and the Chief's factor dismissed.

The background to this situation was described by an independent observer, John Buchanan, who visited the Hebrides in 1782. He wrote that the Chief 'easily perceived the folly, as well as the inhumanity, of lending out the people on his island to imperious tacksmen, for the purpose of raising a fortune to themselves on the ruins of their subtenants'.

It was the familiar story of absentee landownership, and it appears that Mackenzie failed to reach the root of the evil. For Buchanan observed, years after the Chief's visit, that 'the greatest tacksman in Lewis is the Laird's ground officer'. His name was George Gillanders, and his extortions were based on a monopoly of all the produce of the island; fish, grain and cattle. The people had failed to obtain his dismissal, and after he had retired to the mainland with a large fortune his son Alexander remained to scoop another. As an example of his practices, he would pay a fisherman £13 a ton for ling that he had caught and resell it to the merchants for £18.

But meanwhile the Chief had discovered a means of making his island subjects directly profitable to himself. His father's one benefit to Lewis was that he had abandoned his family's Jacobite principles. He supported the Hanoverian cause in the 1745 rebellion, and the son benefited when he was re-created Earl of Seaforth in time to give his name to one of Scotland's most famous regiments. The American war of independence had broken out by the time Seaforth offered in 1778 to raise troops to fight in it. If his islanders wished to cross the Atlantic, he would arrange for them to do so on his own terms.

He reminded the government that his family had ever been able to call out the vassals on their estates 'whenever the Chief required their services', and was authorised to enlist 1082 men between the ages of eighteen and thirty. He was to receive £3 for each as levy money. He travelled personally to Lewis to recruit what became the 78th regiment of Seaforth's Highlanders.

In Castle Brahan a young man named Captain Thomas Mackenzie Humberston waited to receive the troops as they assembled. A cousin of the Earl, he was also heir presumptive since Seaforth did not possess a son. In addition, the Captain was extremely wealthy, having inherited the estate of Humberston in Lincolnshire. He used the one to make certain of the other when he gave Seaforth £100,000 in exchange for a conveyance of his property. The islanders who arrived at Castle Brahan were meeting not only their military commander, but also the young master.

They were long accustomed to the extortionate regime of the Gillanders family in Lewis. The degrading treatment they received as soldiers proved a traumatic experience. In addition to being abused and maltreated, they found the undertakings made to them dishonoured. They did not receive their promised pay. They had enlisted on the definite understanding that they were to be sent to fight in America, where so many of their friends had gone before them to settle, but when they reached Edinburgh it was rumoured that the ships in which they were to embark at Leith would be sailing to India.

To the consternation of Lord Seaforth, the alarm of government and the delight of the citizens of Edinburgh, the regiment mutinied soon after it had reached the capital. Several hundred soldiers marched in an orderly manner to Arthur's Seat, and there ensconced themselves until the representatives of the Scottish Commander-in-Chief arrived to listen to their grievances. The episode has been described most graphically in John Prebble's *Mutiny*.

The mutineers did not refrain from speaking of the 'vices and bad qualities' of the Earl of Seaforth. They demanded a free pardon in writing, the pay that was due to them, punishment of the officers who had treated them with such brutality, and an undertaking that they would not be sent to India. A journalist from Aberdeen wrote a description of the men who exhibited such extraordinary intelligence, discipline and courage in their predicament. 'I had the pleasure of patrolling this morning round the encampment, for though without tents, and not so much as a sergeant among them, they preserve the best discipline, and of a most desolate place make a most elegant summit to Arthur's Seat.'

At a time when soldiers were shot or flogged for a great deal less, the Commander-in-Chief accepted their demands, and their orderly behaviour must have played a part in influencing his decision. From Edinburgh came John Murray, Earl of Dunmore and a member of the ducal house of Atholl, to lead the men back to their duty. This was Seaforth's final humiliation.

The regiment embarked, but the promise regarding their destination was dishonoured and they sailed for India. The Earl of Seaforth never reached his destination. He died and was buried at sea in 1781, and his heir, Thomas Mackenzie Humberston, was killed in India two years later. The Chiefship, the Mackenzie estates and those of Humberston fell into the hands of his brother Francis. Such was the succession of accidents that brought this young man to Lewis as the new proprietor.

Francis seems to have conceived an affection for the island he inherited so unexpectedly. He reversed the order of his names to Humberston Mackenzie and came to live in it for some years with his young family, settling at Seaforth lodge. He and his wife interested themselves in the welfare of the inhabitants, but they also contributed to his, especially when the Napoleonic war broke out. He raised two battalions of infantry, rose to the rank of Lieutenant-General, and was created Lord Seaforth.

It was the second attempt to restore this title, and it proved unsuccessful. Lord Seaforth possessed four sons, but a man named Kenneth Mackenzie, known as the Brahan seer, had foretold that he would outlive them all. Everyone in the Highlands and Islands knew the Gaelic version of this prophecy, and Sir Walter Scott recorded it in English before it was fulfilled. The Brahan seer also predicted that the elder of Lord Seaforth's daughters would cause the death of her sister, and this occurred as well.

She was married to Admiral Sir Samuel Hood, who commanded in the Indian theatre until he died at about the same time as his father-in-law, Lord Seaforth. Lady Hood returned, the childless Chieftainess of the Mackenzies, and took up residence in Castle Brahan. There she went out riding in a carriage one day with her sister. The ponies took fright, she was unable to restrain them, and her sister died of the injuries she received when the vehicle overturned. The event occurred in 1823 and it is commemorated by a memorial which Lady Hood erected at the roadside. More recently, another has been raised to the memory of the Brahan seer at Fortrose, where he is supposed to have died.

Lady Hood made a second marriage to James Stewart, who added Mackenzie to his name when he became the husband of the Chieftainess. He added rather more in 1825, when all of Lewis except for Stornoway was sold in order to pay the entailer's debts and he purchased it for £160,000.

The islanders must have waited with some trepidation to discover the intentions of the latest stranger to become their proprietor. Already Seaforth's deer forest in Park had been let to tenants, and in the early 1820s sweeping clearances had begun in the parish of Lochs, to convert part of its lands into a sheep farm. The people of Lewis could feel reassured when Stewart Mackenzie did not leave the island in the hands of factors, although he led the life of a Member of Parliament in London, but took the management into his own hands, did away with the middlemen and let land direct to the crofters.

But then he vanished from the scene after a few years, as whimsically as he had arrived. He was appointed Governor of Ceylon in 1837, then High Commissioner of the Ionian Isles, an office that he held until his death in 1843. He was fond of islands, it appears, though not especially of Lewis. Neither did the Chieftainess feel a strong enough attachment to prevent her from selling it in the year after her husband's death. So the Mackenzie reign in Lewis came to an end.

This largest of Scottish islands went on the market in the same decade of the Hungry Forties as Islay and Raasay, and was the most fortunate in its purchaser. His name was James Matheson and he had been a lad of twelve, living in the parish of Lairg, when the Countess of Sutherland carried out the second of her many clearances in 1808, to create a sheep farm in his neighbourhood. Five years later he made his timely escape to London, and before he was twenty he had entered the offices of the firm of Macintosh in Calcutta. From there he adventured still farther east, to ally with William Jardine from Dumfriesshire in opening up the China trade. After he had returned to purchase Lewis in 1844, thirty-four years of life remained in which to spend his fortune on the island.

For the past fifty years and more, Lewis had lacked the stable management of a single family living among their people, such as the Campbells had provided in Islay, and the MacLeods in Raasay. Even though ownership had passed by descent, all sorts of people had come and gone as proprietors. If Lewis had later been tossed around in the Roman slave market, as Raasay was to be, it would present a very different aspect today.

A picture of the society which Matheson did so much to transform was being compiled by its parish clergy for the second *Statistical Account* when he appeared in its midst. The Minister of Stornoway completed his report before James Stewart Mackenzie died in 1843 and described him as the sole landowner. He gave the population of the town as a thousand souls, and noted with satisfaction that it contained no prison although he believed the population of Lewis to be 14,000. Actually, Stornoway had more than doubled the Minister's figure as early as 1817, while the entire island contained over 17,000 by 1831.

Perhaps the Minister's figures were more accurate when he stated that 'in Stornoway there are 18 houses regularly licenced for the vending of spirituous liquors'. In earlier times the distillation of whisky had been a home industry throughout the island, so that few people would have needed to come to town in search of refreshment. This had not been an unmixed blessing. Sometimes they had been obliged to pay their rent to the factor or tacksman in whisky, when they could ill afford to sacrifice their precious grain for the purpose.

Illicit distilling continued after it had been forbidden by legislation and the exciseman appeared on the scene. But the two distilleries which the Mackenzies established in Stornoway had already under-mined the profits of the illicit stills by the time Stewart Mackenzie purchased the island in 1825. Matheson closed the Stornoway distil-leries before his death, and Lewis today, in contrast with Islay, is more celebrated for its consumption than for its production of the Water of Life.

There was a less festive liquid in which some people had been paying their rent since the previous century – fish oil. No less than forty boats from the parish of Barvas were engaged in the pursuit of dogfish, and all the tenants of Ness at the northern end of the island were able to meet their rent demands with the valuable oil extracted from them. At that time fishing had been a general source of livelihood throughout Lewis. There had been an average of one boat to every four families in the parish of Stornoway. Three-quarters of the men of Barvas had engaged in fishing, and in the parish of Lochs the proportion was higher.

Dependence on this source of livelihood was bound to have increased as the population rose and the quantity of available land was diminished by the erection of sheep farms. The islanders could see the foreign boats exploiting the riches of their surrounding seas, and the merchants and curers who were equipped to handle their catches. Yet the Minister noted on the eve of James Matheson's arrival that his people possessed neither suitable boats nor nets for deep-sea fishing.

In their inshore waters they caught cod and ling, saithe and sole. The abolition of the salt tax enabled them to salt their haddock, which they also smoked. The periodical herring shoals provided them with their richest source of livelihood, and they learnt to kipper as well as salt this fish. From the many sea-inlets of Lochs the crofter-fishermen took their catches up the coast to Stornoway. Yet the Minister of Lochs reported, 'The poor people are much reduced in circumstances. The fishing, which formerly constituted a chief part of their support, has not been prosperous of late years: but the mainspring of their prosperity was the price of cattle, which has also failed.' The kelp had already failed, though as late as 1850 there were still twenty-five families gaining a small cash income from it beside Loch Roag.

There is no saying what would have occurred if Matheson had not arrived on the eve of the potato blight. He imported meal and seed potatoes which he distributed, half as a gift, and half as payment for public works such as the construction of roads. Stewart Mackenzie had begun road building, but had left only 45 miles of road in an island that possessed no more than one horse-drawn vehicle. By the time Matheson died there were over 200 miles of road with their connecting bridges, used by 87 of such vehicles. As for the lifeline of Lewis, the new proprietor established an efficient steamer service within months of his arrival, bypassing the Post Office as soon as he discovered its unconcerned attitude towards the needs of islanders.

Within ten years he had built most of the seventeen schools with which he endowed Lewis, together with the teachers' homes. Of course their instruction was in English. It was the Church that provided literacy in Gaelic. The Minister of Lochs remarked that fifty years earlier few of his parishioners could read. 'Now the half of them, from the ages of ten to thirty years, can read the Scriptures in their mother tongue.' Since 1843 the overwhelming majority of the people of Lewis have been members of the Free Church. In that year, in what became known as the Disruption, nearly every Minister walked out of the General Assembly of the Church of Scotland in Edinburgh as a protest against the appointment of Ministers by the local landlord. As in Raasay, where the Free Church Minister, Angus Galbraith, was to speak so eloquently on behalf of his flock, the people of Lewis seceded *en masse* with their Ministers.

Sir James Matheson's most imaginative venture was the exploitation of peat. Within a year of his arrival, Alexander Smith, one of the most respected agricultural improvers in Scotland, came to make a survey. A very large area of the island lay under peat. When uncovered, the prehistoric stones of Callanish were found to be buried to a depth of five feet even though they stand on an escarpment.

Much of this peat lies on a layer of boulder clay, spread over the gneiss rock from the glacier age. Where it had been cut for fuel, the soil was improved by crofters with shell-sand and seaweed. One of Alexander Smith's proposals was that the peat moors should be reclaimed systematically to increase the quantity of arable for the land-hungry inhabitants. His other suggestion was that oil and tar should be distilled from the peat that was removed.

Matheson summoned a chemist from London. He built industrial plants, a canal to carry peats to the kiln and a tramway across the bogs. For a time this remarkable activity yielded promising results, and scientists travelled all the way to distant Lewis to inspect the work, reporting enthusiastically on what they saw. But American oil products eventually undermined those of Matheson's enterprise, which was also crippled by the mismanagement of some of his employees. Matheson closed the first industrial undertaking ever attempted in the Hebrides and disposed of all its apparatus. But great patches of green among the dull moors of Lewis attest that the islanders returned to the task of peat reclamation at the first opportunity.

The largest single item of expenditure was the building of Matheson's home in Lewis. In place of the old Seaforth lodge which stood on its slope above Stornoway harbour he erected a great castle in Tudor style. The barren surrounding moorlands were drained, an undulating grass park was created, interspersed with copses of hardwood as though this were an annexe of the Lothians. Along the shore, variegated woodlands of imported trees came into being. Shooting lodges were built and trees planted in other parts of the island.

Such were the activities that provided work for the landless and a means of subsistence for those whose potato crops had failed. But road building and other construction works provide only a temporary cure for unemployment. They could not make Lewis more productive in the long term as peat reclamation did. And Sir James Matheson regarded the fisheries, the most promising potential source of wealth, with curious indifference. Five years after his death his former chamberlain, John Mackenzie, described Matheson's attitude to the Napier Commission. When Mackenzie proposed that the proprietor might promote this industry, Matheson replied, 'The fish curers should do it. The people who are getting the benefit of the fish should do it.'

Yet the steps he did take rescued Lewis at a time of dreadful destitution and wholesale emigration from the Hebrides, and his measures were based on a different attitude from that of the government. In London the Assistant Secretary to the Treasury from 1840 until 1859, Sir Charles Trevelyan, set himself the objective of removing up to 40,000 of what he termed 'the surplus population' to Australia. In 1852 alone, seventeen ships carried 2605 people there in conditions that did Trevelyan little credit. Among all these islanders, there was not one from Lewis.

Over twenty years later, four years before Matheson's death, his chamberlain was a solicitor named Donald Munro, a man who possessed the conventional thought-processes of his kind. The Napier Commissioners became interested in what he had done to provoke a riot on the isle of Bernera, tucked into Loch Roag on the Atlantic coast of the island. Munro explained that he had been attempting to evict the inhabitants on his own initiative. 'I did not consult Sir James Matheson about removing the people, and I issued all the summonses of removing against them without receiving instructions from him to do so. I am not in the habit of consulting Sir James about every little detail connected with the management of the estate.'

One of the Commissioners asked Munro, 'Then you considered the removing of fifty-six crofters and their families too small a matter to trouble Sir James about?' The chamberlain's reply was curt. 'I did.' In the last resort, not even Matheson could beat the system.

He died childless, leaving Lady Matheson in control of Lewis, aided by Chamberlain Munro. In 1882 the lease expired on the great sheep farm of Park, which had been created over half a century earlier out of the old deer forest. The local inhabitants petitioned Lady Matheson to divide it between them, but instead she let the 80,000-acre deer forest to an English sporting industrialist. The natives thereupon took to raiding the sheep farm, a detachment of the Royal Scots was sent to Lewis, and gradually this use of force engendered a spirit of lawlessness throughout the island. The battle of Braes in Skye was no isolated incident in the Hebrides at this time.

The Crofter Act of 1886 gave the islanders security of tenure and immunity from eviction. Sir James Matheson had been largely responsible for the fact that Lewis retained so many of its people, with such a high proportion of them consequently landless. The disappearance of the herring increased their need to gain access to the sheep farms, and they not only raided the district of Park, but also intruded on to Aignish farm, where they threatened to drive all the sheep into the castle policies. The ploy was abandoned after the sheriff had read the Riot Act in Stornoway in English and Gaelic. Nevertheless, Aignish was placed under military protection.

A deputation from Barvas petitioned that Galson farm should be divided among the local people, but Lady Matheson replied, 'These lands are mine and you have nothing to do with them.' At Coll, on the east coast north of Stornoway, the cottars did not seek permission before occupying the farm on the fertile slope that runs down to Broad Bay. Such was the situation by 1888, after the islanders had received the protection of the Crofter Act.

In the far north, the building of the harbour at Ness had been begun in 1883, and although most of the expense was borne by the Fisheries Board, Lady Matheson contributed generously. The women of the fisherfolk would walk to Stornoway for the gutting, and were to be seen knitting in the open as they chatted to one another, waiting for the catches to be landed.

In the wake of the mini-war in the island, another commission was appointed to examine the situation, which it did in the illuminating Brand Report on 'the social condition of the people of Lewis in 1901, as compared with twenty years ago'. In it we learn that although the herring fisheries were three times as valuable as those of white fish, there were far more cod and ling boats, and never as many as 200 herring boats belonging to Lewis before 1900. It is the old story. The land hunger was due predominantly to the fact that the fisheries had not been organised scientifically. On the other hand, landlessness was more acute in Lewis than elsewhere, not so much because much of the arable land had been let out to sheep farmers, but because Matheson had enabled such a large population to remain in the island.

It is sad that the Matheson story should end on a sour note. Lady Matheson was succeeded after her death by her nephew Major Duncan Matheson. When the Board of Agriculture planned in 1913 to form 131 new agricultural holdings on a number of farms, including that of Galson in the parish of Barvas and Gress to the north of Coll, the Major succeeded in blocking it. Towards the end of the First World War the Board was devising a resettlement scheme that would have used every acre of potential arable land in Lewis, in spite of Major Matheson, and this was the explosive factor which faced the new proprietor when the island was sold in May 1918.

——11——
Harris

On a map, Lewis and Harris appear as one island. To the eye of fancy they resemble a gigantic kite that has fallen into the seas off the western rim of Europe, its streamers strung out to the south as far as Barra Head. The whole archipelago is known as the Long Island.

Geographically, Lewis and Harris are divided by obstructive mountains and deep sea lochs, while historically they are separated by the consequences of different ownership. For Leod had bestowed Harris on his son Tormod, and it continued to be the property of the MacLeods of Harris, living in Dunvegan on the neighbouring isle of Skye, for long after the Mackenzies had obtained Lewis.

This clan leadership had been a blessing during the golden age of Dunvegan, when Iain Breac was Chief. But it became a curse after Norman MacLeod succeeded in 1706, still a baby. The estate was then burdened by mountains of debt in addition to the claims of all the widows and daughters of his predecessors. Norman was known as the Red Man, after the portrait of him which hangs in Dunvegan. As soon as he was old enough, he embarked on a lifelong career of drinking and gambling until one of his relatives wrote, 'He has brought an ancient and honourable family from a flourishing condition to the brink of ruin.'

Finally his grandson Norman, the future Chief, persuaded the old profligate to place his property in the hands of trustees and live on a fixed allowance. In 1772 the Red Man died, far from Skye, and it was this grandson who welcomed Johnson and Boswell to Dunvegan in the following year, after they had left Raasay. Here, wrote Boswell, 'Our entertainment was in so elegant a style, and reminded my fellow-traveller so much of England, that he became quite joyous.' There was evidently no risk that the young ladies would interrupt his majestic conversation with Gaelic songs as they had done in Raasay. The bagpipe was still heard but its art was no longer being taught, and even these visitors could remark that the standard of performance had declined.

Each man made a penetrating observation at Dunvegan. Johnson said: 'There is no tracing ancient nations but by language, and therefore I'm always sorry when language is lost, because languages are the pedigrees of nations.' For his part, Boswell wrote in his journal of the benefits that might ensue if 'the lairds were to stay more at home'.

As in Raasay, they described a lifestyle which their hosts could not afford. But in Skye the Chief had been attempting to meet his expenses by rack-renting like the Mackenzie lord of Lewis, and had thereby provoked massive emigration. The new Chief planned to sell Harris, as a means of paying off at least some of the debts he had inherited.

Here lived the grandson of Sir Norman of Bernera, that favourite of Mary MacLeod the poet, in the fertile island in the Sound of Harris that he had received from his father Ruaridh Mór, the great Chief. But Ruaridh had bestowed Bernera on his younger son only in the form of a lease, not with a feu charter that would have given this junior branch a permanent title of ownership. However, Sir Norman's grandson, Donald of Bernera, was approached by the Red Man with a request for a loan which enabled him to rectify this. He agreed to advance the money in return for a charter, and the improvident Chief accepted his terms.

Donald of Bernera himself received the necessary cash from his second son Alexander, captain of the merchant ship *Mansfield*, in which he had won wealth with the East India Company. So it came about that the MacLeod Chief was unable to put Harris on the market with vacant possession of that jewel of the estate, the isle of Bernera, and without this it failed to find a buyer from outside the Hebrides. Captain Alexander himself was consequently able to purchase Harris, with Bernera and St Kilda, and did so in 1779. He left his father in the family island, and his elder brother after him.

The sale occurred a few years after Flora MacDonald sailed to Carolina with so many of her kinsfolk from Skye, while 840 people left Lewis for the same destination. In Harris, by contrast, the Minister reported that 'there has been no emigration, neither has there been any drain of young men for the use of the army or navy'.

The young MacLeod Chief might have attempted to recruit among his clansmen when he embarked on a military career, but he sailed for America in 1776 without playing the part of a pied piper. To his credit, he also refrained from drawing any money from his burdened estate during his years abroad.

Meanwhile, the activities of the new proprietor of Harris were witnessed by a remarkable man. He was a Lowlander named John Knox who went to London, where he earned his fortune as a bookseller in the Strand. He became a leading promoter of the Fisheries Society of which the Duke of Argyll was the first Governor, and published tracts on the ways in which the Scottish fisheries might be developed. These were extremely well-researched, based on no less than sixteen tours that Knox undertook with the encouragement of the Highland Society of London. He was an elderly, knowledgeable man when he came to inspect Alexander MacLeod's enterprise in Harris.

He was particularly impressed by the harbour Alexander had constructed at Rodel, as anyone may be to this day. 'This has water for any vessel to enter or depart at any time of the tide.' Beside it, Alexander had erected buildings designed to transform Rodel into a flourishing centre of activity. 'He has also built a store-house for salt, casks, meal etc., and a manufacturing house for spinning wool and linen thread, and twine for herring nets . . . and has built a boat-house sixty feet long by twenty wide, capable of containing nine boats with all their tackling.' The most impressive building that remains is the house beside the quay, now a hotel. Knox noted that Alexander MacLeod also repaired the church of Rodel, the glory of the Long Island. At the Tarbert of Harris he placed piers on the eastern and western inlets.

Yet all this enterprise was frustrated. Knox described in horrifying detail the crippling effect of the salt tax and of the duty on coal. The difficulties of the islanders were compounded by the swarms of large fishing vessels called busses that invaded their waters from far afield. Two years before Knox surveyed the new works at Rodel, a report described how 'the crews of the busses from the Clyde, etc., attack the poor natives of the West Coast in their miserable canoes, drive them from their best fishing places, destroy their nets, cruelly maltreat them, and then let down their own tackling, in the places of which they had thus robbed the poor natives'. There can be little doubt that the Hebrideans were among their victims.

Both Knox and MacLeod died in 1790, but a few years afterwards the Minister of Harris was able to advocate their cause in the first *Statistical Account of Scotland*. His name was John MacLeod, and he was one of the ablest contributors to this survey. He declared that the entire nation would benefit, 'were a judicious selection made of proper stations on the sea coast for prosecuting the fisheries, and manufactures established for constant employ of fishermen's families'. At present, he wrote, the islanders could only catch saithe and cuddies to eat fresh fish, 'having no access to salt under the present state of the salt laws'.

It appears that the Minister was well aware of the new villages that Campbell of Islay had planted at Bowmore and the Duke of Argyll at Tobermory. He suggested that the poorest people of Harris, those who possessed no stake in the soil and subsisted precariously as day labourers, might 'be collected into villages erected for them in those parts of the coast that lie most contiguous to the fishing grounds . . . They should be free to prosecute the fishing for their own immediate benefit, and made to feel the advantage of working for themselves.' He commented severely on their present activities, neglecting agriculture and the care of their pastures in order to gather kelp. 'Kelp is the staple and, excepting the few cows sold to the drovers, the only valuable article of exportation which the country produces.'

He was living at the time when the landlords of the Outer Hebrides were extracting their enormous fortunes from this source to spend abroad. It is a wonder that his words were printed when he wrote that the system of landownership 'has established over the Highlands and Islands a degree of aristocratical influence entirely incompatible with the liberty of British subjects. While the mutual attachment of the chieftains and their clans subsisted, this evil was neither felt nor complained of'. Whether or not the old bonds of kinship had really operated in such a satisfactory manner, they were doing so no longer in this Minister's judgement.

He did not blame the tacksmen, as John Buchanan had done in print a few years earlier. The explanation is probably that Buchanan had been judging by the extortionate Mackenzie tacksmen of Lewis, whereas the Reverend John MacLeod had been brought up in the time when those of Skye and Harris had been victimised by the Red Man. MacLeod looked upon this middle order of society as assets to their communities, such as the MacLeods of Bernera had proved to be; a cultured class of resident Gaelic gentry menaced by increasingly anglicised and absentee overlords.

In fact, neither Mackenzie nor MacLeod tacksmen enjoyed a monopoly of vice or virtrue, any more than landlords did. Harris was to discover this in the time of Alexander MacLeod's successors, when its inhabitants experienced absentee landlordism in their turn. But for the present the Minister was able to report that here 'the poor have many advantages and, though numerous, are upon the whole well provided for'. If the health of a society can be judged by the condition of its poorest members, Harris was relatively fortunate when the nineteenth century opened.

But this was not to last. Although the salt tax was repealed in 1823, the new regulations enabled Spanish barilla to be imported at a price that crippled the kelp trade. By this time the population of Harris was rising steeply. In 1755 it had been under 2000, in 1792 it was little over 2500, and by 1831 it had reached 3900. People who had earned their livelihood by gathering kelp were driven back for their subsistence on neglected land which hardly sufficed for their numbers.

A reorganisation was taking place during these years, in Harris as in other islands. The old communal run-rig settlements were being broken up in favour of individual crofts. In the past their occupants had earned fortunes for their landlords, and practically nothing for themselves except permission to live on his land. Now their smallholdings yielded hardly enough to feed themselves, let alone any surplus for the proprietor. It was not so much that the Hebrides could not support their inhabitants, as that their inhabitants could no longer afford to support their landlords.

Such was the period of stress in which Harris was mismanaged by the factors of an absentee, until in 1834 the property was sold to the Earl of Dunmore. He was the son of the nobleman who had led the mutinous Seaforth Highlanders back to their barracks in Edinburgh, and whatever his object in buying Harris he had little time to realise it, for he died within two years. The son who succeeded him lived only until 1845, when the potato blight struck the islands. It was not the happiest of times in which to have four proprietors in little over a decade.

The Dunmores soon embarked on the standard practice of removing people who could not pay their rent, and leasing their lands to sheep farmers who could. One such rearrangement was planned in 1836, the year in which Harris changed hands from Dunmore father to son. It involved the fertile machair lands that lie on the Atlantic seaboard of Harris, where the parabolas of silver sand stretch between the waving marram grass and ocean rollers. Here, there was a sheep farmer paying a substantial rent, who sent notice that he would not renew his lease unless the native crofters subsisting on the edge of his property were removed.

These people were treated by their new owner with unusual delicacy. They were given three years' notice to quit, told that their arrears of rent would be cancelled, and that their cattle would be purchased at a price fixed by an independent valuer. Those who wished to emigrate would be given a free passage to Cape Breton Island or elsewhere in Canada, while all who were unable or unwilling to face such a journey would be accommodated elsewhere in the island. These terms were accepted, but during the three-year interval before they were to be implemented attitudes changed. The Dunmores' factor alleged that the Harris folk were incited to resist the proposed evictions by their fellow clansmen in Skye.

When they did attempt to do this in 1839, the Earl of Dunmore called in the Sheriff with a detachment of troops. Two years later the factor justified this action by stating that it 'terminated an outbreak which, but for the prompt measures of government in sending in military, would have thrown the whole Western Highlands into confusion for many years'. Instead, the process continued which cleared the arable and pasture lands of the spectacular Atlantic coast of Harris and planted those who did not emigrate among the barren rocks of the eastern seaboard. The same thing occurred at about the same time in the smaller MacLeod island of Raasay, as well as in far larger Skye.

In such surroundings it would have been virtually impossible to subsist by agriculture, even if the potato blight had not struck, and people turned to fishing in earnest, sailing out of their little creeks and from Rodel with its fine harbour. The Poor Law Inquiry of 1844 reported that nearly all the crofters of Harris possessed a boat and tackle, a far higher proportion than in Lewis. The people crammed on the rock of Scalpay in East Loch Tarbert lived, indeed, in something approaching urban conditions as they gradually earned for themselves a reputation for seamanship that made them famous throughout the country. In the east-coast fishing port of Wick, men would pretend that they came from Scalpay in order to be taken on as crew members. For the womenfolk of Harris, the Dunmores helped to make their tweed fashionable, and to enlarge its export market. They even caused their Murray tartan to be manufactured in Harris tweed.

The proposed destination of Cape Breton Island which the Earl of Dunmore offered to his islanders suggests that he had taken the trouble to study the most important work in print, recommending a humane and scientific policy of controlled emigration and colonisation to the government. Its author was the Earl of Selkirk, the seventh son of a Border nobleman who succeeded to the title at the age of 28, after all his brothers had died of tuberculosis. He ranks with John Knox among the Lowland philanthropists who tried to help the distressed Gaels, and, like Knox, he received little support from the politicians.

While the sons of the Chiefs were learning, in so many cases, the curious form of English sometimes known as County Cockney at such seminaries as Eton, Selkirk was studying Gaelic. His grand design was to transport whole communities of those who wished to emigrate to an environment in which they would enjoy ample lands and security of tenure. The landlords opposed such an exodus at a time when kelp gathering was still profitable, and when young men were required to fight in the Napoleonic War. But there was a brief period of peace in 1803, and during it Selkirk succeeded in obtaining a grant of land in Prince Edward Island, Nova Scotia, near to Cape Breton Island where others had settled already. Without delay he set sail with three ships, filled with islanders for whom he tried to make all the provisions which he considered emigrants were entitled to expect.

The ship containing folk from Skye arrived first, Selkirk himself two days later, and finally the boat filled with the people of Uist. Selkirk had spent five weeks at sea with Hebrideans, learning their needs and capacities, filling his notebooks with details that were to serve him when he divided the land amongst them, and ensured that each pioneer was adequately equipped. His enterprise was a model of its kind, and helps to explain why Nova Scotia contains the one Gaelic-speaking society outside Scotland to this day.

In 1811 Selkirk obtained a larger grant of land in the region of the Red River, which runs into Lake Winnipeg. But here his scheme of colonisation on a more massive scale was frustrated by the fur traders, fearful for their profits. They gained the ears of politicians at the Colonial Office who obstructed Selkirk's enterprise, and he finally died of tuberculosis in 1820, heartbroken and almost ruined. Yet he had left behind him his blueprint on emigration, while the Canadian lands which he had dreamed of settling with evicted Gaels became transformed into the bread-basket of the world as he had foreseen, in spite of fur traders and politicians. The offer which the Earl of Dunmore made to the Harris crofters in 1836 bears the mark of his inspiration.

The Uist islanders who had not sailed with Selkirk in 1803 experienced very different treatment. These still lived under the descendants of King Somerled; Lord MacDonald of Sleat of North Uist, and MacDonald of Clanranald of South Uist. No islands had yielded larger fortunes from kelp than these, or witnessed a greater rise in population during the boom period. After it had ended, a factor for the Clanranald property stated in 1823 that it was 'entirely a kelp estate', and that now the price of kelp was declining 'the population is excessive much beyond what the lands can maintain'. What they could least afford to maintain were the extravagances of Clanranald in London and Paris.

But this was precisely what they were compelled to do when South Uist and Benbecula were sold in 1827 to a proprietor who embarked on a policy of wholesale eviction. This time the inhabitants of Uist sailed away in conditions very different from those that Lord Selkirk had provided.

It is impossible to determine the extent to which the Chief of Clan Donald, Lord MacDonald of Sleat in Skye, impoverished himself in attempting to relieve his destitute islanders, and to what extent his family had frittered away the fortune the people had laboured to win him during the kelp boom. But he, too, resorted to the remedy of evicting them in favour of sheep farmers. North Uist, beyond Bernera in the Sound of Harris, offered a particularly attractive proposition to them. Since prehistoric times its relatively high fertility and comparatively low rainfall had attracted the settler. Here, from 1823 onwards, large farms began to replace the densely populated townships as these were cleared by eviction.

The process culminated in one of the most notorious episodes in this age of horrors, at Sollas in 1849. MacDonald had already swept away his superfluous clansmen in the peninsula of Sleat in Skye when he embarked on the task of removing about 1300 people from North Uist in 1838, the venture that led to the Sollas incident. This involved over 600 people who had already suffered extremes of hardship in the wake of the potato blight. When an attempt was made to remove them by force, they set up the pathetic and unsuccessful resistance that was remembered as the battle of Sollas.

The destination of many of these people, as of the emigrants from

Harris and Skye at this time, was to be South Australia, and the conditions in which they travelled might well have caused Lord Selkirk to turn in his grave. Parties of them were dumped in various places of transit, and left without food or shelter while they awaited their passage. An eyewitness in Inverness described an all too typical example of this. 'The sight of these creatures, old men hugging their children to their bosoms to protect them from the weather, and women sitting on the cold wet stones on a winter night suckling their infants with perhaps little nourishment to give them, and all without a single morsel of food, was sufficient to raise the sympathies of the most hardened.'

Many died on the long voyage, and most of the survivors arrived in a state of debility. They were sustained only by the mutual support they gave one another in their tight-knit kinship groups, behaviour cemented by centuries of farming in the communal nexus of the run-rig townships.

The immigration agent at Adelaide, Handaside Duncan, was well aware of this peculiarity of the Hebrideans. 'Removed by their insular position from almost any intercourse with the mainland, they have been from their earliest childhood accustomed to intercourse with none but their own families; the stranger who appeared amongst them was the infant newly-born, and he who left them was, in general, carried to the grave. It is in vain to ask such people to emigrate except in entire families.' Duncan gave a striking example of the binding force of their kinship loyalties. 'Their social and domestic attachments lead them to remain together, so that inducements which would tempt many others to the gold fields are powerless on the Highlanders.' An Adelaide newspaper mentioned another reason why they were unwilling to stray from their own flock. 'They cannot converse freely except in Gaelic.'

It was not only a deep need of the Hebrideans that they should remain together after they had reached their destination, it was also their expectation. Through all their privations they had been sustained by the hope of rebuilding a communal life in this great empty continent. Their disappointment, when they discovered that no such provision had been made, must have been shattering. A petition to the Governor from the heads of a kinship group newly disembarked at Adelaide in 1855 throws light on their state of mind.

These men, in passable English, 'humbly beg your Lordship, that government would grant each family of us more or less land, in a manner that we would be able to live by it, as we would pay the whole amount to government by instalment. In the next place, we the undersigned, as all head of families, should we scatter here and there in search of work, we don't know what to do with our families, as we have no money to uphold them during our absence. We do humbly expect to have better prospect through your Lordship's influence.' Had proper arrangements been made here for the reception of the Hebrideans, their language and culture might have taken root in Australia as occurred in Nova Scotia, and as the Welsh language has done in Argentina.

But it is Australia that has produced, in Professor Eric Richards, the outstanding scholar of the Highland Clearances and publisher of this evidence of the fate of the emigrants. Among them was one Christina MacAskill from Harris, who died in 1853 aged thirty, only a few weeks after her arrival in Adelaide. Her two little children, probably unable to understand English, had to be placed in an asylum for the destitute while their father went up country to seek work. Such a dreadful climax to their previous sufferings might have been avoided if the immigrants from Harris had not been forced to separate. Statistics of human misery cannot strike the heart so sharply as the fate of those two motherless children from Harris.

———12———
Leverhulme

The stories of Harris and Lewis, divided by Leod between his sons, Tormod and Torcuil, in the thirteenth century, were drawn together in the twentieth by an Englishman who purchased both.

William Lever was born at Bolton in Lancashire, and laid the foundations of a world-wide commercial empire with a capital of over £46 million by the manufacture of soap. A pious Non-conformist, he expressed his devotion to his wife by joining her maiden name of Hulme to his own when he was raised to the peerage. He was a sixty-seven-year-old widower by the time he purchased Lewis in May 1918. He did not come in search of social status or the recreations of a sporting proprietor or a tranquil place of retirement. He was moved by an ambition to solve the Hebridean problem, using his vast wealth and outstanding talents. No enterprise of his had ever failed in the past: to this one he devoted the last seven years of his life.

He acquired Lewis a few months before the armistice released all the servicemen to return home. In January 1919 he purchased south Harris from the Earl of Dunmore. By this time north Harris was owned by Sir Samuel Scott, living in the great castle of Amhainnsuidh, built in 1868. Leverhulme bought him out in June, thus becoming proprietor of the whole island.

The islanders were accustomed to noblemen of all sorts, millionaires, and owners of their land who could not understand their language. They had not encountered one who retained the virtues of the *petit bourgeois*, austere in his personal life, addicted to hard work, egalitarian in his social intercourse, yet autocratic in pursuit of his objectives. When he moved into Matheson's castle at Stornoway Leverhulme did not occupy one of the large bedrooms, but an attic open to the leads. He enjoyed dancing, and when he invited the local people to his parties he was punctilious in taking as his partner every elderly woman among his guests.

His insights were remarkable, and transcended his ability to persuade the public to buy his soap, or anything else that he determined to sell them. He was an early advocate of the six-hour working day and of a decimal coinage. It remained to be seen whether he would succeed in comprehending the habits and aspirations of Hebrideans and in communicating his own to them, across a divide symbolised by the language barrier.

Leverhulme did not discover his mission in Lewis; he brought it with him. He was determined to implement the policy that the Fisheries Society, John Knox the bookseller and so many others had attempted to promote in the past. During the year from October 1917 to September 1918, the catches of herring landed at Stornoway consisted of 54,000 crans preserved on ice, 30,000 that were kippered, and 2700 pickled. The figures were promising, but Leverhulme was concerned to find a solution to the problems of scarcity and glut, and in so doing he became the pioneer of fish canning in Britain. More remarkable still, he was thirty years ahead of his time in experimenting with methods of quick freezing.

He used himself, his family and guests as guinea-pigs. 'I had the frozen herring for breakfast yesterday, and neither myself nor any of our guests could distinguish the difference.' Before the end of 1918 he had already registered his Stornoway Fish Products and Ice Company, and Lewis Preserved Specialities Company.

There was to be no waste of the produce of the sea. Dogfish had been caught in the past for their oil. He declared that their flesh was delicious and that they should be processed into fish cakes. The offal should be converted into fish-meal and fertiliser, bones and heads into jelly and glue. Work was begun on a canning factory in Stornoway and the machinery for it was ordered from Stavanger in Norway. Although this was to be the industrial base, there were to be satellites in other parts of the island.

On his arrival Leverhulme found that the local line-fishing was still being destroyed by illegal trawling. But he planned that the islanders should man ocean-going boats of their own, 'the best-equipped fishing fleet the world has ever seen'. Anticipating radar, he intended that spotter planes should report on the location of shoals of fish. Before the end of 1918 he had set up the Mac Line Drifters and Trawlers Company.

He approached Duncan Maciver, a successful fish merchant in Stornoway, saying to him, 'Whatever I do in the way of trawlers and drifters, I desire to be associated with yourself.' But Maciver declined to go into partnership with him, insisting that he must retain his independence. 'One of the features that one enjoys most, and it should be jealously guarded.' Maciver was, nevertheless, to become his most trusted colleague among the islanders.

Yet Leverhulme failed to realise the extent to which the rest of them shared the same jealousy. It was no part of his plan that they should become owners of the ocean-going boats, as they were of the small craft which they operated at present. They were to be wage-earners as members of his crews. Leverhulme believed in controlling his labour-force.

This approach soon led him into a confrontation over the land of which he was now the feudal Superior. The Board of Agriculture had drawn up its scheme for dividing all the farms of Lewis into crofts in 1917, before the island was put up for sale, and the then Secretary of State for Scotland was committed to its implementation. His name was Robert Munro, of a Clan belonging to Easter Ross, from where he took his title as Lord Alness. Although he knew less about Lewis than Leverhulme did, and found it unnecessary to visit the island in order to discover more, his knowledge of Highland history was deeper. He knew that the splitting up of those farms for the landless cottars to whom they had been promised was an emotive issue; the righting of an ancient wrong that had festered since the clearances.

Leverhulme believed that the crofting way of life was outmoded, and that to extend it would be 'a gross waste of public money'. He found the black houses primitive and filthy. He would build people better homes and offer them a more prosperous future. In the summer of 1919 he employed an acknowledged agricultural expert, Dr Hardy, to make a land-use survey with the help of Arthur Geddes. Their exemplary report went far to confirm conclusions that Leverhulme had reached already. In particular, Hardy stressed that 'a remedial policy based on extension of land for crofters is clearly no solution, since at best it only affects seven per cent of the sufferers'.

Yet Hardy did not support Leverhulme in his belief that fishing offered the sole solution. He accepted the fact of land hunger, and postulated that 'rural reconstruction of the island must rest upon the improvement of the land', since the farmlands already improved were wholly inadequate to the demand. He used terms that Leverhulme may have found hard to comprehend when he wrote that it was 'imperative to revive the traditional community spirit, the essential feature of Hebridean civilisation'. This was a treasure hidden in the smoke of the black houses, transmitted in a language the new proprietor could not understand.

But the facts of reclamation were clear enough. Lewis contained 710 million tons of peat, Hardy pointed out, 20 feet deep in some places. Everywhere in Europe arable land had been reclaimed from peat in the past, and much of the soil of Lewis had been won in the same manner. There was no reason why the process should not be continued on a more systematic basis. The paradox was that Leverhulme could not legally interfere with the common grazings, which were precisely where much of this improvement should have been undertaken. Perhaps he was thankful. He permitted two half-hearted schemes, but when his heart was in a project there was generally more to be seen than that.

In the circumstances it is greatly to his credit that he did promote the cottage industry of weaving. This had been a part-time employment, like line-fishing, fitted into the intervals between seed-time, harvest and winning the peats: but it had languished in Lewis by the time Leverhulme bought the island. Harris tweed, by contrast, was already world-famous, nursed by the Dunmores, and there was a boom in this product after 1918.

Despite his horror of the black house, from which the tweed derived its distinctive odour, Leverhulme helped to revive the activity, though he offered what he conceived to be more salubrious surroundings. 'My intention is to erect at convenient centres in Lewis and Harris small power-driven dyeing, carding and spinning industries to prepare the crofters' wool for the handloom weaver to work into cloth in or near their homes.' Preferably near them rather than in them, he seems to be suggesting. With this alternative in mind, he introduced steel looms from Yorkshire in sheds that he built at Ness, Barvas and Carloway. Here he was encouraging crofters in their traditional way of life. Nevertheless he set up these work sheds on the west side of the island, far from the fishing centre of Stornoway. They have been dismantled since, and weaving is once more a genuine cottage industry in Lewis.

But as for the farms, he was determined that these should not be divided into crofts. He had been scandalised to discover that milk was imported from the mainland and that many families could not afford to buy it. Neither did they enjoy a nourishing meat diet. The farms would provide the milk for a dairy that he began building at Stornoway, and become a sufficient source of beef and mutton as well. 'If the farms are taken, I shall be forced,' he warned, 'to stop the development work.' The autocrat had reared his head.

During 1919 the Land Settlement (Scotland) Act was passed, which gave the Board of Agriculture two and three quarter million pounds to spend on the acquisition of such properties, with compulsory powers of purchase. In the district of Back, north of Stornoway, cottars moved into the farms of Coll and Gress, staked out their claims and began to build themselves dwellings. These were the farms that Leverhulme coveted above all, to provision Stornoway.

His response to the raids was to visit the district in person and make an appeal to the culprits. He stood on the end of the bridge of Gress, facing about a thousand people, the disputed green slopes rising behind them to his left, the waters of Broad Bay to which he wished to lure them on his other hand. He was a stocky man, plain and direct in his speech, and the words with which he unfolded his plans for their future prosperity have been recorded. His audience cheered him loudly when he had finished.

But at that moment a member of the crowd made a short speech in Gaelic to his companions, before turning to Leverhulme with a question that evoked an even louder burst of applause. Leverhulme asked his interpreter for a translation, and discovered that the crofter had been warning the crowd against his promises, saying all the people wanted was the land. Perhaps there were not many dissenting voices, but the farms contained only enough land for a few. Leverhulme drove back from the bridge of Gress, and waited to see whether the majority would persuade them to change their minds.

By November Dr Hardy's report was in his hands, and in that month he gave an address in Edinburgh in which he declared, 'The new Lewis and Harris must be full of thriving and prosperous cities, towns and harbours, and of happy, rich, contented men and women, ten, twenty or one hundred times in number that of the present population.' By the end of 1919 much of the infrastructure could be seen already. In Stornoway the dairy had been completed, the canning factory remained only to be roofed, an ice factory and power house were under construction, the gas works were being renovated. A housing estate was being laid out, containing the kind of suburban home that Leverhulme assumed the islanders would be delighted to exchange for their black houses. Hundreds of men were finding work and wages on the roads he was building south to Arnish, and up the coast beyond Coll and Gress towards North Tolsta.

The islanders could see that Leverhulme had not been delivering empty promises. But still more was going on beyond their field of vision. He was also laying the foundation for the marketing of their produce through Fleetwood on the west coast of England. Refrigerated carriers were to transport their catches to this distribution centre, and a Mac Fisheries chain of shops were to sell them throughout the country. By 1921 the number of these shops had risen to 360.

But still there were those who did not desire to move into a suburban home or become regular wage-earners. They preferred the traditional, independent crofting life the farms could give them, and the government had promised them. 'We fought for this land in France,' they declared, 'and we're prepared to die for it in Lewis.'

When these had not left the farms by the following spring, Leverhulme called a halt to work on the Arnish and Tolsta roads. He dismissed from his employment everyone from the Back district, whether they were among the Coll and Gress raiders or not. He suspended work on the canning factory, so near completion. He informed the Secretary of State that he would resume operations only when the farms had been evacuated, and received support from leading members of the community. Councillor John Morrison declared: 'The present situation has been brought about by the Board of Agriculture.' Provost Roderick Smith warned: 'If the government persists in a policy which would involve the cessation of the development schemes they will be injuring Lewis for political reasons.'

Majority opinion was veering in favour of Leverhulme in the country areas as well. For instance, a resolution came from where his uncompleted road still faces an empty landscape. 'This mass meeting of the men of North Tolsta heartily approves of the schemes of Lord Leverhulme for the development of Lewis and strongly disapproves of the attitude of the raiders of Coll and Gress farms.' But Robert Munro was bound by a government undertaking, and Whitehall was not the best of places in which to assess attitudes in Lewis. 'The Board feels that the time has now come,' he wrote from London, 'when it is their clear duty to proceed with a partial scheme of land settlement in Lewis.'

Faced with this illiterate reading of the situation, Leverhulme conceded the farms on the west side of the island. But he would not give up Coll and Gress, which he considered essential for the needs of Stornoway.

It was high time the Secretary of State visited the island to examine the state of affairs for himself, and he had at last determined to do so when his wife died. He sent the Lord Advocate instead. This man was called Morison, one of the most common names in Lewis, but in fact he was Edinburgh born and bred. Presumably he was a competent lawyer, since he became a judge of the Court of Session, but he proved unfit to cope with the situation that faced him when he landed in Lewis in October 1920. He persuaded the raiders to withdraw from the farms pending a settlement, which they duly did. But either because he was known to be committed to the crofting system, or because he was the spokesman of an administration that had passed the Settlement Act, or even because he failed to express himself with the clarity of a Leverhulme, his words were interpreted by different people in different ways.

This proved fatal when Leverhulme appealed to Munro in December to postpone any division of the remaining farms for ten years, a proposal that was accepted everywhere in the island except in Back where Coll and Gress lay. Munro agreed in January 1921, saying, 'From the numerous resolutions which have reached me from meetings held throughout the islands, I think I am entitled to assume that your policy is endorsed by a very large section of the community.' But a smaller section of the community felt entitled to assume, after listening to the Lord Advocate, that they had been asked to withdraw from the farms pending an immediate division of them. The game of musical chairs soon began again.

In May 1921 Leverhulme brought all development works to a halt once more, and this time he announced that he would not be entertaining his relatives and friends at the castle during the summer. He informed Munro again that operations would be resumed when the raiders withdrew, and the Secretary of State wrote: 'It does seem a pity that the whole future of the island for years to come should be jeopardised and indeed wrecked, on account of a difference of policy regarding two small farms.'

A tragedy indeed. It was not really of fundamental importance whether milk and meat reached Stornoway from Coll and Gress or from the mainland. But it was a matter of principle to Leverhulme that the economy of the island should be planned from the start in a rational manner, just as it was a point of principle to the raiders that they should recover their ancestral lands.

'We want work, not crofts. We have had enough of crofts,'

somebody had called out to Lord Morison during a meeting he held in Stornoway. But the politicians had promised them crofts, and so crofts were what they got. Leverhulme wrote to Munro: 'Sooner than have to submit to these two farms being taken piecemeal, I have decided not to oppose your taking the whole of the farms of Coll and Gress subject to satisfactory terms being arranged.' He threw in two more farms, out of which 120 new crofts were created, in addition to 81 that were enlarged.

That autumn Leverhulme unveiled the war memorial on its eminence above Stornoway, and paid generous tribute to the islanders in what proved to be his speech of farewell. In the evening he paid a visit to his uncompleted canning factory with Duncan Maciver's son. There, in the presence of this sole witness, he broke down and wept over the wreck of his dream. Then he sailed away in the darkness, never to return.

But he did bequeath a final legacy to Lewis, a free gift of the island to its inhabitants, with its castle, and all the houses and installations he had erected. No such act of munificence was ever seen in the Highlands and Islands, before or since. The inhabitants accepted the town, and the Stornoway Trust was established to administer it. The castle was let profitably to sporting tenants until after the Second World War, when it was converted into a Technical College. The surrounding woods and parklands have provided some of the town's finest amenities, including its golf course.

Some 3000 statutory tenants were offered their crofts as a gift, but only forty-one of these accepted. In this, they showed their awareness of what Leverhulme had asserted in the first place, that crofting was not a viable way of life any more, but depended on external subsidy. Unemployment and destitution returned to Lewis after his departure, leading to massive emigration.

But Leverhulme did not sail so far when he left Lewis. After he had wiped his eyes, he turned them towards Harris. In 1919 he had announced in Edinburgh that this island was to share in the golden future, and it was already rumoured then that he was planning to construct a harbour at the southern end of Harris, far larger than that of Rodel. In Harris he provided work for everyone in need of employment at a time of acute depression, much of it at Obbe, which was renamed Leverburgh. The population of Harris had been culled since it stood at about 3900 in 1831, but by now it had reached 4750.

The advantage of Leverburgh as a fishing port was that it faced the Atlantic as well as the Minch. The channel was beset by rocks, but Leverhulme planned to blast some of these away and to mark the remainder with buoys. He moved much of his plant here, built warehouses, homes in which his employees could live, and another for himself with a round, walled garden. A kippering industry was started here successfully in 1924, and in the following year the islanders started trawling for white fish as well as drifting for herring. The barometer was set fair when Leverhulme died suddenly in May 1925. His executors instantly halted all his Hebridean projects. Leverburgh, which had cost a quarter of a million pounds to construct, was sold off to a demolition company for £5000. Those who had been unwilling to surrender their hard-won statutory rights for the undertakings of an elderly man were, to some extent, vindicated. On the other hand, those who would have preferred the island to be purchased by the Board of Agriculture had the experience of Raasay to reflect upon in due course.

So ended a tragedy that can be compared, at one level, to the one Galsworthy staged in his play, *Strife*. Leverhulme may have seen this long before he purchased Lewis and Harris, for he was addicted to the theatre. There is some evidence that he saw his own conflict as a personal one between himself and Munro, the Secretary of State. But like the protagonists of Galsworthy's play, both of them were at the mercy of forces beyond their control.

After the great war, Britain lost her export markets in Russia and eastern Europe. A recession hit the entire Scottish fishing industry. As Dr Hardy's colleague, Arthur Geddes, was to write, 'Knowing how much local fishing depended upon international policy, particularly the resumption of trade relations with the chief customers of the past, Leverhulme, one feels, should have dealt no less outspokenly with these,' than he did with the government when it failed to support his Hebridean project. Lewismen who regarded the project warily were influenced by the fact that in the past they had found employment in east-coast fishing boats. When Leverhulme arrived on the scene, the number of places in these boats had sunk to a few hundred.

Another factor was that the new steam drifters required smaller crews. Most ominous of all, there were occasions during the dispute when Leverhulme curtailed work in Lewis, not because of the raiders, but because of a financial crisis in another sector of Lever Brothers' gigantic empire.

Geddes was to write: 'There are men and women of insight in Lewis today, to whose judgment a lifetime's disinterested work with the people gives some authority, who believe that in the end Leverhulme's incursion brought little lasting good.' But if it achieved nothing else, it did evoke a surge of vitality, a lively debate, a questioning of values. When the islanders referred to Leverhulme in Gaelic as 'the old soap man', they were not sneering at him. Rather, they responded to him in their varying attitudes with a dignity, a strength of character and a clarity of expression that matched his own.

Two decades later, Sir Frank Fraser Darling commented in his *West Highland Survey* on the 'punch and power to overcome difficulties which is the strength of Lewis'. No doubt the islanders possessed this weapon before Leverhulme appeared, but he certainly gave the islanders a whetstone on which to sharpen it.

──── 13 ────
Catholic Islands

Barra, South Uist and Benbecula, at the southern tail of the Long Island, are the principal Catholic strongholds of the Scottish islands, in a country whose established national church is a Calvinist one.

South Uist and Benbecula originally belonged to the MacDonald of Clanranald who succeeded to his estate in 1794, when it yielded an untaxed income of considerably more than a quarter of a million pounds a year at the modern value of money. After this had been diminished by the collapse of the kelp boom he resorted to the capital, selling South Uist and Benbecula in 1827, Canna in 1828 and Eigg soon afterwards. These were merely the adjuncts of a mainland estate based on the great castle of Tioram in Moidart, which also went under the hammer to pay for his extravagance abroad.

By contrast, the small island of Barra contained the very seat of its MacNeil Chief, the castle of Kisimul on its rock in Castlebay. This castle had been built as early as the fifteenth century, and the last Chief to inhabit it before it fell into ruin was General Roderick MacNeil. He was reputed to be a choleric individual, but perhaps his temper was affected by the worries he inherited in 1822 with the chiefship. The estate was burdened with settlements in favour of other members of the family, just when the price of kelp was starting to collapse.

General MacNeil might have evicted his clansmen in order to sell their land to a wealthy sheep farmer, as others were doing at this time. In fact, he tried to keep them in their homeland, though he certainly extracted all the labour he could from them, in a desperate attempt to meet the financial obligations that had been laid on his shoulders. It was not for the islanders' benefit that he promoted the fisheries and established a glass factory at Northbay, nor were they protected from the danger of eviction for long. MacNeil was ill-served by his mainland agents, who mismanaged his affairs until the isle of Barra had to be sold in 1838 to pay his creditors.

Barra was purchased by John Gordon of Cluny for £38,050, and he also acquired South Uist and Benbecula. Gordon belonged to an Aberdonian family which already possessed a reputation for meanness and rapacity. When he died in 1858 he was said to be the richest commoner in Scotland. Charles Fraser-Mackintosh, the Inverness Member of Parliament and landowner who participated in the Napier Commission of 1883, referred to him as 'the unlamented Aberdonian', and recalled how he had wished to turn Barra into a convict settlement, and was ready to dispose of it as such to Government, no doubt first by clearing off the whole population. He evicted his islanders by the thousand, with a cruelty that became a national scandal.

Towards the end of 1850 *The Scotsman* reported that his vassals in Barra 'received notice to remove from their homes in March, but were allowed to remain in them till May, when they were ejected from them. The only recourse in the circumstances was to erect tents by means of blankets raised on sticks, while some of them took refuge in caves and in their boats. From these places also they were subsequently warned to remove, and shortly afterwards, under the warrant of the Sheriff Substitute, their tents were demolished and the boats broken up'. John Gordon was generally resident in Edinburgh, where he could read such news over his breakfast. Evidently it left him unabashed.

Public indignation was inflamed by the sight of ragged, starving islanders who trailed into the mainland towns. The eccentric re-porter, Thomas Mulock, suggested that the new-found sympathy for 'maltreated Celtic serfs' was influenced by a fear that the towns-people might become liable for their support. Gordon received a query from Glasgow, asking him what he intended to do for the relief of his destitute islanders who had arrived in the city: 'Of the appearance in Glasgow of a number of my tenants and cottars from the parish of Barra I had no intimation previous to my receipt of your communication; and in answer to your enquiry . . . I say, "Nothing".'

A succession of writers have cast doubts on the accounts of atrocities. But the Australian historian, Professor Eric Richards, has unearthed reports from the distant destinations of emigrants which corroborate them in all too sickening detail. Canadian depositions tell of Gordon's victims, hunted by factors and policemen when they hid in the hills, handcuffed and forced aboard the ships, families divided. Those who had been promised that Gordon would provide for their passage abroad were described by the quarantine officer at

Grosse Isle on their arrival. 'I never, during my long experience at the station, saw a body of emigrants so destitute of clothing and bedding; many children of nine or ten years old had not a rag to cover them . . . One full-grown man passed my inspection with no other garment than a woman's petticoat.' The unlamented Aberdonian need not concern himself. The law was on his side and his policy was approved by Sir Charles Trevelyan in London.

After John Gordon's death, the surviving islanders passed under the heel of Lady Gordon Cathcart and her husband Sir Reginald Cathcart who, according to one of the parish priests, 'Ground down the tenants until they were little better than slaves.' When the Napier Commission arrived in 1883, it received a reply to one of its questions which helps to explain the continuing presence of these natives. One of the inhabitants of a township in an arid corner of South Uist was asked why it had not been cleared of its people. 'You must understand,' he said, 'that the land was not thought good enough for clearing.'

The commissioners faced a particular problem here, outlined by a letter from the Bishop. 'I refer to the way in which the Catholics (the great bulk of the population) of South Uist and Barra have been dealt with in educational matters, in being refused Catholic teachers in schools attended almost exclusively by Catholic children.' He expressed the surprise he had felt on taking up his appointment in 1878. 'The whole management of educational matters was practically in the hands of a very small non-Catholic minority, who in no ways represented the feelings or wishes of the immense majority of the people.' He had written to the absentee, and Protestant, proprietor Lady Gordon Cathcart about this, but to no effect.

By this time the population of Benbecula, South Uist and Eriskay had been reduced to 5821, of whom only 289 spoke no Gaelic. Among these were the majority of Protestants, including the estate agent of Lady Gordon Cathcart. The Bishop informed the Napier Commission that people were 'deterred by fear' from exercising their right to demand Catholic teachers. As soon as the Crofter Act had given them protection from the threat of eviction, the islanders appointed an English Catholic named F. G. Rea as teacher in Garrynamonie school, the first in which a vacancy occurred. He was welcomed to South Uist in 1890 by Father Allan MacDonald, who had himself been appointed to the island six years earlier. It was a meeting of two very remarkable young men.

Over their first meal together, Father Allan listened carefully to Rea's speech and expressed his satisfaction. 'Your English is so clear, and anyone can easily understand every word you say.' At first Rea was taken aback. 'But when Father Allan went on to explain that most Englishmen he had met were visitors who came to the hotel for the salmon and trout fishing, I had a shrewd idea what he meant; for often the exaggerated accent and drawl affected by some of my countrymen when visiting abroad is appalling.' A plain-spoken townsman from Birmingham, Rea not only taught his children conscientiously but left a rare picture of their little world with all the attention to detail of a sympathetic outsider.

'The scene of the children of all ages entering at the doors, each with a piece of peat which was deposited on the floor near the fire, was quite novel. Though it was winter time, none of the children wore shoes or stockings and all the boys, with the exception of a few of the biggest, wore kilts of home-spun cloth.' It was his first encounter with about a hundred children, many of whom could speak no English, while he had not a word of Gaelic. Two girls who were Gaelic-speaking student teachers assisted him.

Rea described the winter hardships of these children who, 'with a very few exceptions, had nothing to eat from when they left home in the morning till they returned in the evening. Often they were wet through before they arrived at school, and remained all day in their damp clothes, for it would have been an impossible task to have dried all their clothes by the fires.'

As for the weather in which they sometimes travelled to school, he recalled a gale in which, 'When I ventured out of my door to go to the school, it was as though I was being pushed by a board to the wall and pressed hard against it. By dint of holding on to the stones and pulling myself sideways, the wind pressing me tightly against the wall all the time, I managed to reach the opening into the playground where I was at once torn from my hold and whirled right past the school door.' When lessons were over, he found men in oilskins peeping round the lee side of the school wall. He took two of their children by either hand. 'When we reached the opening through which I had passed in trying to get into school that morning, they were lifted right up in the air.' Rea himself crawled home on his hands and knees.

He tells us: 'There was only one policeman for South Uist and two other islands containing altogether a population of seven thou-

sand, but his post was a sinecure as the people were most peaceful.'
He suggests their staple diet by mentioning that he was given salt
herring for breakfast on his arrival and salt ling for high tea. One of
his greatest services was to open evening classes in seamanship, so
that this society of fishermen would have access to Mates' Certificates
when they went away to sea.

He witnessed the waulking (hand-fulling) of the tweed, now a
thing of the past, and heard the songs that accompanied this labour.
Donald MacCormick, Rea's school attendance officer, was making
a collection of these waulking songs, so helping to preserve what the
poet, Sorley Maclean, has described as one of the finest achievements
of Scottish culture.

Like MacCormick, Father Allan was a poet himself. But he also
made a dictionary of the special meanings of words and phrases in
South Uist, as well as keeping a Gaelic diary and collecting folk-tales.

Such interests were not new to his island, but they had received
a stimulus from John Francis Campbell, the pioneer of systematic
folklore studies. Known as *Iain Òg Ile*, Young John of Islay, he was
the heir who failed to inherit the island, though his memorial still
overlooks Islay House. Before his death in 1885 he had published
his four volumes of Gaelic folk tales, his collection of Ossianic
ballads, and had inspired other scholars by his example. Father
Allan came to South Uist in the year before the death of *Iain Òg
Ile*, and was among the worthiest of his successors.

Father Allan travelled everywhere on foot, ministering to his
scattered parish. The 400 inhabitants of Eriskay were especially
inaccessible. It is an extremely barren island, on which all these
people had been flung during the clearances, and where they could
only support life by fishing. In 1893 Father Allan was moved to
Eriskay, where he built a new church and where he died in 1905, at
the tragically early age of forty six.

Before he did so, his island suffered a novel form of exploitation.
An unscrupulous charlatan named Ada Goodrich Freer wheedled
his papers out of him and used them to publish articles and a book
in which she was able to pose as an expert on Hebridean folklore,
although ignorant of its very language. Much of Father Allan's
material was rendered valueless by this treatment, and many of his
papers went missing. At the same time, the very existence of Donald
MacCormick's collection of waulking songs would have been unknown after it had disappeared without trace, but for Father Allan's

reference to it. As for Rea's account of his sojourn in South Uist, it remained the secret of his family in England.

However, the living arts continued to flourish though their records were lost. 'Father Allan,' Rea assures us, 'was a lover of bagpipe music and he often invited different pipers to his house to play for him.' This was a contrast to what occurred in the Calvinist islands, where the pious were encouraged to burn their pipes. Here the very children danced to their music, as Rea described. 'The pipes were playing and many of the older children were dancing reels, the rest of them clapping hands and laughing – it was a happy scene.' Pipe music was being transmitted by oral tuition, like the stories and the songs. 'I found that a number of boys had brought their "chanters", and the piper held a competition to ascertain the best player. It was amazing to me to see and hear how well these lads played.'

So it was that the extreme poverty of these islands was compensated by a cultural wealth. In the early Thirties the musicologist Margaret Fay Shaw celebrated the little world which she found in her wonderful book, *Folksongs and Folklore of South Uist*. She tells of the traditional cycle of the seasons, preserves the music and words of the songs that lightened labour, depicts the people who sang them, the houses they lived in and the tasks in which they engaged. Dr Shaw also made a film of this way of life, shown to television audiences fifty years later.

The islanders have received other compensation for the scourge of John Gordon, the larceny of Ada Goodrich Freer, and the loss of Father Allan. In the year after his death, John Lorne Campbell was born. He met Margaret Fay Shaw at Lochboisdale in South Uist and in 1935 they were married. This was a time when the waulking songs were still to be heard in the home. Dr Shaw would take down both the words and the music by the light of a storm-lantern, for the fulling of the cloth was a winter activity, and later correct her texts with the singers.

John Lorne Campbell brought his first recording apparatus to Barra in 1937, and later recorded live waulkings in South Uist. It is likely that by 1955 the activity had died out throughout the Hebrides. So, by this narrow margin, a great part of this unique repertoire was saved.

Dr Campbell's activities were far-reaching. Rea's family sent him their secret treasure, which he edited impeccably and published as *A School in South Uist* in 1964. Through the post came Donald

MacCormick's lost collection, and it forms the first volume of Campbell's monumental *Hebridean Folksongs*, published in 1969. The original manuscript contained none of the airs, but from live singing he traced those of all forty songs except one, and included all their variant versions in his text. These revealed the liberties Marjory Kennedy-Fraser had taken in the art songs she had composed on their basis.

Rescuing what he could of the pilfered work of Father Allan, Campbell published the latter's dictionary in 1958 and an edition of his poetry in 1965, *Bardachd Mhgr Ailein*. It was the network of scholarly associates whom all this activity attracted that helped to bring to light the seventeenth-century papers of Edward Lhuyd and John Beaton. The presses of Oslo and Dublin, London and Oxford shared the honour of publishing this wealth of material.

Campbell has added the living as well as the dead to his island choir. In particular, he recorded the life story and the repertoire of songs and stories of Angus MacLellan, who was already fourteen years old when the Napier Commission came to hold its hearings in South Uist in 1883. Here was a man whose retentive mind at the age of eighty-five preserved a priceless picture of his folk during that span of time. Campbell assembled 'much the longest text in colloquial Scottish Gaelic', and published two volumes in English translation, comprising less than a quarter of this material, as well as a Gaelic text. For this achievement Angus MacLellan received the MBE, the first award ever bestowed for services to Gaelic culture.

Angus lived well into his nineties, strong in mind and body. 'We used to have bread and tea in the morning, potatoes and fish for our midday meal, and porridge and milk for supper.' Boats from the Isle of Man and Ireland used to come and buy their potatoes at seven shillings a barrel. But when Angus's father went with others to plant potatoes on the offshore isle of Calvay, his companions received a sentence of six weeks' imprisonment in Edinburgh. He had received an interdict from Lady Gordon Cathcart's factor, and was not on Calvay when the others were caught, so he escaped.

The family also escaped death when, one after another, they all contracted typhus. People incurred a dangerous risk of infection when they tended their sick neighbours, and Angus was warned by his mother not to enter a house to which she sent him with milk, butter and bread that she had baked. But he disobeyed her. 'I went and poured the milk into a vessel for him, and put some water in it, and gave it to him. When he had drunk it he said: 'Oh, may your soul and the souls of your people be rewarded for that in heaven; but I hope to God you won't catch anything I have.' Angus did not, and his patient recovered.

Angus enlisted in 1889 in the Queen's Own Cameron Highlanders, and one of his anecdotes relates how an officer who was a son of Lord Lovat rescued him from unfair punishment by a harsh sergeant. He went on to work, generally as a ploughman, on mainland farms and his description of those years is a contribution to social history without equal.

He returned to South Uist in about 1900 and obtained the status of a crofter eight years later. About half a century passed before John Lorne Campbell met him walking along a road. 'I said, "Where are you going?" "I'm going to collect my sheep at Loch Eynort for the shearing." I thought he was a man of about sixty-five, but I learnt to my astonishment he was twenty years older.'

Campbell had begun his voyage of discovery in the western isles when he sailed to Barra in 1928. Here he found a society no less unaffected by the English-speaking, industrialised mainland. It was rich in many-sided personalities of whom John MacPherson was a remarkable example. He had become Postmaster of Northbay in 1923 and was elected a County Councillor for many years. With the advent of the motor-car, he introduced the first into Barra in 1928. When the tourists began to arrive he opened a guest-house, and it attracted politicians and peers, scholars and sportsmen, people who came as much to savour his company as to explore his island. He was known as the Coddy, and it was he who helped Campbell to perfect his Gaelic.

Compton Mackenzie came to live on Barra in 1933 when he was fifty years old and at the height of his fame. He invited Campbell to visit him and one of their earliest joint ventures was to assemble all the historical evidence they could find about the island, which they published in *The Book of Barra*. As for Compton Mackenzie's association with the Coddy, millions must have seen the film that was made of his novel *Whisky Galore*, in which John MacPherson eclipsed the professional actors by his performance in a major role, as though he had been a film-star all his life. His rarest gift was the ability to tell stories with equal art both in English and Gaelic, adapting his style to the scope of these two very different languages.

Croft in South Uist
Castlebay, Barra

Goat Fell, Arran

Brodick Castle, Arran

Glen Rosa, looking towards Goat Fell, Arran

Lochranza Castle, Arran
Cathedral of St Magnus, Kirkwall, Orkney

Earl Patrick's Palace, Kirkwall, Orkney

Kitchener's Memorial on Marwick Head, and cliffs of Orkney's western mainland

Lerwick fishing boats, Shetland

Oil tanker at Sullom Voe, Shetland
Scalloway Castle and harbour, Shetland

Campbell recorded him extensively in both and after his death in 1955 published examples of his bilingual skill in *Tales from Barra, told by the Coddy*. The two men, with enthusiastic help from others, also recorded as many as their time and means permitted, after Campbell had introduced his first wire recording apparatus to the island.

But in 1933, that first year in the long, fruitful association between Compton Mackenzie, the Coddy and Campbell, an event occurred which goaded them into action in a different field. During the summer a government Minister visited the island, in a warship that was actually lying in the bay when some trawlers sailed in and began to fish illegally. The islanders' protest to Whitehall met with a bland denial of what everyone had witnessed with their own eyes. Thereupon, Sir Compton Mackenzie founded the Sea League, the Coddy became its active spokesman and Campbell its secretary. Its activities were not confined to Barra. Meetings were arranged from one end of the Long Island to the other.

This wrong was an ancient one, but it contained a novel enormity. A Sea Fisheries Regulation (Scotland) Act had been passed in 1895 to protect the essential livelihood of the islanders, and it lay dead on the statute book. Had it been implemented, the Minch would have been closed to foreign trawlers in the same way in which the Vestfjord, between the Lofoten islands and the Norwegian mainland, was protected.

The profits of *The Book of Barra* were devoted to the expenses of the Sea League, whose broadsheet, published in English and Gaelic, is a notable contribution to the Hebridean literature of protest. Campbell was to write later, 'I have never been more thoroughly convinced of the justice of any cause than I was of the Sea League. The situation was a revelation of the attitude of the Westminster Government and the Scottish office towards the Hebrides. The islands were despised because they were poor, and they were poor because their economic interests in the greatest source of wealth accessible to them, the sea, had been sacrificed to those of the English trawling monopolies.'

This was what Leverhulme had set out to rectify a decade earlier. By the time the Minch was closed in 1964, over a generation later, the traditional occupation of the island fishermen, using ring nets and long lines, had been destroyed.

The Sea League broadsheet publicised other scandals, including that of the roads. In 1936 all the car-owners on Barra refused to pay their road fund licences. The twenty miles of road on their island consisted for the most part of cart tracks that had been laid during the potato blight of the 1840s. 'To get to the populous settlement of Eoligarry at the north end of the island it is necessary to take to wet salt sand for nearly a mile across the Traigh Mhór.'

The culprits received such a savage sentence, coupled with a threat of imprisonment, that they appealed to the High Court of Justiciary. Here the Lord Justice Clerk ruled: 'It is illegal, apart from express power conferred by statute, to fence the payment of expenses with the sanction of imprisonment. I cannot regard an illegality of this kind as in any sense a trivial matter, and I have felt the greatest doubt as to whether it is not the duty of the Court to set the sentence aside.' The legal expenses had been costly, but at least the islanders received justice on this occasion. Their roads received attention as well.

It was in 1936, while the islanders were preoccupied over illegal trawling and the condition of their roads, that a MacNeil Chief reappeared in Barra. He was an American architect named Robert Lister MacNeil, who had been recognised as such by the Lyon King of Arms in Edinburgh and waited until the death of the absentee Lady Gordon Cathcart in order to purchase her share of the island. Albany Herald hailed his achievement in restoring the ruin of Kisimul, on its rock in Castlebay. 'It is often complained that some Chiefs have sold their old clan territory and emigrated. Here is an outstanding example of the reverse: of a Chief who has devoted his whole life and fortune to returning from the New World to rebuild the ruined home of his forefathers.'

Many of the Barra folk failed to share his enthusiasm. Theirs was an egalitarian, Gaelic, crofting society free from the tartanic flummeries associated with Caledonian balls and clan gatherings. They would have preferred their castle to remain a ruin than to be restored as a base for junketings that had no intrinsic connection with their lives. In any case the islanders, who knew their genealogy at least as well as the Lord Lyon in Edinburgh, were well aware of the rival claim of a Canadian MacNeil, which he did not receive long enough notice to advance. But, as Dr Campbell suggests, 'Various outside clan societies and political interests in Scotland, including one important Highland paper,' were determined to reimpose a Chief of Barra, and not surprisingly they succeeded.

The real Chief, the Coddy, died and was buried near the ruins of St Barr's church. Compton Mackenzie left the island after twelve years. He wrote: 'It is my hope that one day I shall rest near him and the other old friends in the last *céilidh* of all.' He has had his wish. John Lorne Campbell and his wife went in 1938 to live on the isle of Canna, where they have remained ever since. It was the Coddy who told them it was for sale, before this had become public knowledge. Here they have created a mecca for Hebridean studies, to which scholars from all over the world have been coming for decades. And in 1981 they placed it in the custody of the National Trust for Scotland, with their priceless archive of recordings and their library. Unlike the records of Iona, the muniments of the Lordship of the Isles and the Beaton library, what the Campbells have retrieved of the Hebridean heritage is safe.

14
Arran and Bute: Islands in the Royal Domain

The two largest islands in the Firth of Clyde flaunt monuments that proclaim a different history from any of the other Scottish islands. One is Rothesay castle, dominating the capital town of Bute. It is among the country's oldest, and consisted originally of a circular wall built on a flat-topped mound surrounded by a moat, the only structure of its kind in Scotland. Four round towers were added in the thirteenth century projecting from its walls, which still stand to a height of thirty feet. The central tower was added in about 1500.

Visitors who sail into Brodick harbour on Arran set eyes on another castle that dominates the bay, not a ruin like Rothesay, but a palace that has been inhabited and enlarged over the centuries until it passed, during the present one, into the custody of the National Trust for Scotland. Brodick castle is unique among the Scottish islands, and like Rothesay castle it is a reminder that Bute and Arran were the property of the Stewart kings; their personal property, not territory which they acquired by inheriting the Crown.

How early the family of Walter the High Steward acquired Bute is uncertain, but his son Alan was in a position to bestow its church of Kingarth on Paisley abbey in 1204. So evidently they were established here before Alexander Stewart, co-Regent of Scotland in 1255, laid claim to Arran through marriage with the island's heiress. She was a descendant of King Somerled, who had given Arran to his son, Angus. When the male line failed, Somerled's family contested the Stewart claim. They asserted the traditional Celtic rule that the assets of a kindred should be redistributed within it in such circumstances, not alienated by marriage with a stranger. This was to remain a source of strife for centuries.

Meanwhile the people of Arran received visits from two most distinguished kings long before their owners acquired royal status. The first of these was Haakon of Norway, who sailed round the Mull of Kintyre in 1263 on his expedition to assert his sovereignty, and anchored his fleet in the bay of Lamlash. Although all the islanders were probably speaking Gaelic by this time, they were still surrounded by many mementoes of their Viking past when their legit-

imate King from Norway arrived in their midst. There were conspicuous Norse graves. Broad Vik, now called Brodick, and Sandy Vik,
now Sannox, were still identified in the old tongue: so was their
highest peak, Geita Fjell, Goat Fell. Haakon's expedition failed,
he died in Orkney on his way home and three years later his successor
ceded all the western isles to the King of Scots, together with the
overlordship of Man.

Scarcely more than a generation later the Arran folk found another
King in their midst, in no less dramatic circumstances. The Scottish
royal house had died out in the direct line, John Balliol had become
King as the senior collateral heir, and then been deposed when he
tried to resist the bullying demands of the King of England. The
next in line of succession, Robert Bruce, was crowned in 1306, and
led the resistance to Edward of England's attempt to subjugate the
country. At the outset he was defeated and forced to flee the land.

The next claimant after Balliol and Bruce was John Hastings,
Lord of Abergavenny. The three men descended from three sisters,
Balliol from the eldest, Bruce from the second and Hastings from
the youngest. Hastings submitted that the Scottish kingdom was
divisible between the heirs of the three of them like any other

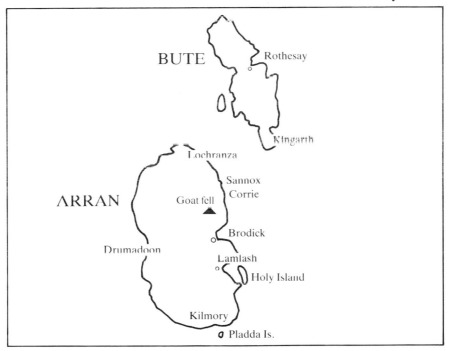

property. But now Balliol had been deposed and Bruce had fled, Hastings had larger expectations, which King Edward encouraged when he gave Hastings a Scottish earldom including Arran and Bute. That is how he came to be holding the castle of Brodick in 1307. Only a small part of its present structure, known for no good reason as the Bruce's room, could possibly date from that time.

King Robert's staunch companions, Douglas and Boyd, rowed secretly to the island with a band of supporters, and went into hiding beside Brodick bay. When three boats arrived from the mainland, bringing supplies for the garrison, they pounced. Some men rushed to the rescue from the castle, but the patriots chased them back again. During this interval the supply boats put to sea, but the wind was against them and they were wrecked. The party of Douglas returned to the assault, and secured a precious consignment of arms, food and wine. Then, since the castle was too strong to attack, they found a remoter hiding-place where they remained for ten days, wondering what to do next.

Unknown to them, Robert Bruce had set out from Rathlin island off the coast of Ireland, and landed on Arran. He found an old woman who told him of the fracas on the shore at Brodick and led him to his friends' secret lair. The episode raises a strong presumption that he had been taught Gaelic by his Celtic mother, although he must have spent most of his life speaking French. The sole account of all these events is the verse chronicle, written in Middle English, of John Barbour, Archdeacon of Aberdeen.

Barbour's narrative does not mention the King's cave at Drumadoon as being Bruce's hiding-place on his return to Arran, let alone the spider. The attribution of the King's cave is dismissed by Arran's historian, Robert McLellan, though this does not discourage visitors from the long walk along a shingle beach below the great iron-age fort to visit this shrine. Nor are they disappointed by what they find. The cave is large enough to hold hundreds of people and on its walls are carvings which, if authentic, date from long before Bruce's time. One depicts a man holding what appears to be a bow over his head, another a cross rising out of foliage, and there are also pictures of animals. McLellan accepts the controversial verdict that these are authentic murals of the Scots of Dalriada.

When the King had rejoined his devoted supporters, they decided to row back across the Firth to his former home of Turnberry castle and resume their guerilla warfare on the mainland. The islanders saw no more of royalty until Bruce had won his throne, his son King David II had died childless, and his Stewart grandson succeeded in 1370 as Robert II, King of Scots.

Robert II was fifty-four years old when he inherited the Crown, a fair age by the standards of the day. But he had employed his more active years in fathering at least twenty-one children, legitimate and illegitimate, whom he endowed with paternal indulgence. Naturally the islands that were his family's personal property were pressed into service. Arran and Bute were privileged to support his bastard son known as Black John Stewart, whose family were created hereditary Sheriffs of Bute and Keepers of Rothesay castle. This had been dismantled during the war of independence, but it was now restored. Both Robert II and his son Robert III loved to retire there, as though it was a favourite holiday home. In Arran, the land of Corrygills, on the broad peninsula between Brodick and Lamlash, was earmarked to maintain the Sheriff's baillie, who resided in Brodick castle.

Robert III detached other lands of Arran for a bastard son of his own, another John Stewart. He was planted in Kildonan, whose castle ruins can still be seen facing towards the little isle of Pladda off the south coast. He was also endowed with the fertile lands of the Shiskine district, extending inland from Drumadoon bay up the Black Water and the Clauchan Water. But much of Arran still remained directly within the royal domain.

Here as elsewhere, the native cultivators had lost the status of peasant proprietors which they had enjoyed under Norse udal law. The treaty under which they passed to the Scottish Crown in 1266 stipulated that 'the men of the said islands, as well lesser as greater, shall be subject to the laws and customs of the realm of Scotland'. What this entailed for the large majority who comprised the 'lesser' folk can be glimpsed in references to the affairs of the royal burghs, to whose number Rothesay was added in 1401. Their regulations stipulated that a thrall who succeeded in living in such a burgh for a year and a day unchallenged should remain free. Likewise, no bondsman could be captured while he was attending a fair in any of them.

The burgesses and guilds of craftsmen in the royal burghs were apt to adopt a hostile attitude to such infiltrators. But the Clyde islanders did possess a more accessible potential asylum from this early date than any in the Hebrides beyond, where fugitives from feudal serfdom might just possibly find safety. They might wish to escape either because their rents and the personal services demanded of them were oppressive, or because they fell victims to the quarrels of their masters.

The career of Ranald Mac Alasdair illustrates their predicament. He appears to have been a survivor of the old Gaelic aristocracy, paying rent for Crown lands under the new dispensation. He was tenant of nine farms for a period of fifteen years, and for four years he was the lessee of the whole island. Consequently he was a prime target for the MacDonalds of Islay, who had never accepted the Stewart title to Arran, and claimed that its rents should be paid to themselves as the true owners. The royal accounts of 1446 describe the losses suffered by tenants in the Lochranza area at the hands of raiding MacDonalds, where Ranald Mac Alasdair was the most substantial farmer.

The King's solution was to place a baron from the nearby mainland in the castle whose ruins still dominate Lochranza bay, that vulnerable place of entry in the north of the island. His name was Montgomery – a name which belonged originally to a castle in the French parish of Lisieux. While this gave the islanders another feudal overlord to support, it does not appear to have increased their safety. In 1455 the leader of the MacDonalds arrived with over 5000 men in seventy galleys, harried the island, and even destroyed Brodick castle. The extent of the damage may be gauged by the fact that Ranald Mac Alasdair was excused his entire rent. Three years later he died in debt.

Presently a family arrived that was to dominate Arran as no other had done in the past. In about 1474 James III married his sister to Lord Hamilton, and thirty years later their son was created Earl of Arran. Plenty of princesses were betrothed to Scottish subjects with generous dowries to support them. But by chance it happened that for generations the descendants of this pair were heirs presumptive to the Crown, as one child sovereign succeeded after another, and there were intervals of years before they were old enough to beget an heir apparent who extinguished the Hamilton claim until the same thing occurred again.

To complicate matters further, the Hamilton claim was contested by the Stewart Earls of Lennox, whom the Sheriffs of Bute supported out of loyalty to their name and clan. The people of Arran and Bute were dragged into a vortex of savage in-fighting beween these semi-royals, at least as barbarous as any of the conflicts in the western isles. A difference was that in the Hebrides the islanders were related to their quarrelsome patriarchs, while here they were simply the vassals of alien overlords.

The details of their conduct do not make edifying reading, but the predicament of islanders living in the royal domain cannot be envisaged without them. In 1526, when James V was a minor, his guardian Stewart of Lennox was murdered by a Hamilton known as the Bastard of Arran. Gang warfare spread to Bute, where Rothesay burgh was burned and its castle besieged in 1527, and to Arran where Brodick castle was burned and its keeper killed in the following year. This was the work of the Sheriff of Bute's own sons, the local source of authority.

After James V had reached an age to embark on his personal reign he visited the damaged castle of Rothesay in 1536, and gave Sir James Hamilton 3000 crowns with which to repair it as a royal residence. On this occasion a Hamilton found himself at the receiving end of royal justice, to his extreme surprise. When he failed to carry out his instructions, and could not account for the money, he was executed.

But James V died in 1542, leaving only a week-old baby, Mary, Queen of Scots. Her brothers had died and she was described as sickly and unlikely to live. The contest between the Stewarts and the Hamiltons for the succession now reached ferocious proportions. The destiny of Queen Mary was a major concern of the courts of Europe. It was also a religious issue, exercising Catholics and Protestants at this critical juncture of the Reformation. Hamilton of Arran and Stewart of Lennox offered themselves to the highest bidder, with as little concern for any religious belief as for the safety of the country or the welfare of their islanders.

Arran became regent, as heir presumptive, joining the Catholic party of the French Queen Mother. Hereupon Lennox brought an armada from England to devastate the island. In 1544 he arrived with a dozen ships from Bristol, utterly destroyed Brodick castle and carried fire and sword throughout Arran. He crossed over to Bute, seized Rothesay castle and let loose his English soldiers on a similar rampage, although this was Stewart property.

But the fatality for both rivals was that Mary had lived, not died. Worse still, she married the heir to the French throne and no son of theirs. For Arran there was a yet more serious one when the

Protestant Queen Elizabeth succeeded her Catholic sister Mary on the English throne in 1558. In that year the English associates of Stewart of Lennox stepped up their pressure on the pro-French party in Scotland. The Earl of Sussex sailed north from Dublin, and according to the official report he 'burned the whole of Kintyre; from thence went to Arran and did the like there'. It gives an appalling description of the manner in which the island peasantry were stripped of their livestock and their small possessions.

Too late, Hamilton of Arran discovered that he had backed the losing side. Queen Mary's French husband died. In 1560 her mother died in Edinburgh, defeated by an invading English army. His final humiliation came with the marriage between Queen Mary and Henry Stewart, Lord Darnley, the son of his arch-enemy Lennox. His own son declined from weak-mindedness into total imbecility.

When Queen Mary was deposed and her baby son was crowned King James VI, Arran became heir presumptive once more. He returned expectantly to Scotland, but this time he did not obtain the regency. He was placed in confinement while the ex-Queen's bastard brother, the Earl of Moray, assumed this office.

Soon the islanders had cause to wonder how many of the country's ruling élite were sane. The Stewart Earl of Moray was murdered by a Hamilton, and revenged by the assassination of John Hamilton, Archbishop of St Andrews. He was a notable reforming prelate and an old man, yet he was hanged with the greatest indignity. Stewart of Lennox succeeded as Regent and was killed in the following year. When the Earl of Arran died a natural death in 1575, Stewart of Bothwellmoor became guardian to his lunatic son, whom he induced to resign all his titles into Stewart's hands. He was a favourite of James VI, by whom he was created Earl of Arran in 1581. Yet it was a Douglas who murdered him and mounted his head on a spear, leaving his corpse to be devoured by dogs. While the earldom now lacked an incumbent, Stewart of Bute obtained the office of Keeper of Brodick castle.

He soon parted with it. A younger brother of the idiot Hamilton heir succeeded in recovering his family's lost property and in 1593 Lord Hamilton appointed John Hamilton 'captain and keeper of his castle of Brodick in Arran and all his lands on this isle of Arran in the sheriffdom of Bute'. James VI went on to create him Marquess of Hamilton. Rarely had the islanders witnessed such kaleidoscopic changes of ownership as during the previous twenty years.

They narrowly escaped a still more bizarre dispensation in 1600. Queen Elizabeth of England's military expedition to Ulster under her favourite, the Earl of Essex, had ended in failure. She proposed that 'the Hamilton Scots be sent to Ireland with their followers out of the Isle of Arran'. There was almost nothing James VI would not have done to ingratiate himself with her and her ministers, as he waited hopefully to inherit her throne. But on this occasion the islanders were not called upon to fight their fellow-Gaels at England's command.

Evidently, conditions at home were far from peaceful at this time. The Privy Council took notice that murder, mutilation and theft had become 'very frequent' in the island. Its Marquess turned into a recluse and his son became an absentee. In 1622 the Privy Council actually attributed the high incidence of crime to 'the non-residence of the Marquess'.

But the greatest hazard to the islanders continued to be the dynastic status of the family that had been planted in their midst. This proved to be a scourge once more when the great rebellion broke out against Charles I. By now there was little prospect that a Hamilton would become heir presumptive again, yet King Charles treated the young third Marquess with all the privileges of a near relative. He created him a Duke, and when the Scots revolted against the King's high-church policies, Charles sent him north to negotiate. Hamilton's arrogance and stupidity were largely responsible for the war which followed.

The Campbell Earl of Argyll stepped forward as leader of the Covenanters, the Calvinist opposition, and the Clyde islands were among the earliest victims of the strife. In 1639 the Campbells invaded Arran and seized Brodick castle. At Lochranza the Montgomeries, now Earls of Eglinton, joined the Covenanters of their own accord, fearful of an invasion by the Catholic, royalist, anti-Campbell MacDonalds. Ancient sources of discord governed the new alignments. Old wine was poured into new bottles.

In 1645 the MacDonalds, under their leader, Montrose, descended on Bute. It appears that although the Stewart Sheriff was holding Rothesay castle for the King, most of the islanders favoured the Covenant. Such was the damage inflicted by the invaders that the levy on Bute was suspended for as long as two years, on the grounds that the island was too crippled to pay it.

The Montgomeries had retired from Lochranza castle to the

mainland, where the Countess of Eglinton wrote to her husband of the panic in their island, as they awaited the arrival of Montrose. 'I assure you they are looking every night for him in Arran, for man, wife and bairn is coming over to this side, and all their goods that they can get transported, both out of Arran and Bute.' They feared the Macdonalds, but it was the Campbells who came.

According to an indictment that was upheld after the Restoration, the Campbells laid Arran waste so thoroughly that it remained a wilderness for the next six years. They carried off all the livestock their boats could contain, and the remainder they killed and flayed for their hides. In Bute, the Campbell atrocities during 1646 involved people as well as property. Two hundred members of the garrison at Toward were bound after they had surrendered, then murdered. Other royalists were hung from trees. These enormities occurred after King Charles had surrendered to the Scots, and his supporters had consequently laid down their arms.

The execution of King Charles and his cousin, Hamilton, was followed by two novelties in Arran. The first was government by a woman, for the Duke left an only daughter, who was recognised as Duchess in her own right after the Restoration and did not wait until then to act in this capacity. Her portrait hangs in Brodick castle, and depicts a woman who was not beautiful, but appears shrewd and masterful.

The other novelty was the arrival of an English garrison in 1652, after Cromwell had placed Scotland under what was probably the most just and efficient administration it had ever enjoyed, a military dictatorship. The Duchess Anne's castle was surrendered without a blow. 'They within granted admittance with these compliments: that our men were very welcome because they were not in a capacity to avoid it, for they told them in plain terms that if they could have prevented it, our men should not have come in there. Yet after about two hours' stay, the chief tenants in the island came and were very civil to the Captain and the soldiers.'

The Protectorate regime imposed a fine on the Hamilton family for their part in the late war, and Anne had paid it in full by 1657, before Cromwell's death. Her castle had been destroyed and rebuilt as often as any in the British Isles, and very much less of its earlier structure remains today than Cromwell's deputies now added to it. A battery was erected at one end of it, whose guns commanded the slope that runs down to Brodick bay. Beside this a well-constructed block of three storeys was added to house the soldiery. All this building activity seems to have inspired the Duchess Anne. She was the first proprietor of Arran who began the construction of its roads, and at Lamlash she built a pier.

In Bute the hereditary keeper of the royal castle of Rothesay surrendered his charge to an English garrison that remained until the year after Cromwell's death. Here, in May 1655, the town clerk, Donald MacGilchrist, was appointed teacher of Rothesay school. He may not have been the first schoolmaster there, but he is the earliest on record, and from his time the records of this famous school are continuous. So is the line of the Sheriffs of Bute. Sir James Stewart lived to see the Restoration and to seek compensation for his losses before his death in 1662. His family astutely avoided the political pitfalls of the years ahead, and received an earldom from Queen Anne.

But it was her namesake the 'Duchess Anne' who dominated the fortunes of the Clyde islands for the remainder of the century and beyond. She lived until 1716, so that she ruled for over sixty-five years, giving her islanders a longer period of stability than any of them could have remembered. Plenty of events occurred in the course of it that might have plunged Arran into turmoil if she had acted with less discretion. The Episcopal establishment was restored after the return of Charles II, and the faithful remnant of the Covenanters endured savage persecution rather than recognise an un-Covenanted King. Duchess Anne was a devout Presbyterian, and she gave her co-religionists what succour she could. But she did not allow the excesses of religious bigotry to cross the water.

Its ripples surrounded her island in 1685 when the Catholic James VII succeeded to the throne and the Earl of Argyll sailed to Islay, Mull and Kintyre, raising recruits for a rebellion on behalf of the Protestant Pretender, the Duke of Monmouth. He landed on Bute, where the Campbells 'committed many abuses, by plundering people's houses and hocking kine, sheep and lambs'. He burned down the only remaining inhabitable portion of Rothesay castle, and his own son was accused by the Minister there of having directed many of the outrages, which included stealing the Rothesay poor-box. It is noteworthy that Argyll did not call upon the redoubtable Duchess Anne, although she was an equally devout Presbyterian.

After their religion had triumphed in the revolution of 1688, she busied herself openly in supporting the reformed ministry, providing communion cups and building churches. For the people of Kilmory, Gaelic religious texts were ordered in 1704. 'The Session has recommended to the Moderator to buy twenty Irish psalm books for the use of the parishioners.' These translations of the psalms were very largely the work of the Campbell clergy of Argyll.

Soon afterwards the Clyde islands, like the others, experienced Edinburgh's attempt to use religion to destroy their Gaelic language. The Society for the Propagation of Christian Knowledge boasted openly in 1716 that their objective was 'rooting out their Irish language, and this has been the care of the Society so far as they could, for all the scholars are taught in English'. Arran possessed no such school as that of Rothesay, but it possessed its village teachers. One of these received adverse comment from the Session of Kilbride in 1714. 'The said Neil being interrogated anent this report confesses that he was intemperate upon Wednesday was a fortnight, with rum, being a kind of liquor with which he was not acquainted and which deceived him.'

The SPCK failed in its mission to the extent that Arran reared a notable Gaelic scholar in the eighteenth century. He belonged to Clachaig, joined the Ministry, and in 1778 published a pioneering *Analysis of the Galic Language*. He possessed the knowledge and the integrity to expose the bogus poems of Ossian as a fraud at a time when Dr Samuel Johnson pronounced them a hoax, and it became a patriotic duty in certain Scottish circles to defend their authenticity. William Shaw was persecuted almost as though he had committed treason, until he left the country. He found asylum as a clergyman of the Church of England, perhaps through the good offices of Dr Johnson.

The Welsh scholar Thomas Pennant visited Arran while William Shaw still lived there and observed that 'the men are strong, tall and well-made: all speak the Erse language'. But the impression of cultural and physical fitness was an illusory one. By now the Dukes of Hamilton were for the most part absentees, supported like nabobs by their island subjects. 'A deep dejection,' Pennant wrote, 'appears in general through the countenance of all: no time can be spared for amusement of any kind; the whole being given for procuring the means of paying their rent; of laying in their fuel, or getting a scanty pittance of meat and clothing.'

Here as in the other islands, people had lived since time immemorial in a state of interdependence, employing a run-rig system of agriculture, distributing shares in their arable land, common grazings and fishing banks so as to provide a fair livelihood for all. When the increasing population imposed too great a strain on these resources, many looked for work elsewhere. By the time of Pennant's visit, three hundred young men from the parish of Kilbride alone were serving in ships at sea. Here, as elsewhere, no effective steps were taken to develop the fisheries scientifically, although there was such a large potential market beyond the Firth of Clyde.

As for agricultural improvement, the leading exponent of the age, Sir John Sinclair, wrote towards the end of this century, 'The misfortune of being without resident proprietors is greatly aggravated when they wantonly expend, in foreign countries, the income derived from the labour of their tenantry.' His observation applies to Bute, whose Earl spent most of his life involved in London politics or travelling abroad, though his corpse was brought to Rothesay in 1792.

But Sinclair's strictures apply as severely to Arran as to any of the Hebrides, and the beautiful, empty glen of Sannox remains today a particularly poignant memorial to the evictions carried out by the estate managers of the Hamiltons. Among those who left here was Daniel Macmillan, founder of the great publishing house which bears his name, and ancestor of the Prime Minister, Harold Macmillan, now Earl of Stockton. A barytes mine was opened in the glen in 1840, but when the 11th Duke succeeded he ordered it to be closed as a blot on the landscape, not that he came here often to feast his eyes on the wilderness his family had created. He spent far more of his time gambling in Paris, where he was killed in a quarrel at the age of fifty-two.

The Sannox clearances were conducted by a particularly dreadful factor named John Paterson. He wrote a book about Arran in 1837 in which he deplored the fact that he was unable to evict anyone who took in relatives he had rendered homeless. He also recommended that the Gaelic language should be stamped out, and received a silver medal for his writings. In the event, the ancient language expired during the present century, with all the folklore and traditions that it enshrined.

The population of the island diminished to under 5000. For the islanders who stayed the Hamiltons built some attractive houses, forming linear coastal villages that can still be seen at Catacol, Corrie and Lamlash. The people grew potatoes, gathered kelp until the market collapsed, and fished. But tenants of the Duke's houses were forbidden to take in paying guests at a time when tourism was beginning to offer a new source of livelihood. Brodick castle had been enlarged to accommodate the latest Duchess, who was a German princess, and her surroundings were not to be vulgarised by *hoi polloi* from the mainland towns.

But Arran could not be sealed off as a private playground. Its magnetic attraction, its accessibility and the improvements in transport and communications prevented this. Thomas Telford had laid out the first road to cross the island in 1817, linking Brodick with the west coast. The first steamboat sailed from Greenock to Arran in 1829. Sir Walter Scott's poem, 'The Lord of the Isles', which made Arran famous for its scenery, has been luring sightseers ever since its publication in 1815.

Visitors have finally gained access to Brodick castle itself. Its last Hamilton owner was the wife of the late Duke of Montrose, and after her death in 1957 it passed into the custody of the National Trust for Scotland complete with its treasures. In addition, visitors can enjoy the wonderful gardens created by the last Duchess to live in Brodick. The other Scottish islands contain nothing to compare with them, and they have few rivals on the mainland. To these her daughter, the Lady Jean Fforde, has added a further gift of over seven thousand acres of hill and glen, including Goat Fell, and these are also administered today by the National Trust for Scotland.

Today such village communities as that of Lochranza in the north are dying, while the tourist centres expand and flourish. The island is ringed with golf courses, while bracken creeps over the run-rig undulations on deserted hill slopes. At Brodick the Hamiltons have left behind them a unique and priceless souvenir of the royal connection that governed this island's destiny from the day when a Stewart first married into the family of King Somerled.

———15———
Shetland and Orkney: Islands in Pawn

The story of Shetland and Orkney ought to be very different from that of the Hebridean isles. Both remained under Norwegian sovereignty for two centuries longer, until the fifteenth century. Here the Norse tongue took root and continued in popular use for upwards of a thousand years. It was still being employed in administrative documents when the seventeenth century opened.

But the most fundamental difference was that the Hebrideans were deprived of the benefits of Norse udal law in 1266, when they passed to the Scottish Crown. This law gave to the cultivator an absolute right of ownership in the land he tilled, and in the northern isles it has never been formally repealed. Had the Hebrideans continued to enjoy such titles of landownership after 1266, instead of being placed under Scottish feudal law, they might have made fortunes for themselves out of kelp, rather than for their landlords. The means by which the northern islands were reduced to the same condition of serfdom can only be described as rape.

The dynasty of Thorfinn the Mighty became extinct in the male line in 1231, when the earldom of Orkney with its lordship of Shetland passed through an heiress to the Scottish Earl of Angus. The same occurred a second time, then a third, when Henry Sinclair won the prize in 1379. There had been close connections between the Orcadians and the people of Caithness beyond the Pentland Firth since Viking times, and the succession of the Scottish earls helped to increase them. The fertility of those islands, beyond such a narrow stretch of water, naturally attracted the Scottish settler.

Henry Sinclair became the first Earl of Norway when he succeeded to Orkney, while still a subject of the Scottish King in his original possessions. He was also invested as Lord of Shetland; but here circumstances were different, for Shetland lay directly on the route from Norway's political and commercial headquarters at Bergen to the Norse islands of Faroe, Iceland and Greenland, and the Shetlanders were involved in the affairs of this far-flung maritime kingdom, rather than with those of Scotland.

As early as 1194 the Shetlanders took part in a plot to overthrow

King Sverre, the Faroese comb-maker's son who had usurped the Norwegian throne. Sverre prevailed, and detached Shetland from the Orkney earldom as a reprisal. During two centuries of Scottish infiltration into the Orkney islands, Shetland was ruled directly from Norway, until it was bestowed on Earl Henry Sinclair in 1379. The differences between the two island societies are visible to this day, despite their common heritage.

By the time of Earl Henry's succession Norway was threatened by dynastic hazards. During much of the fourteenth century she was linked by a union with the Crown of Sweden. By its close, Denmark had joined them for a brief period in which all three Scandinavian peoples were ruled by a single sovereign, but they had been separate since prehistoric times and the union could not last. However, Christian I of Denmark came to Bergen in 1450, and there imposed a treaty which established a 'perpetual and inviolable union' between his country and Norway. In this case the union lasted until 1814, and it was not an equal partnership. Norway was reduced to the status of a Danish province, with profound consequences for her Atlantic islands.

Bergen, their natural capital, the most splendid city in the north,

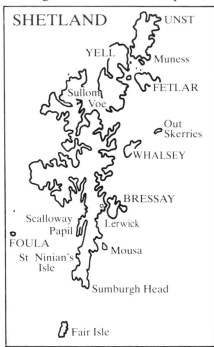

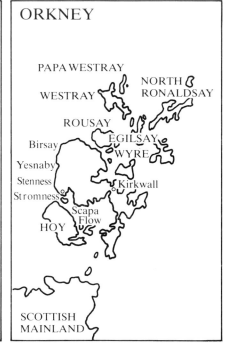

was an early casualty. Here stood the fine hall of King Haakon after whom Kyleakin takes its name. Here was the earlier castle of King Sverre, a great abbey, the wooden mansions of the merchants along the quay. Creditors of Christian of Denmark, with pirates in their wake, descended on this rich store of loot. Sverre's castle, the abbey and the houses of the merchants were ransacked and destroyed. The Bishop tried to protect refugees in the abbey church by raising the sacred Host before the altar. German raiders hacked off his hands, then murdered him.

Bergen had been Shetland's seat of government until a few generations earlier and would remain a magnet for her mercantile activities during centuries to come. Today Bergen possesses one of Shetland's nearest railheads, and the Norwegian flags that flutter from so many different sorts of craft in Lerwick harbour still proclaim the ancient connection. But during Christian I's reign Bergen was crippled, and the Shetlanders suffered accordingly.

A Norwegian king would have defended the most precious jewel in his crown: the Danish one regarded the fate of Bergen with apparent indifference. The interests of the rival German Hanseatic ports were evidently of greater concern to him. Above all, it is inconceivable that a Norwegian king would have pledged Shetland and Orkney as securities for a royal dowry, and taken no steps to redeem them. This is what King Christian did when his daughter Margaret was betrothed to James III, King of Scots, in 1468.

The relative values set upon the two properties is startling. Margaret's dowry was agreed at 60,000 golden florins, of which 10,000 were to be paid immediately in cash. Christian's sovereign rights in Orkney were pledged for the remaining 50,000. When he found himself unable to raise more than 2000 in gold, he pawned his rights in Shetland for the remaining 8000 florins in 1469. It is tempting to speculate on what might have occurred in the Faroe islands if Christian had had to mortgage these as well, lying as they do nearer to Scotland than to Norway, and far nearer than to Denmark.

The transaction differed fundamentally from the surrender of the Hebrides and Man in 1266. Orkney and Shetland had been pawned only until they could be redeemed. There was also a difference in precisely what the Danish King had surrendered, 'our lands of the Orkney islands'. What James III had obtained as his security were simply the rents of the northern isles that belonged to the Norwegian Crown.

Their islanders were to continue to live under udal law. This was recognised by the Scottish Parliament in 1504, in an Act which stated explicitly that Scots law was not applicable to Orkney and Shetland. As late as 1567 Parliament ruled again that the islanders 'ought to be subject to their own laws', and, by implication, not to Scots law. Between those two dates, a judgement of a Shetland court in 1538 was upheld in Bergen as correct according to the Norse code.

At the time of the mortgage William Sinclair was Earl of Orkney and Lord of Shetland. Two years later James III induced him to part with all his rights of property and administration in the islands in return for a grant of land in Fife. So the emoluments of the earldom became vested in the Crown, in addition to those of the kingdom of Norway. Even if the islands were to be redeemed, the King of Scots would remain Earl of Orkney, in the same way as the English sovereign held the Channel Islands as Duke of Normandy. And just as the Channel Islands continued to enjoy their French laws and institutions, so the northern isles ought to have retained their Norwegian ones.

The bishopric of Orkney still belonged to the metropolitan See of Trondheim in Norway, though its current incumbent was a Scot as some of his predecessors had been. James III arranged the transfer of the bishopric to the See of St Andrews, with all the revenues and privileges that belonged to it.

But the magnificent cathedral of Kirkwall with its endowments was in an anomalous position. It was held to be the private property of the descendants of Earl Rognvald, who had begun its construction and had been canonised in Rome. Whether or not Earl William Sinclair could be deemed to have conveyed the legacy of a Saint to James III as part of the total package, the King assumed that he enjoyed the disposal of it, and he bestowed the cathedral of St Magnus upon the 'Provost, Magistrates and Community of Kirkwall'. How well the citizens of Kirkwall have discharged their trust may be seen to this day by the admiring visitor.

The Shetlanders and Orcadians had been turned from Scandinavian into Scottish subjects only a few decades before the abolition of the Hebridean Lordship of the Isles. In the Hebrides it had been possible to lop off the head of a hierarchical society, depriving it in one blow of its source of law, administration and rights of property. There was no such simple means of reducing the free peasant proprietors of the northern isles, none very rich or very poor, to a similar condition of serfdom. Yet this is what the Edinburgh policy makers succeeded in achieving.

The most conspicuous memorials to their achievement are the colossal palaces and castles that the islanders were compelled to build for their new and alien masters. None is more astonishing than the huge fortification of Noltland on the Orcadian isle of Westray. It possesses triple tiers of gunloops, to which the expert Douglas Simpson drew particular attention. 'Nothing like them, no provision for firearm defence upon so lavish a scale, and with such consideration, exists, so far as I am aware, in any British castle – or indeed, I believe, in any castle on the Continent.' Yet this virtually impregnable fortress was erected on a small island that belonged to the bishopric of Orkney.

The Bishop of Orkney at the time when it was built was Adam Bothwell, no villain by the standards of his day. He displayed zeal in visiting his parishes among the islands and in supplying their clergy, but he held his office after the Roman Catholic Church had been abolished in Scotland, when many of his brethren were embezzling church property for themselves or conveying it to their relatives. Bishop Adam possessed a sister, Margaret, who married Gilbert Balfour, and he was doing nothing exceptional when he bestowed the isle of Westray on them for their maintenance. If the islanders were surprised to find themselves paying their church tithes to this pair, it was something they were to become accustomed to, here as elsewhere.

Gilbert Balfour was a Fife Adventurer on the loose long before James VI launched others on to the isle of Lewis. He became Master of the Household to Mary, Queen of Scots, and was deeply implicated in the murder of her husband Darnley. Noltland castle was completed in the final year of her reign, and evidently she was informed of this. After she had married the Earl of Bothwell, she created him Duke of Orkney and ordered Noltland to be prepared for their reception. In the event, she was deposed and Bothwell fled to the northern isles. Balfour was there before him, and refused him admittance to Kirkwall castle. He sailed on to Shetland, his enemies in pursuit, and thence to Bergen where he was arrested and ended his days in a Danish prison.

Gilbert Balfour joined the unsuccessful rising on behalf of the exiled Queen Mary, and was compelled to flee to Sweden. Here this incorrigible conspirator was executed for his plot against the life of the Swedish King. The fortress of Noltland proved in the end of no service to anybody, though the Balfours remained in possession of the isle of Westray for generations to come.

The islanders were already plagued by a far greater menace. Among the Queen's bastard brothers was Robert Stewart, for whose upkeep she provided in 1564 by leasing to him the Orkney earldom for a rent. By this arrangement he would augment her revenues and make what he could for himself in addition. He arrived in Kirkwall late in 1567 and at once set about adding church properties to those that had been granted to him by his sister. In a matter of months Adam Bothwell had surrendered all remaining episcopal rights and revenues to him.

Robert Stewart's enterprises were made easier by the Queen's deposition, as he moved in on the properties that Bishop Adam had earlier presented to his relatives. He occupied Noltland, where the Privy Council ordered him in vain to surrender 'the house and fortalice of Westray'. But the principal prize he was after was the church property of Birsay, where Thorfinn the Mighty had built his palace and established the first minster in Orkney. Bishop Adam had bestowed Birsay on his cousin Sir John Bellenden, a man who never visited Orkney in his life. Warned by his factor that Robert Stewart was 'bent to have the superiority of this country, as well of the bishopric as the rest', Bellenden found it wise to accept some church lands near Grangemouth in exchange for his swag in the north.

At Kirkwall, Robert Stewart enjoyed the amenities of the Bishop's castle, whose ruins stand near the cathedral. But he conceived a grandiose plan to establish himself in the seat once occupied by Thorfinn the Mighty. No sooner were his transactions with Bishop Adam and Bellenden concluded than he began the building of his new palace at Birsay. He employed the forced labour of islanders who were given neither food, drink nor wages for their work, and the skill of masons who had recently completed Noltland castle. This is revealed by the marks they incised in the stones. As at Noltland, only ruins remain of this gigantic undertaking.

Compared to Birsay palace, the house Robert Stewart built for himself in Shetland is comparatively modest. He planted it at Sumburgh, on top of the ruins of Viking homes, and of the broch and the wheelhouses, whose stones doubtless contributed to its construction. When Walter Scott came to survey the ruins he gave them the romantic name of Jarlshof, and this has become attached to the entire site.

In twenty-five years Robert Stewart more than doubled the revenues of the Bishopric, but little of these funds were used for any religious purpose, or reached the pockets of native islanders. Robert placed his own dependants from the south in the livings, whether or not they were ordained, and there were even disputes between rival claimants to the spoils of a parish. By the time of Robert Stewart's death in 1592 only a single surviving native Minister remained, in Shetland's northernmost isle of Unst. It is doubtful whether any of the others could understand the language of their parishioners.

The emoluments of the Crown estate were increased by a third during the same period. Robert's step-brother Laurence Bruce was his chief instrument of extortion, in the office of Foud, or chief magistrate. The burdens of the islanders were increased by altering the weights and measures by which they were assessed, increasing dues in a coinage of Robert Stewart's own valuation, and multiplying grounds for fines and confiscation of property by arbitrary edicts. Most serious of all, the udal titles to property were undermined in courts to which Robert appointed the judges. Professor Gordon Donaldson, who has analysed the surviving court records, has written: 'Instances were not wanting when landed property was extorted not merely by fraud, but by force.'

Yet it was not the udallers who protested to the central government in the first instance, but Scottish feudatories in Orkney who owed no allegiance to the Lord Robert. When they submitted their articles of indictment in 1576 he was summoned to Edinburgh and warded in the castle, while a flood of complaints from native islanders followed in the wake of the formal charges. The response resembled that of requests for justice from the western isles. There was no trial, no redress, and in 1581 he was invested as Earl of Orkney.

After James VI had come of age and embarked on his personal rule, there was a second enquiry into Earl Robert's oppressions in 1587, when the King took back his earldom and annexed the bishopric of Orkney to the Crown. But if the islanders hoped they would now obtain relief, they were soon disillusioned. King James bestowed a fresh charter on Robert Stewart, to which his son Patrick succeeded on his death in 1592. The tyranny of Earl Patrick was such that even the monumental iniquities of his father were largely erased from folk memory.

Patrick inherited the Bishop's castle at Kirkwall and his father's palace at Birsay, but they did not satisfy him. He put the Orcadians to work on a palace more splendid still, only a short distance from Kirkwall cathedral. Such a man was unlikely to be satisfied with the more limited accommodation of Jarlshof in Shetland, especially when Laurence Bruce upstaged him by building himself a stout castle on the island of Unst. But in any case, Earl Patrick required an intimidating fortress in Shetland to which the islanders could be summoned to sample his justice, with a dungeon below the court-room.

Bruce's castle of Muness on Unst was erected in 1598, and work began on Earl Patrick's at Scalloway soon afterwards. The forced labour that built it was conscripted from considerable distances. In 1602 one man from Dunrossness in the extreme south of Shetland, and another from Delting in the far north, were prosecuted for 'non passing to my Lord's work to Scalloway as they were directed'.

In former times the Foud of Shetland or his deputies had travelled on circuit throughout the islands, administering justice, and at mid-summer the central court, or Lawting, had assembled at Tingwall. This was located approximately in the centre of the long, narrow mainland, on an island in a shallow loch like that of the Council of the Isles in Islay. As soon as Scalloway castle was fit for use, the proceedings of the Lawting were transferred to it.

Evidently the Law Book of Shetland had not yet disappeared, because in 1602 mention was made that it had been consulted in a case before the Lawting. But at about the time when the seat of justice was moved from Tingwall to the grim castle of Scalloway, Shetland's Norse code of laws vanished. And while Laurence Bruce manipulated the ancient office of Foud, his nephew the Earl used the Scottish offices of Justice General and Sheriff Principal to make up what laws he chose and apply them through either system, whichever served him the better.

In Shetland the first udal estate had been alienated during Earl Robert's reign, in 1577. Since then others had been driven into debt so that they were forced to sell their properties, while some were terrorised into doing so. The average value of their estates at this time ranged from £300 to £700, while the possessions of more humble folk might be worth no more than £20 or £30. When Laurence Bruce of Muness castle died in 1617 he bequeathed an estate valued at £4000.

This is less surprising than the wealth of some of the clergy. James Pitcairn, the Minister of Northmavine, left property worth £3000 at his death in 1612. As for what his parishioners thought of this, one of them was prosecuted for striking him with a spade. But he fared better than Earl Patrick's toady Harry Colville, the Minister of Orphir in Orkney, who had been hunted to a brutal death by the islanders in 1596.

The inventory of Pitcairn's goods reveals how he spent his time among parishioners to whom he could not preach because they were unable to understand his language. He possessed 35 horses and mares, 154 cattle beasts, 782 sheep and five boats. The Minister of Walls, Robert Swinton, possessed only three boats, besides four herring nets, and we know his brother organised the fishing for him because they took a dispute to court.

The surviving records of the court reveal the petty extortions of Laurence Bruce the Foud in all their diversity. On one occasion he exacted a heavy fine for an offence that had been passed over, thirty years earlier, because it was of an entirely technical nature. He imposed a levy on all who kept pigs, as a result of which many people killed their stocks, and did not replace them after the regulation was withdrawn. One who did continue to keep swine was fined for allowing his pigs to injure the field of a neighbour, while the victim was fined for erecting an 'unlawful dyke' to keep them out. It is thought to have been Bruce who first demanded an ox as his payment for dividing the property of dead people among his heirs. In Earl Patrick's time every parish was paying an annual levy of an ox and twelve sheep in addition. He enforced an exclusive right to wrecks, and on one occasion a man of Yell was prosecuted for attempting to conceal a piece of iron from a Danish boat among his peats.

One of the most bizarre of money-making devices was prosecution for slander. Fines were exacted whether or not a criminal allegation had been made, or the defamation amounted to personal injury on which a price could be set. The money was paid as a rule to the King, though on one occasion at least it went to the injured parties. This occurred when a man was sentenced for saying that in Lunnasting 'there was not an honest man within the whole parish except three', and was ordered to pay four marks to each person slandered, however that might be assessed. Perhaps the object in this case was to ruin the careless talker.

Today crime is rare in Shetland and there are well-populated islands that contain no resident policeman. It is not surprising to discover that under Earl Patrick theft was common. One victim was William Bruce, to whom the Earl granted the custody of Jarlshof in 1604, after he had completed the building of Scalloway castle. In the same year there was a mammoth theft of its peats, presumably gathered before Bruce took up his residence. William Fermour the local Foud was found to be responsible, though he tried to shift the blame to Orcadian settlers in the parish of Dunrossness. Unscrupulous masters are rarely served by honest underlings.

The gradual proliferation of Scots in lands formerly owned by the udallers is well exemplified by the Bruces. There was Andrew Bruce in Unst, who also owned lands between there and Fetlar; and another William Bruce whose base was Whalsey, though he also gathered rents from his properties in Unst in the far north and Dunrossness in the extreme south. As for the Orcadians in this parish who were accused of stealing the Earl's peats, it may be that some of them had been driven from their own islands by the same process of expropriation as the Shetlanders were experiencing.

They were prohibited from trading without a licence from the Earl. This was among the complaints that had been lodged in the time of Earl Robert, and since no action had been taken in Edinburgh the regulation was allowed to continue. It inhibited what ought to have been the most lucrative occupation of the islanders. They were natural seamen, descendants of the Vikings, using boats of a superlative design evolved in Norway a thousand years earlier. Even a man whose total estate was worth little more than £26 owned a boat, although the smaller craft rowed by four oarsmen cost from £4 to £20.

The fish they caught were converted into scat and landmails, girsum, wattle and teinds, every kind of levy that could be devised and then increased under Norse or Scots law; and they could only dispose of their catches through merchants who were generally landlords, with a monopoly that enabled them to dictate the price.

As usual, it was the Orcadians who were the more articulate in their protests against the villainies of Earl Patrick. In 1606 they succeeded in causing a bill of indictment to be brought against him in Edinburgh. It was quashed through the influence of powerful courtiers, but in that same year King James appointed James Law to the long-vacant See of Orkney that Patrick had been exploiting so lucratively. Law came from Fife, the son of a family of lairds of long standing, and he was no adventurer. After collecting evidence of the oppressions in the islands he wrote directly to James VI in London.

'Alas, dear and dread Sovereign,' the Bishop told him in 1608, 'truly it is to be pitied that so many of your Majesty's subjects are so manifoldly and grievously oppressed; some by ejection and banishment from their homes and native soil, others by contorting the laws and extorting their goods, the most part being so impoverished that some of them neither dare nor may complain, but in silent and forced patience groan under their grievance.' Law stood high in the estimation of the King, and as a result of his accusations the Earl was summoned in that same year 'to answer the complaints of the poor distressed people of Orkney'.

At last the Scottish Privy Council was obliged to take notice, after forty years, of the fact that 'some persons bearing power of magistracy within the bounds of Orkney and Shetland have these divers years bygone most unlawfully taken upon them for their own private gain and commodity to judge the inhabitants of the said countries by foreign laws, making choice sometimes of foreign laws and sometimes of the proper laws of this kingdom, as they find matter of gain and commodity'. The Councillors were evidently in error as to which of the two were 'foreign laws' in the northern isles.

Earl Patrick's outrageous response to the attack on his authority was to invest his bastard son Robert, a lad under twenty-one years of age, as his Sheriff and Justiciar and send him to the islands to hold courts and collect rents. Robert returned to inform his father, now confined in the castle of Dunbarton, that the islanders had ejected him. Patrick rounded on him in a fury, and drove him back to restore his father's authority. With a mere handful of accomplices, Robert Stewart established himself first in the palace of Birsay, then in the new palace of Kirkwall. Finally he was driven into the Bishop's castle, where he was taken prisoner. Earl Patrick's last, despicable act was to attempt to save himself by denouncing his son, before they were both executed in 1615.

It was treason that had cost them their lives, not any crime they had committed against the islanders. These did not recover the lands which the Stewarts and their friends had seized from them, nor the illegal taxes and dues that had been squeezed out of them. To make matters worse, James VI now leased the islands to a succession of farmers-general, a new order of men on the make. A Minister described the condition of the surviving udallers in 1627. 'In respect of the great duty paid to his Majesty out of this udal land, and the augmentation of it so oft, and of the great number of people sustained upon this land, these mean udal people are not able to live.'

There was a further danger that some sovereign would grant the royal earldom again to one of his relatives or favourites. It occurred in 1643, when the great rebellion against Charles I had spread throughout Scotland, England and Ireland. The King granted the northern isles to the Earl of Morton, doubtless hoping that this would attract funds and soldiers to the royalist cause.

It is hard to believe that the islanders could have felt any desire to support another Stewart, but they were given no option. When the King's general, Montrose, took the field they were compelled to supply £40,000 and 2000 men for his army. The Earl of Morton died, but his brother hastened to the islands to enforce his family's feudal power. After the death of King Charles a further £60,000 and 300 horse were exacted from them in 1650. Montrose himself arrived in Kirkwall early that year, with a commission as Viceroy which Charles II sent him from Jersey. He took his raw levies from Orkney to the mainland, where they reached the Kyle of Sutherland before the enemy dragoons caught up with them. Here the young islanders faced a cavalry charge, without support. Those who were not cut to pieces fled homewards.

In the following year they supplied an entire regiment as well as further cash, when Charles II paid his sole visit to Scotland as a Covenanted King. So they contributed to the carnage of the battle of Worcester in 1651. But if they hoped to be compensated for their hardships and sufferings after the restoration of Charles II in 1660, they were disappointed. He squeezed £182,000 out of them, then handed the islands back to the Morton family to gather their own reward for their loyalty to the Crown. This the Mortons did with a thoroughness that must have reminded the inhabitants of Earl Patrick.

Between the battle of Worcester and the death of Oliver Cromwell in 1658 the inhabitants of Orkney and Shetland sampled English rule, like the Arran islanders. The arm of the great dictator extended as far as Lerwick, where he built the first fort above the sound of Bressay and sent troops to garrison it, as well as others to Scalloway castle. His object was not to overawe the islanders, who must have been delighted when he sent the Morton family packing, but to protect them against the depredations of the Dutch.

The Hollanders' Knowe, midway between Scalloway and Lerwick, is marked by a monumental stone that commemorates the massive Dutch presence in Shetland's fishing grounds during this age. They had been coming since the sixteenth century in large sailing vessels such as the islanders could not afford, exploiting the wealth of the herring shoals, and coming ashore to buy fresh meat, vegetables and woollen stockings at the market on the Howe. By Cromwell's time the booths established by the sound of Bressay formed the nucleus of the village of Lerwick, while so many Dutch busses (two-masted vessels of burden) lay in the sound at one time that it was possible to walk over them to the isle of Bressay. The poverty in which the fishermen of Shetland were kept by their landlords prevented them from acquiring such fishing boats for themselves until the nineteenth century.

Conditions on land had continued to deteriorate. By Cromwell's time only one representative of the older prominent udallers remained in the Orcadian parish of Deerness, with a dozen smaller ones, some in a very small way indeed. The great estates, by contrast, had burgeoned. The descendant of Bellenden, who had surrendered Birsay to Earl Robert, possessed an estate valued at £1400 a year in 1653. The Balfours still flourished on the isle of Westray, in the possessions they had inherited from their infamous ancestor, Gilbert. These two properties had been the largest ever carved out of the former lands either of the Church, the Crown or the Earldom, and were very much more extensive than the average feudal estate created in Orkney.

Yet there were many besides those of the Bellendens and Balfours, far larger than any udaller of the previous century had owned. Their numbers were still increasing. In 1653, when Cromwell's regime made its valuation, a certain David MacLellan was found to have risen from the rank of servant to that of a landlord worth £1700 a year.

After the restoration of the monarchy conditions returned to normal, but at the outset of the eighteenth century two new factors contributed to the further degradation of the northern islanders. The high tax imposed in 1712 on foreign salt drove away the merchants who had come from abroad to cure and export the catches of the native fishermen. The monopoly in this enterprise passed to the landlords, and a change in the system of land tenure resulted. From now on they either granted no lease at all, or made it short and precarious, subject to a stipulation that the tenant must fish for the landlord and pay his rent in fish. If he was caught selling his catch elsewhere, he was punished by instant eviction. In these circumstances he had no further incentive to improve his land.

The second circumstance, which completed the servitude of the islanders, was an alteration in the habits of fish in their surrounding seas. The great quantities of them that could be caught by line in inshore waters began to diminish towards the end of the seventeenth century, so that fishermen were forced to adventure into the ocean beyond. The Scandinavian word for ocean is *hav*, so that this became known as the haaf fishing, and it required boats larger than the islanders could afford. The landlords provided them and compelled their tenants to man them, rewarding them so meagrely for the dangers of their calling that their utmost labours failed in most cases to pay their rents. Few of them were ever out of debt to their masters.

'Those masters are as absolute as some princes, for if these poor people do but murmur, they and their families are banished for ever out of their territories.' So wrote the visiting Dr Campbell in 1753, and such comments became more systematic when Sir John Sinclair's Statistical Account of Scotland was compiled in the 1790s.

The Reverend John Menzies, Minister of Bressay, observed: 'Many services, the sad marks of slavery, are demanded. They must fish for their masters, who either give them a fee entirely inadequate to their labour and dangers, or take their fish at a lower price than others would give.' The Minister enquired, 'Why not let them have leases upon reasonable terms, and dispose of their produce to those who will give them the best price? Why not let them fish for themselves? Why should the landlord have any claim except for the stipulated rent?'

There was a route of escape for such skilled seamen and many of them took it, as the Minister of Birsay in Orkney remarked. 'Most of the people of the barony and Marwick are bred fishermen, and multitudes of our young men go to sea, both in merchant and in his Majesty's service; few in proportion of whom ever return to settle here.'

As for the Royal Navy, a quota of young men were compelled to enlist in every district, under threat that their families would be evicted if they refused. Despite that, men who remained were menaced by the press gangs both ashore and on land. The Minister of Birsay could give no exact figures. 'Doubtless many entered or have been impressed, that have not come to our knowledge.'

During the eighteenth century the northern islanders finally lost their native language, though not before a curious visitor had salvaged a small fragment of its ballad literature. The Reverend George Low belonged to Edzell in Forfarshire, and visited the northern isles as a young man in 1774. His passion was natural history, but his intellectual curiosity fed on anything that caught his attention. In Orkney he came across a Norse version of the Lord's Prayer, and when he reached the remote Shetland isle of Foula and found its inhabitants still speaking the ancient tongue he invited one of them to recite the Lord's Prayer to him again. He noted that it was in a relatively pure form of Norse compared to the corrupt Orcadian version.

Then he struck gold. One of the Foula folk recited to him thirty-five verses of a ballad that he wrote down as best he could, although he did not understand the language. Yet he succeeded so well that any Faroe islander can read his words at a glance, although they are not to be found in the immense Faroese ballad literature. For the language that Shetland lost is identical to the one that still flourishes in those neighbouring Faroese islands.

George Low discovered no Norse texts in Orkney. Yet even here, where Scottish influence had penetrated so much earlier, the retentive power of memory was discovered by a Minister in one of the remote islands during his time. The Minister thought to entertain his parishioners in North Ronaldsay by reading an English poem by Thomas Gray to them about the fate of Earl Sigurd of Orkney who died at the battle of Clontarf in 1014. It was a loose translation from the Norse of the macabre song sung by the Norns as they wove his destiny, using human heads as the weights, and their entrails for the warp and weft. To the Minister's astonishment, the islanders knew the original by heart.

The society these Ministers described was about to be shaken, like those of the other islands, by the Napoleonic War which removed so many of their young men, and by the clearances that gained momentum in its aftermath. But Shetland reared an island champion unlike any other in this epoch. His name was Arthur Anderson, and he was born in 1792 in a house north of Lerwick that is now preserved in his memory. As a boy he tended the salt fish laid out to dry on the beach of Bressay, until he joined the Royal Navy at the age of sixteen, to fight in the Napoleonic War which, fortunately for his compatriots, he survived.

Outside his islands Anderson is celebrated as one of the founders of the P. and O. Steamship Company, which still remains a world-wide enterprise. But before it came into being he had been concerned that a steamship service should be established between Scotland and Shetland, and to this day it is a P. and O. steamer that sails between Aberdeen and Lerwick.

Most urgently, he was determined to rescue his islands' principal source of livelihood from the stranglehold of the landlords. He established his own fish-curing enterprise, introducing the wooden frames that are used in Norway for drying the fish. It was not until 1872 that his influence brought a commission of enquiry which investigated the way in which landlords and merchants were exploiting the islanders, as a result of which it was stopped by Act of Parliament. His authority there was increased when he became the first Shetlander to sit as Member of Parliament for the northern isles. Hitherto his society had enjoyed no say in the choice of their representative at Westminster.

Their fine knitwear, product of the soft wool of the Shetland sheep, was also in the grip of the landlords. Anderson sent knitted stockings to Queen Victoria which created a vogue for them in the fashionable world, and soon such products, including the gossamer-like shawls, were being marketed in London, beyond the clutches of local vultures. For widows who were in so many cases the creators of these now world-famous articles, he built a block of handsome homes in Lerwick.

But his most conspicuous gift to his people is the Educational Institute he established in the island capital in 1862, now known as the Anderson High School. He did not neglect outlying communities either. Today, perhaps the most vital community of its size in any of the Scottish islands is the remote Out Skerries, where fewer than 100 people support their own missionary and schoolteacher, and man their own boats and factory while their knitting is amongst the most intricate and beautiful anywhere. Anderson stepped in when their education was neglected, supplying them with a teacher.

Before the time of Arthur Anderson the Shetlanders were amongst the most deprived of all Scotland's islanders. It was very largely due to his efforts that this was far from so by the time the Crofter Acts gave security to them all from the tyranny of feudal landlordism.

16

Islands in Transition

All islands have their individual characters, but among the Scottish ones the Orkney isles are more different than the rest. Except for mountainous Hoy they are carpets of farmland lying on old red sandstone, scattered beyond the agricultural corridor that extends north from the Moray Firth, through Easter Ross and Caithness. No such fertile islands lie in the Atlantic seas beyond them. From the earliest times they have lured the settler like a crock of gold at the end of the rainbow, and the quantity and quality of their monuments celebrate this unique magnetism.

No island capital in the north possesses buildings comparable to those of Kirkwall. Its cathedral and its palace are unique in their magnificence. Even the relatively modest seventeenth-century mansion, Tankerness House, now a museum, would do credit to a far larger mainland metropolis. The prosperous farms of the surrounding countryside are owned by those who work them, and represent a triumph over the Scottish feudal landlordism which reduced the Orcadians to poverty in an earlier age.

A metropolitan spirit prevails here, and a sense of particular identity that has survived the mobility of modern life. The population has fallen below 20,000, and today only one farmer on Egilsay is a native Orcadian. The rest have emigrated over a period of time from an island whose 14 farms, ranging in size from 50 to 300 acres, were served neither by a public water supply nor by electricity. While these sought richer pastures on the mainland, strangers have moved in to take their place. But the natives have not abandoned the control of their affairs to influential settlers or distant authorities, as they demonstrated recently in no uncertain manner.

Early in 1977 the South of Scotland Electricity Board decided to prospect for uranium along the spectacular cliffs of the Orkney mainland, between the port of Stromness and Yesnaby headland. Edwin Eunson's response on behalf of the Orkney Islands Council was uncompromising. 'The Council must declare its total opposition to uranium mining in Orkney and there is therefore no point in proceeding with exploratory drilling.' Had the Electricity Board decided to prospect in Raasay, it would merely have had to negotiate with an absentee landlord in the south of England who would have leapt at such a promising overture, and with a Council dominated by residents of the eastern mainland whose attitude might not have reflected that of the islanders.

In Orkney the Board had been obliged to approach local working farmers, who signed concessions to drill on their land before they were fully aware of the implications. Soon a majority of these had offered their signatures again, this time to the petitions of protest. The Orcadians are notoriously undemonstrative but this issue brought them out in crowds, marching through the narrow streets of Kirkwall and waving placards. They protested that uranium mining would wreck their finest coastline, spoil some of their best agricultural land, leave unsightly spoil-heaps and send radioactive dust on the prevailing wind across their largest centres of population.

Neither the Scottish Office nor the passage of time could wear down the opposition of the islanders. Two years after the initial proposal had been rejected, the Secretary of State Bruce Millan instituted a public enquiry. Edwin Eunson warned that if it recommended overruling the islanders, the result would be civil disobedience. As a last resort, the Orcadians resolved to invoke Norse udal law, and lodge an appeal in the International Court at The Hague. In 1979 there was a change of government, and a new, Conservative Minister was asked in vain for an undertaking that no mining for uranium would be permitted in Orkney.

An annual midsummer festival of the arts had been instituted in Kirkwall in 1977, which was dominated in 1980 by the uranium crisis. A concert of 'Uranium Songs', composed by Peter Maxwell Davies who lives in the isle of Hoy, was among the entertainments. So was an orchestal cantata called *Black Pentecost.* It may be that the final battle remains to be fought, but from that day to this there has been no exploratory drilling along the Yesnaby cliffs.

The island most similar to Orkney in a number of ways is Islay, far to the south-west. Here there was also a seat of island government in an earlier age, as well as a degree of fertility that attracted the settler. Its rulers erected the buildings of Iona, administered justice at Finlaggan and held sway in the castle of Dunyveg. The monuments of Islay suffered more severely than those of Orkney, but its language has survived, though the number of those who speak it is diminishing.

Islay was relatively fortunate in its landlords from the coming of the Campbells of Shawfield in 1726. They created the urban centres of Bowmore, Port Ellen and other coastal villages. They gradually transformed the pattern of landholding so that Islay escaped the worst horrors of the clearances. Today its farming structure bears a closer resemblance to that of Orkney than of the Hebridean islands with their crofting townships.

But what if the MacDonalds of Islay had succeeded in their repeated attempts to follow the example of the Isle of Man, and exchange English for Scottish sovereignty? Today the British sovereign is Lord of Man, just as she is Duchess of Normandy in the Channel Islands, but Jersey, Guernsey and Man are all self-governing. Islay and Man are of approximately equal size and comparable fertility. In both of them Gaelic is still spoken. Each possessed roughly the same degree of autonomy until the Norwegian sovereign surrendered his ownership of both to the King of Scots in 1266.

By 1766 Man contained 14,000 inhabitants, subsisting mainly by fishing and agriculture like the 6000 people of Islay at that time. In 1851 the Manx population had risen to 52,000, that of Islay to a little over 15,000. By the 1970s the numbers in Man had risen to over 60,000 while those of Islay had fallen below 4000. All the inhabitants of Man elect representatives who sit in their own island Parliament, a body to which the Hebrideans sent members until the year 1266. After that date the Hebrideans were represented by their tribal Chiefs and churchmen in the Council of the Isles that convened at Finlaggan in Islay, until the Lordship of the Isles was abolished in 1493. Today the inhabitants of Islay are governed by mainland authorities and island landlords whom they have not elected. Indeed, the relationship between them resembles that of Oliver Twist with Mr Bumble the workhouse beadle. It is not surprising that more people choose to live in Man than in Islay.

To some extent it is not even a matter of choice. Among the mainland bodies whose net is cast over island affairs is the Civil Aviation Authority. Recently the Authority announced its intention to sell Islay's little airport, either on its own or as a package with those of Tiree, Benbecula, Sumburgh in Shetland, Kirkwall in Orkney, and Wick on the northern mainland. All have incurred losses, but they provide essential social services. This is on a par with the decision of another mainland authority in the 1960s, which refused to build a road to the township of Manish in Harris, on the grounds that it was 'becoming extinct'.

The largest landlords in Islay are the Morrisons, successors and descendants of the Campbells in one of the most stable and well-conducted of the Hebridean estates. But it has been paying off its workers gradually in recent years, and in 1984 it was announced that the home farm was to be displenished and its employees dismissed. Islay House itself has been advertised for sale. This has occurred at a time when there is a recession in the whisky industry, on which the inhabitants are heavily dependent.

Meanwhile another outside body has been taking an interest in the island, the Royal Society for the Protection of Birds. Vast flocks of barnacle geese land here on their seasonal migrations, destroying the pastures like a plague of locusts. Although the welfare of the human population might be thought more important than that of a species which is in no danger of extinction, it is not the responsibility of the Royal Society for the Protection of Birds. This body is discharging its functions by urging the government to forbid the shooting of geese, no matter what damage they do to the essential livelihood of the farmers. It would be impossible to diminish their numbers appreciably by shooting them, for they assemble in dense clouds.

However, the interests of nature conservancy have generally been preferred to those of the inhabitants throughout the Scottish islands, and those of tourists and the armed forces have enjoyed a similiar priority. The story of St Kilda illustrates this.

The 36 remaining inhabitants of this island were evacuated in 1930, by decree of a distant authority that they could not be maintained there. The landlord, Sir Reginald MacLeod of MacLeod, received over 400 requests by others to settle on St Kilda in their place, which he refused. Instead, the island passed to the National Trust for Scotland which leased it to the Nature Conservancy. By the late Fifties the armed forces were moving in with tractors, diesel generators and helicopters, all the assets that might have maintained a native population there. While proper hospital services could not be provided at this time for far more accessible islands such as Canna, they were available here.

In some islands the natives have not been removed before all this money and apparatus arrives on their doorstep, and they are able to share in the benefits. One of these is Shetland's northernmost island of Unst. The fertility of its soil and the wealth of its fishing grounds attracted Laurence Bruce to settle here in the sixteenth century, that rogue who tyrannised the islanders under the regime of Earl Robert Stewart. The ruins of his castle at Muness still stand as a souvenir of his presence.

Unst contained over 3000 inhabitants in 1861, and still held over 1000 in 1961. Its weather conditions qualified the island better to become the site of Shetland's principal airport than Sumburgh in the south, because fog occurs less frequently here. This the RAF recognised when they established a station on Unst, which had become the largest employer on the island by the 1970s. But such a source of prosperity, not being indigenous to the locality, is as precarious as the benevolence of landlords who come and go.

Benbecula, between South and North Uist, has been a recipient of comparable favours. The building of a guided missile range at Balivanish caused a forty-five-per-cent increase in the population, and has given the natives limited access to such novel luxuries as a squash court and a swimming pool. It need not be supposed that any distant authority, devoted to the well-being of Hebrideans, decided that their happiness consisted in learning to play squash.

The comparison between Islay and Man at the southern end of the chain of Scottish islands is outdone by another in the far north. Beyond Shetland lie the Faroe islands, roughly equal in dimensions, considerably less fertile, their weather stormier, but enjoying the same wealth of fish in their surrounding seas. For centuries the population of Faroe had not risen above 5000, and it remained at this figure in 1800, at a time when Shetland contained 22,000 people. Today there are 46,000 Faroe islanders living in their homeland, and several thousand more who speak the Faroese language have settled overseas. This is precisely the language that the Shetlanders have lost, and the importance they attach to it is curious and significant. They define a Faroe islander as someone who speaks Faroese, not anyone who wears their national costume or claims Faroese descent. It is as though the Hebrideans based their identity on their Gaelic language, rather than the wearing of the kilt or pride in a Gaelic clan name.

The Faroe islands were granted self-government by Denmark in 1948. Elected representatives from their eighteen inhabited islands sit in the Parliament of Tórshavn, their capital, with powers to raise their own taxes and manage their own economy. Everyone here is consequently involved in the decision-making process and shares in the management of their own affairs.

This has enabled them to implement the policies that the fifth Duke of Argyll had sought to promote in the Scottish islands at the end of the eighteenth century, and Leverhulme in Lewis in the twentieth. They have been challenged to do this for themselves, not as the recipients of paternal benevolence from some remote authority, and they have achieved a spectacular success. At a time when the Sea League was campaigning ineffectually for the protection of Hebridean fisheries by the British government, the Faroese were assembling the largest trawler fleet in Scandinavia. Today they enjoy the highest per capita national product in the world, a lower inflation rate than Britain's, and no more than seasonal unemployment.

Their prosperity has provided them with the means, as well as the will, to achieve a cultural renaissance that borders on the miraculous. Every Faroe islander is fully bilingual in Faroese and Danish, and many speak English as well. This small society has created a flourishing literature where they had only their traditional poetry a century ago. The most distinguished of their living novelists, Heðin Brú, was published in English translation as early as 1948, and other Faroese authors have been translated since. A hundred years ago the islands had never produced a native artist. Today they contain no less than six who are supported exclusively by their sales at home, apart from their exhibitions abroad.

The Faroese have had to adapt to changing conditions, as other countries have extended their fishing limits, depriving them of their more distant fishing grounds, and compelling them to exploit their own 200-mile zone. They have found a new use for their distant water fleet through an agreement with Senegal. Here they have arranged to build a factory capable of employing up to 300 of the inhabitants, supplied by Faroese purse-seine netters fishing in their waters.

They have fish factory ships at home, and at Grimsby in Britain, where they provide haddock for the fried-fish trade, cod fish-fingers and canned and frozen products for the luxury market. At home they have established 22 factories dispersed among their inhabited islands. It would have been far more economic to concentrate these in a single centre, but Tórshavn already contains some 15,000 people, and it is one of their prime objectives to maintain the scattered communities in the remotest corners of their country. To this end they have spared no expense in maintaining ferry services, spanning wide waterways with electricity cables, and building local hospitals and schools.

A remarkable example of Faroese policy is the northernmost village of Viðareiði, which contains only about 200 people and possesses no natural harbour. A road has been built to it, involving two long tunnels through the mountains, and a paper factory planted there. The raw material must be imported, since the islands are treeless except for one precious plantation at Tórshavn. There is also a new hotel for visitors to one of the most spectacular places in Europe. The village is buttressed by a cliff with a sheer drop of 2500 feet, one of a line of them, like the prows of gigantic battleships heading towards the Arctic.

Viðareiði's only natural source of subsistence is a portion of the scanty cultivable land of these islands. But while every possible patch of soil is tended here, with a care that makes a mockery of the bracken-covered wastes of some Scottish islands, the care for this township is based on quite other considerations.

Viðareiði might well have been considered a suitable site for a guided missile range, justifying all the expense that has been lavished on it on those grounds. Since Denmark has retained control of foreign affairs, Faroe is included in NATO, and a radar station has been built in a remote spot on one of the islands. But there are only about 150 Danish servicemen here, most of them involved in fishery protection, and it is inconceivable that the Faroese would welcome the kind of largesse that has reached Unst with the RAF or Benbecula with its squash court.

Their amenities are paid for out of the 250,000 tonnes of fish that they export, the proceeds of their fishery agreements with the European Community (of which they are not a member), with Canada and the Soviet Union, East Germany and other Scandinavian countries. They also build boats for themselves and for export, and every kind of marine tackle, including technical inventions of their own devising.

These developments were far advanced by 1959, when there were no more than twenty-five boats of 40 feet or more in length in all the Hebridean ports, and Norwegian, French and German craft filled their waters, many of them factory ships. The Shetlanders witnessed a stirring sight in 1965 when a Norwegian fleet of new purse-seine netters sailed into Bressay Sound, to use Lerwick as their base for operations in the surrounding waters.

In that year the Highlands and Islands Development Board was established. It had been proposed originally in 1939 by Sir Alexander MacEwen, sometime Provost of Inverness, and by John Lorne Campbell of Canna, secretary of the Sea League. They had suggested that the chairman should be a Highlander and at least one member a Gaelic speaker. In the event it consisted of Lowlanders except for one islander, Prophet Smith, who had been the unsuccessful Labour parliamentary candidate for the northern isles. Paternalism was to remain the order of the day. But although the Board was to demonstrate more than once that Daddy does not always know best, it did bring timely relief when the island fisheries were in decline, boats out of date, and 50 young men in Stornoway alone waiting on the quay, their names down for a boat of any kind.

The HIDB has proved to be a milestone in the rejuvenation of the islands. Another milestone was passed when the first oilfield off Shetland was discovered in 1971. Acting with an initiative worthy of their cousins the Faroese, the Shetlanders drew up a development plan to prepare for the disruption that was bound to follow when they became the principal base for the North Sea oil industry. They set aside Sullom Voe for its main complex, a comparatively remote site already disfigured by the RAF. This new source of employment has helped to increase the population of Shetland from under 18,000 to over 22,000, though this has been achieved by immigration, not, as in Faroe, by a natural increase of the native islanders.

In 1974, Shetland County Council received statutory powers of unprecedented dimensions. They received the right to acquire land, license construction work, act as the harbour authority of Sullom Voe. In that year the Council signed its own agreements with major oil companies. To a lesser degree the County Council of Orkney was called upon to face the same challenge. The advantage they both enjoyed was that each possessed its own elected Council, based in the islands. Had the oil been discovered off the Long Island, the fate of its inhabitants would have been governed by mainland authorities based on the east side of Scotland, and their representation would have been a weak, minority one.

This situation was remedied in 1975, in the reorganisation of local government that was introduced thoughout Britain. The Long Island was at last given its own council, with the same enlarged authority as Orkney and Shetland were to enjoy. Unlike the northern isles, the Hebrides lacked previous experience of such local responsibilities, so that the manner in which the Council of the Isles, Comhairle nan Eilean, has discharged its responsibilities is the more remarkable. At last the western isles have their own, self-financed, Radio nan Eilean, their own publishing house, and a bilingual education policy which their council adopted in the very year it was constituted.

It is a remarkable fact that an altogether disproportionate number of Scotland's most distingushed poets today are those who compose in Gaelic. Prominent among both poets and prose writers are natives of Lewis: Derick Thomson, Iain Crichton Smith and Donald Mac-Aulay. In Lewis, seat of Comhairle nan Eilean, are those who may succeed in implementing the principle which Samuel Johnson once enunciated in the Hebrides, that languages are the pedigrees of nations, as the Faroe islanders have done.

One of the hardest tasks of the Long Island Council has been to integrate all the isles within its charge between Lewis and Barra Head through improved communications. As long ago as 1920 Lord Leverhulme wrote of the Hebridean sea-transport services, 'Anything more callously indifferent to the interests of a section of the community I have never experienced.' Since then, the belated improvements have, as a rule, been planned on an east-west basis, connecting the different islands with the mainland. The Council's 1983 report recognised the part which inadequate transport facilities had played in the past as a cause of depopulation, and members of it who visited the Faroe islands could study their policy in searching for a remedy.

But it is a costly one. It has involved linking the 107 inhabitants of Vatersay south of Barra by ferry with their neighbours and the 132 people of Eriskay with South Uist. This involves a reversal of the old mainland attitude to the people of Manish, when they were denied a road to their township on the grounds that they were becoming extinct. As a matter of fact, far healthier societies than that of Manish are at risk.

In the 1930s the isle of Scalpay off Harris contained a vigorous fishing community of 950 souls, with 150 children in its school. The population has declined to 456, and there was considerable controversy recently when it was decided to transport the children of Scalpay across the sound to the school at Tarbert. The removal of school-children from their home environment is one of the potential causes of depopulation. On the other hand, as the Council pointed out in its 1983 report, education bills are high because 'the insular and rural nature of the area necessitates the duplication of services'. But it does so just as much in Shetland, where the parents of Out Skerries successfully resisted a proposal to send their children to school in Lerwick without their consent, although there are less than 100 parents in Out Skerries.

The 1981 census gave the population of the Long Island as 30,713. This was roughly the population of the Faroe islands when they gained self-government in 1948. The consortium of Comhairle nan Eilean would be more numerous still if it included Scotland's second largest island, Skye, whose links with Lewis and Harris date back to the MacLeod mini-kingdom and are far older and closer than those of the Catholic isle of Barra. Skye, Lewis and Harris share the same Calvinist faith, a powerful binding force in these islands.

In addition, Skye is linked to the Long Island by the fast ferry route across the straits of Kyleakin and thence by a second car ferry from Uig to Tarbert in Harris. Skye contains the school at Portree which generations of scholars from the Outer Hebrides have attended. Today they have begun to enrol in the newly established Gaelic business college in Skye, Sabhal Mór Ostaig. Yet for reasons best known to the planners, Skye has been absorbed into the mainland administrative district of Lochalsh, which belongs to the Highland Region beyond. The island shares a Member of Parliament with Ross-shire.

Skye is another island which invites comparison with Faroe. It is of about the same extent and by no means more mountainous or barren. It is a great deal more compact, with only Raasay as a significant satellite. In 1840 there were about 20,000 people living in Skye, speaking a language with an ancient literature. At that time the Faroese numbered 8000 people, speaking a language that had never been seen in print, and which was not even used in their churches. Today the Faroese population of 46,000 is to be compared with Skye's residue of less than 10,000. The quality of life of the Gaels here does not compare favourably with that of the Faroese, neither does the status of their language.

It is possible that the mainland authority will prove more enlightened than others in the past in remedying this, but the initiative does not lie with the native islanders. They possess only a minority voice among English-speaking people of a different background and environment. It seems more likely that Skye will become transformed gradually into another Mull, Scotland's third largest island

and a favoured place of retirement for the English-speaking gentry and for young people from the industrial towns who have opted for island life.

Skye, like Mull, attracts a seasonal tourist trade, while the Cuillins are a favourite resort for mountain climbers. The Highlands and Islands Development Board were among the promoters of a more skilled and permanent form of employment when the Gaeltec factory was built in the island. Here the young, trained in micro-technology, make electronic products that are marketed across the world. However, the highest employer of skilled industrial workers in the Hebrides is Lewis Offshore Limited. On the Arnish peninsula to which Leverhulme built the first road from Stornoway, its heavy steel fabrication yard has employed upwards of a thousand local people as welders, pipe fitters and other skilled technicians serving the offshore oil industry. Unfortunately the demand for its products fluctuates, with the same hazards for local employment as the distilleries of Islay have experienced. Although this is a world-wide phenomenon, its effects on small island societies can be especially damaging.

The present political response contains elements of paradox. In all Scotland, the western isles constituency is one of only two represented by a Scottish Nationalist Member of Parliament, Donald Stewart. In the European Parliament the only Scottish Nationalist Member is Mrs Winifred Ewing, representing the Highland Region which includes the northern isles. Yet neither the Hebrides, Orkney nor Shetland could possibly retain grateful memories of government from Edinburgh in the old days of Scottish independence. At the time of the Scottish referendum on national devolution there were some Shetlanders who actually threatened to pronounce a UDI from Scotland if the union with England were to be severed. The Shetlanders and Orcadians do not consider themselves to be Scots, although many of them descend from the Scots who have been settling in their islands over a period of centuries. As for the ethnic identity of the Hebridean Gaels, these islanders bear about as much resemblance to the inhabitants of Edinburgh as the Basques do to the Parisian French.

Those islanders who supported the Nationalist representatives in the British and European Parliaments may have been doing so largely on ethnic rather than political grounds. At least it is clear that they were asserting their individuality, a special identity. In our densely urbanised, highly industrialised society, the inhabitants of our offshore islands comprise only a tiny minority. They have had no means of protesting effectively when their homelands were treated by a nation of townspeople as sporting playgrounds, suitable sites for military installations and oil terminals, or places in which to protect and study animals rather than protect the welfare of humans.

In the past the islanders have had little remedy. Only a few decades ago they were powerless even to protect their home waters from foreign trawler fleets, especially those of the large English companies. For the present generation the situation is different. The young of today do not yet enjoy all the privileges which have created such wonders in the Faroe islands and made them such an object of envy. But they do possess new powers to govern their own destiny and to restore their ravaged islands, and they may yet realise the dream of Sorley Maclean, the Raasay poet who saw the dead returning to Hallaig, the fair township from which his forbears had been evicted.

> each one young and light-stepping,
> without the heartbreak of the tale.

> a chuile té òg uallach
> gun bhristeadh cridhe an sgeòil.

Select Bibliography

Anderson, A. O. and M. O., *Adomnan's Life of Columba*, 1961.

Anderson, Peter, 'Birsay in the 16th Century,' in *Orkney Heritage* II, 1983.

Balfour, David, *Oppressions of the 16th century in the Islands of Orkney and Shetland*, 1859.

Balfour, J. A. (ed.), *The Book of Arran* II, 1910.

Banks, Noel, *Six Inner Hebrides*, 1977.

Bannerman, John, 'Scottish Entries in the early Irish Annals,' in *SGS* XI, 1968.

    Studies in the History of Dalriada, 1974.

    and K. A. Steer, *Late Mediaeval Monumental Sculpture in the West Highlands*, Appendix II, 1977.

    and Ronald Black, 'A 16th century Gaelic Letter,' in *SGS* XIII, 1978.

Boswell, James (ed. Frederick Pottle and Charles Bennett), *Journal of a Tour to the Hebrides*, 1963.

Brand Report, *Parliamentary Papers*, Command 1327, 1902.

Bristol, N. Maclean, *Hebridean Decade: Mull, Coll and Tiree*, SWHIHR, 1983.

Brøndstet, Johannes, *The Vikings*, 1982.

Brown, George Mackay, *An Orkney Tapestry*, 1969.

Cameron, Alexander, *Reliquiae Celticae*, 1892–4.

Campbell, John Lorne, *Tales from Barra, told by the Coddy*, 1960.

    and Thomson, D. S., *Edward Lhuyd in the Scottish Highlands*, 1963.

    and Hall, Trevor, *Strange Things*, 1968

    and Collinson, Francis, *Hebridean Folksongs*, 3 vols., 1969–81.

    (ed.) *A Collection of Highland Rites and Customs*, 1975.

    Canna: the Story of a Hebridean Island, 1984.

Clapperton, Chalmers M. (ed.), *Scotland: a new study*, 1983.

Clouston, J. Storer, *A History of Orkney*, 1932.

Collinson, Francis, *The Traditional and National Music of Scotland*, 1966.

Cooper, Derek, *Hebridean Connection*, 1977.

Crawford, Iain, and Switsur, R., 'The Udal, Uist,' in *Antiquity* 51, 1977.

Cregeen, Eric (ed.), *Argyll Estate Instructions*, SHS 1964.

Cregeen, Eric, and Mackenzie, Donald, *Tiree Bards and their Bardachd*, SWHIHR, 1978.

Darling, F. Fraser, *West Highland Survey*, 1956.

Donaldson, Gordon, 'Norse and Scottish Law in Shetland,' in the Nevis Institute, *The Shetland Report*, 1978.
  Shetland Life under Earl Patrick, 1958.
  'The Scots Settlement in Shetland,' in Donald Wittrington (ed.), *Shetland and the Outside World 1469–1969*, Aberdeen University Studies 157, 1983.

d'Oyly, Elizabeth, *Orain le Baintighearna D'Oyly*, 1875.

Duncan, A. A. M., 'Bede, Iona and the Picts,' in *The Writing of History in the Middle Ages*, 1981.
  'Argyll and the Isles in the early Middle Ages,' in *PSAS* XC, 1956–7.

Fenton, Alexander, *The Northern Isles: Orkney and Shetland*, 1978.

Geddes, Arthur, *The Isle of Lewis and Harris*, 1955.

Giblin, Cathaldus, *Irish Franciscan Mission to Scotland 1619–46*, 1964.

Grant, I. F., *The MacLeods: the History of a Clan*, 1959.

Gray, John Morgan, *Lord Selkirk of Red River*, 1963.

Gray, Malcolm, *The Highland Economy 1750–1850*, 1957.

Hamilton, J. R. C., *The Excavations at Jarlshof*, 1956.

Henderson, Isabel, *The Picts*, 1967.

Hewison, J. K., *The Isle of Bute in the Olden Times* II, 1895.

Holmer, Nils, *The Gaelic of Arran*, Dublin Institute for Advanced Studies, 1957.

Hunter, James, *The Making of the Crofter Community*, 1976.

Jackson, Kenneth, 'The Britons in Southern Scotland,' in *PSAS*, 1954.
  'The Pictish Language,' in F. T. Wainright (ed.), *The Problem of the Picts*, 1955.

Johnson, Samuel (ed. R. W. Chapman), *Journey to the Western Islands of Scotland*, 1930.

Jones, Gwyn, *A History of the Vikings*, 1968.

Kinvig, R. H., *The Isle of Man*, 1975.

Knox, John, *Tour of the Highlands of Scotland and the Hebride Isles in 1787*, 1787.

Lamb, R. G., 'The Cathedral of Christchurch and the Monastery of Birsay,' in *PSAS* 105, 1972–4.

Lamont, William D., *The Early History of Islay*, 1967.
    Ancient and Mediaeval Sculptured Stones of Islay, 1972–4.

Lavelle, Des, *Skellig: Island Outpost of Europe*, 1976.

Low, George, *Tour through the Islands of Orkney and Shetland*, 1879.

Lucas, A. T., 'The Plundering and Burning of Churches in Ireland,' in Etienne Rynne (ed.), *North Munster Studies*, 1967.

MacCodrum, John (ed. and trans. William Matheson), *The Songs of John MacCodrum*, SGTS, 1938.

MacDonald, Allan (ed. and trans. J. L. Campbell), *Bardachd Mhgr Ailein*, 1965.
    (ed. J. L. Campbell) *Gaelic Words and Expressions from South Uist and Eriskay*, Dublin Institute for Advanced Studies, 1958.

MacDonald, Angus and Archibald, *The Clan Donald*, 3 vols. 1896–1904.

MacDonald, Finlay J., *Crowdie and Cream*, 1982.

MacDonald, James, *General View of the Agriculture of the Hebrides*, 1811.

MacDonald, John (ed. and trans. Annie M. MacKenzie), *Orain Iain Luim*, SGTS, 1964.

MacDonald, Kenneth, 'The Rev. William Shaw – Pioneer Gaelic Lexicographer,' in *TGSI* 50, 1979.

MacKenzie, Alexander, *History of the Clan MacKenzie*, 1879.

MacKenzie, Alexander (ed. Elizabeth Sutherland), *The Prophecies of the Brahan Seer*, 1977.

Mackenzie, Compton, J. L. Campbell and Carl Borgström, *The Book of Barra*, 1936.

Mackenzie, W. C., *History of the Outer Hebrides*, 1903.
    The Book of the Lews, 1919.

Mackinlay, J. M., *Ancient Church Dedications* II, 1914.

Maclean Bards (ed. Colm Ò Baoill), *Bàrdachd Chloinn Ghill-Eathain*, SGTS, 1979.

Maclean, Loraine (ed.), *The Middle Ages in the Highlands*, Inverness Field Club, 1981.

Maclean Sinclair, Alexander, *The Clan Gillean*, 1899.
    (ed.) *Na Baird Leathanach*, 1898–1900.

Maclean, Sorley, in Donald MacAulay (ed.) *Nua-Bhàrdachd Ghaidhlig*, 1976.

MacLellan, Angus (ed. and trans. J. L. Campbell), *Stories from South Uist*, 1961.

(ed. and trans. J. L. Campbell) *The Furrow Behind Me*, 1962.

McLellan, Robert, *The Isle of Arran*, 1970.

MacLeod, Calum, in *Gairm* 125–9, 1983–5.

MacLeod, Mary (ed. and trans. J. Carmichael Watson), *Gaelic Songs*, SGTS, 1965.

MacPhail, J. R. N., *Highland Papers*, SHS, 1914.

MacQuarrie, Alan, *Iona Through the Ages*, SWHIHR, 1983.

MacTavish, Duncan (ed.), *The Gaelic Psalms 1694*, 1934.

Martin, Martin, *A Description of the Western Isles of Scotland*, 1934.

Marwick, Ernest, *Orkney Poems*, 1949.

The Folklore of Orkney and Shetland, 1975.

Matheson, Angus, 'Documents Connected with the Trial of Sir James MacDonald of Islay,' in *TGSG* V, 1958.

Megaw, Basil, 'Norsemen and Natives in the Kingdom of the Isles,' in *SS* 20, 1976.

Menzies, Gordon (ed.), *Who Are the Scots?*, 1971.

Mooney, John, *Charters and other Records of Kirkwall*, 1952.

Morison, Roderick (ed. and trans. William Matheson), *The Blind Harper*, SGTS, 1970.

Munro, Jean, *The Founding of Tobermory*, SWHIHR, 1976.

Munro, R. W., *Munro's Western Isles of Scotland*, 1961.

New Statistical Account of Scotland, 1845.

Nicolson, Alexander, *History of Skye*, 1930.

Nicolson, James, *Shetland*, 1975.

Nicolson, Nigel, *Lord of the Isles*, 1960.

Oftedal, Magne, 'On the Frequency of Norse Loan-words in Scottish Gaelic,' in *SGS* IX, 1962.

Orr, A. M., *Rothesay Public School*, 1955.

Pennant, Thomas, *A Tour in Scotland and Voyage to the Hebrides 1772*, 1790.

Piggott, Stuart, *Scotland Before History*, 1982.

Prebble, John, *Mutiny*, 1975.

Rea, F. G. (ed. J. L. Campbell), *A School on South Uist*, 1964.

Renfrew, Colin, *Investigations in Orkney*, SAL Research Report 38, 1979.

Richards, Eric, *A History of the Highland Clearances*, 1982.

'Highland Emigrants to South Australia in the 1850s,' in *Northern Scotland*, 1982.

Ritchie, Graham and Anna, *Scotland: Archaeology and Early History*, 1981.

Ross, Anne, *Pagan Celtic Britain*, 1967.

Ross, Neil, *Heroic Poetry from the Book of the Dean of Lismore*, SGTS, 1939.

Royal Commission on the Ancient and Historical Monuments of Scotland, Argyll I 1971, II 1975, III 1980, IV 1982: Outer Hebrides, Skye and Small Isles 1928.

Sharpe, Richard, *Raasay: Documents and Sources*, 1978.
    Raasay: a Study in Island History, 1982.

Shaw, Frances J., *The Northern and Western Islands of Scotland*, 1980.

Shaw, Margaret Fay, *Folksongs and Folklore of South Uist*, 1977.

Sinclair, Sir John (ed. Reid Tait), *Statistical Account of Shetland*, 1925.
    (ed. Storer Clouston) *Statistical Account of Orkney*, 1927.
    The Statistical Account of Scotland, 21 vols, 1791–9.

Small, Alan, 'Excavations at Underhoull, Unst,' in *Aberdeen University Review* XL, 1963.

Smith, David, 'Udal Law,' in the Nevis Institute, *The Shetland Report*, 1978.

Steel, Tom, *The Life and Death of St Kilda*, 1965.

Stevenson, David, *Alasdair Mac Colla and the Highland Problem in the Seventeenth Century*, 1980.

Storrie, Margaret, *Islay: Biography of an Island*, 1981.

Taylor, A. B. (trans.), *The Orkneyinga Saga*, 1938.

Thom, Alexander, *Megalithic Lunar Observatories*, 1971.

Thompson, Francis, *Harris and Lewis*, 1968.

Thomson, Derick S., 'The MacMhuirich Bardic Family,' in *TGSI* XLIII, 1963.
    'Gaelic Learned Orders and Literati in Mediaeval Scotland,' in *SS* 12, 1968.
    (ed.) *The Companion to Gaelic Scotland*, 1983.

Thomson, William (ed.), *Orkney Heritage* II, 1983.

Wainright, F. T. (ed.), *The Problem of the Picts*, 1955.
    (ed.) *The Northern Isles*, 1962.

Walker, John, *Report on the Hebrides of 1764 and 1771* (ed. Margaret McKay), 1980.

Wallace-Hadrill, J. M., *Early Mediaeval History*, 1975.

Watson, William, *Scottish Verse from the Book of the Dean of Lismore*, SGTS, 1937.

West, John, *Faroe, the Emergence of a Nation*, 1973.

Western Isles Structure Plan, Comhairle nan Eilean, 1983.

Wheeler, Philip, *The Island of Unst*, Nottingham University Studies, 1964.

Whitelock, Dorothy (trans.), *Anglo-Saxon Chronicle*, 1961.

Wilson, David, *The Vikings and their Origins*, 1970.

Abbreviations

PSAS	*Proceedings of the Society of Antiquaries of Scotland.*
SAL	Society of Antiquaries of London.
SGS	*Scottish Gaelic Studies.*
SGTS	Scottish Gaelic Texts Society.
SHS	Scottish History Society.
SS	*Scottish Studies.*
SWHIHR	Society of West Highland and Island Historical Research.
TGSG	*Transactions of the Gaelic Society of Glasgow.*
TGSI	*Transactions of the Gaelic Society of Inverness.*

Picture credits:

Between pages 22–23: BARNABY'S PICTURE LIBRARY Tobermory, HIGHLANDS AND ISLANDS DEVELOPMENT BOARD Jarlshof & Kildalton Cross; ROBERT T. SMITH Broch of Mousa; SPECTRUM COLOUR LIBRARY Duart Castle; JAMES WEIR Iona Abbey; TOM WEIR Callanish Stones & home interior Skara Brae.

Between pages 86–87: BARNABY'S PICTURE LIBRARY Tarskavaig; HIGHLANDS AND ISLANDS DEVELOPMENT BOARD Dunvegan Castle & Laphroaig distillery; SPECTRUM COLOUR LIBRARY sheep on Raasay; JAMES WEIR Loch Coruisk, Porthnahaven, Bowmore Harbour, Tarbert Pier; TOM WEIR scything, Stornaway, Rodel Church, & spinning.

Between pages 150–151: BARNABY'S PICTURE LIBRARY Goat Fell & Glen Rosa; JANET & COLIN BORD Lochranza Castle; HIGHLAND AND ISLAND DEVELOPMENT BOARD Brodick Castle & Marwick Head; DON MacCASKILL South Uist croft; ROBERT T. SMITH Lerwick fishing boats; SPECTRUM PICTURE LIBRARY oil tanker; JAMES WEIR Earl Patrick's palace, St Magnus cathedral, Scalloway Castle; TOM WEIR Castlebay.

Index